CLARENDON LAW SERIES

Edited by

PETER BIRKS

CLARENDON LAW SERIES

AN INTRODUCTION TO

CONSTITUTIONAL LAW

ERIC BARENDT

University College London

Oxford University Press

*This book has been printed digitally and produced in a standard specification
in order to ensure its continuing availability*

OXFORD
UNIVERSITY PRESS

Great Clarendon Street, Oxford OX2 6DP

Oxford University Press is a department of the University of Oxford.
It furthers the University's objective of excellence in research, scholarship,
and education by publishing worldwide in

Oxford New York

Auckland Cape Town Dar es Salaam Hong Kong Karachi
Kuala Lumpur Madrid Melbourne Mexico City Nairobi
New Delhi Shanghai Taipei Toronto

With offices in

Argentina Austria Brazil Chile Czech Republic France Greece
Guatemala Hungary Italy Japan South Korea Poland Portugal
Singapore Switzerland Thailand Turkey Ukraine Vietnam

Oxford is a registered trade mark of Oxford University Press
in the UK and in certain other countries

Published in the United States
by Oxford University Press Inc., New York

ISBN 978-0-19-876254-6

Preface

There are many books about the constitutional law of the United Kingdom. Some are comprehensive textbooks, while others are monographs concerned with particular areas. In writing an introduction to constitutional law, I have adopted a different approach. This book looks at the principles of the United Kingdom constitution from a critical, comparative perspective. It introduces readers to general themes, for example, the separation of powers and judicial review of legislation. Reference is made in some chapters to the protection of basic rights in liberal constitutions. But I do not discuss particular civil liberties in detail; they are well covered elsewhere. Rather, this book is concerned with the structure of the constitution. In particular, it examines the distribution of power between the branches of government—legislature, executive, and judiciary—and the provisions and procedures in the constitution for its control.

A critical examination of the principles of constitutional law in the United Kingdom is now more imperative than ever. At long last the terms of its uncodified constitution—in some areas, little more than flexible conventions or political practices—have been searched and found wanting. The government elected last year has put constitutional reform at the top of its agenda. Measures have already been introduced in Parliament to devolve power to Scotland and Wales, and to incorporate the European Human Rights Convention into United Kingdom law. Other reforms are expected soon. Freedom of information legislation will be enacted. There will probably be radical changes to the composition of the House of Lords; it is likely that the funding of political parties will be regulated, and there may be a change to the electoral system.

This book is largely concerned with an exposition of the general principles of the constitution of *the United Kingdom*. It also discusses matters, in particular the role of political parties, on which for the moment its constitution is silent. One chapter discusses the constitution of the

European Union (or Community). It is obviously right to devote a chapter to this topic. In the first place, membership of the Community has required modification of the rule of parliamentary supremacy, the most fundamental constitutional principle in the United Kingdom. Secondly, it compels commentators to think afresh and with more urgency about the merits of federalism and the role of judicial review in a liberal constitution.

Some chapters (or particular sections of them) examine aspects of other constitutions when they afford illuminating comparisons with United Kingdom law. These constitutions are principally the United States Constitution, the oldest and certainly the best known constitution in the world, and those of France and Germany, our leading partners in the European Union. The most influential writer on our constitutional law, Albert Dicey, highlighted characteristics of the constitution by copious references to the very different texts and principles in other countries. As is well known, Dicey thought the uncodified, common law arrangements here far superior to documentary, particularly federal, constitutions. I do not share his view. Parliamentary legislative supremacy means in practice that the constitutional checks on government are feeble. The United Kingdom constitution fails to provide that balance of power between different institutions which, albeit in different forms, is to be found in the constitutions of France, Germany, and the United States.

I am grateful to the Leverhulme Trust for the award of a Research Fellowship, which relieved me of normal teaching and other duties in 1994–5. The Fellowship also enabled me to spend some time at the Max-Planck Institute for International and Comparative Public Law in Heidelberg to study German constitutional law. Some of the chapters first took shape in lectures given at La Sapienza University, Rome, at the invitation of Professor Alessandro Pace. Conversations with him, and with Professor Dieter Grimm, have enriched my understanding of constitutional law in continental Europe. I am indebted to Trevor Allan, Peter Cane, Andrew Le Sueur, Dawn Oliver, and Jane Stapleton, for their comments on chapters of this book. They drew my attention to many points I had overlooked. I am responsible for the errors that remain. I would also like to thank Andrew Fenney and Sylvia Lough for their invaluable help.

Normally, authors of law books worry whether their work will already be out of date by the time it is published. This is less of an anxiety with a book of this character, concerned as it is with matters of principle rather than the details of statutes and case law. I have, however, anticipated the future by assuming that the legislation devolving power to Scotland and Wales and the Human Rights Bill 1997 will be enacted this year. I have also given references in Chapter 4 to provisions of the Treaty of Amsterdam which requires the ratification of all Member States of the European Union before it enters into force.

ERIC BARENDT
February 1998

Contents

A Note on Abbreviations

A few of the abbreviations used in the footnotes in this book may be unfamiliar. A list is appended.

FRENCH ABBREVIATIONS

Rec.   Recueil des décisions du Conseil constitutionnel
RJC   Recueil du jurisprudence constitutionelle

GERMAN ABBREVIATION

BVerfGE   Entscheidungen des Bundesverfassungsgerichts (Decisions of the German Constitutional Court)

EUROPEAN CONVENTION ABBREVIATION

EHRR   European Human Rights Reports (unofficial)

Secondly, a number of books are referred to frequently, so for reasons of space reference in the footnotes is given only to the author. These works are:

Bagehot   W. Bagehot, *The English Constitution* (introd. by R. H. S. Crossman, London, 1963)
Bell   J. Bell, *French Constitutional Law* (Oxford, 1992)
Bradley and Ewing   A. W. Bradley and K. D. Ewing, *Constitutional and Administrative Law* (12th edn., London, 1997)
de Smith and Brazier S. de Smith and R. Brazier, *Constitutional and Administrative Law* (7th edn., London, 1994)
Dicey   A. V. Dicey, *Introduction to the Study of the Law of the Constitution* (introd. by E. C. S. Wade, 10th edn., London, 1961)
Favoreu and Philip   L. Favoreu and L. Philip, *Les grandes décisions du Conseil constitutionnel* (7th edn., Paris, 1993)

Table of Cases

Table of United Kingdom Statutes

I

Constitutions

1. WHAT ARE CONSTITUTIONS FOR?

THE opening pages of textbooks on constitutional law frequently pose the question: what are constitutions? A standard answer is that the word has two meanings. In the first, the constitution of a state is the written document or text which outlines the powers of its parliament, government, courts, and other important national institutions. Almost every country in the world has a documentary constitution of this type. Some of them also set out fundamental rights, such as the right to freedom of speech and the right to a fair trial. It is characteristic of documentary constitutions, particularly those guaranteeing fundamental rights, that they impose constraints on the powers of the legislature and the government. In some cases such limits may be enforced by the courts. Their decisions comprise the central part of constitutional law. Moreover, there are special procedures for constitutional amendment; a documentary constitution cannot usually be changed by ordinary legislation.

On this definition the United Kingdom does not really have a constitution; there is no text or document which can clearly be identified as having that status. Although there are many laws which in terms of their content have a constitutional character, they have never been incorporated or codified in a single authoritative text. Moreover, it is probable that the United Kingdom Parliament is always free to amend laws which in other countries would be found in the constitutional text and which, therefore, could not be changed by ordinary legislation. This is one aspect of the principle of parliamentary supremacy or sovereignty, that Parliament is always free to make any law it likes. Although modified by membership of the European Union, this principle remains a fundamental aspect of United Kingdom law.[1]

It seems unsatisfactory, however, to conclude that there is no United Kingdom constitution. For politicians, courts, and commentators in Britain frequently refer to the rules or principles of 'the constitution' or

[1] See Ch. 5 for further discussion.

argue that some course of conduct is 'unconstitutional'. So the second, broader meaning of the term is that it refers to the collection of legal and non-legal rules which compose the system of government, for example, the rules outlining the powers of ministers and Parliament and regulating the relationship between them.[2] Legal rules are those which are interpreted and enforced by the courts, while non-legal rules are the customs or conventions regarded as imposing obligations, although they are not enforceable by the judges. An example of a British constitutional convention is the rule requiring the Monarch to assent to legislation which has been approved by the House of Commons and the House of Lords. The particular characteristics of the United Kingdom constitution will be discussed in Chapter 2, as will be the important role played in it by constitutional conventions. The first chapter of this book explores some general features of constitutions, in particular their role in constraining the exercise of political power and the part played by the courts in enforcing constitutional law.

Obviously it is important to have some idea of what a constitution is, and what (in most countries) the constitutional text contains, in order to appreciate the distinctive character of constitutional law. But it is also essential to ask another question: what are constitutions for? The answers to a question of this type will almost always shed light on the significance of a legal or social institution. We have a richer understanding of contract law, for instance, if we appreciate that the purpose of making a contract is usually to make clear provision for aspects of the parties' commercial relations, and to determine what is to happen if their promises are not performed. Equally, we cannot understand why the family is an important institution, unless we consider what its functions are with regard, say, to the personal development of adults or the education of children.

It is relatively easy to suggest some answers to questions about the functions and purposes of constitutions. We can look at the political circumstances in which they were drafted and adopted. First, a common occasion for framing a constitution is the emancipation of a country from a colonial regime. So it became usual for Commonwealth countries, such as India in 1950 and Nigeria in 1963, to adopt a constitution when they achieved independence. One early and well-known example of this type of constitution was the American Articles of Confederation 1776, subsequently replaced by the federal United States Constitution

---

[2] See K. C. Wheare, *Modern Constitutions* (2nd edn., Oxford, 1966), 1.

in 1787. One function of post-colonial constitutions is to give moral authority, or legitimacy, to the institutions of the newly independent state. In some cases the constitution may also aim to bring together the citizens of a state (or group of states) by providing a common or shared sense of purpose, while protecting the rights of individuals and of the distinct communities which comprise it. In Chapter 4 we will see that it is possible to regard the Treaties of Rome and Maastricht as the constitution of the European Union, although the Union is not a state, nor likely to evolve into one in the foreseeable future. This view of these Treaties as constitutional texts emphasizes the intention of their framers to bring the peoples of Europe together, or to integrate them, into a single Union, just as the United States Constitution integrated diverse communities in, say, Virginia and New York. (This object is not always successful, as is shown in different ways by the constitutions of Belgium, Cyprus, and, most recently, Yugoslavia.)

Secondly, constitutions are drawn up to establish the fundamental principles of a new system of government subsequent to a revolution. That was the case with the first French Constitution of 1791. Recent examples are the modern constitutions of Portugal, adopted in 1974, and of Spain, adopted in 1978, which signalled the transition of those countries from Fascist regimes to liberal parliamentary democracies. Something similar has happened in South Africa where the change from a white supremacist regime to a genuine multi-racial society has been followed by the promulgation of a constitution with a comprehensive Bill of Rights. Thirdly, after the Second World War, Germany, Italy, and Japan all adopted new constitutions, in order to make a fresh start following their defeat and experience of totalitarian government. These constitutions are characterized by their strong protection of individual liberties, and by the restraints imposed on fascist parties and (in the case of the German Basic Law, 1949, and the Japanese Constitution, 1946) upon the raising or deployment of armed forces.

Although constitutions vary enormously in terms both of their content and historical background, some common purposes can be detected. This is true at least of the liberal constitutions of the United States, most European countries in both the West and, after 1989, the East of the continent, and many members of the Commonwealth, for example, Australia, Canada, and India. A liberal constitution is not simply a power-map, identifying for its readers the institutions and persons entitled to exercise political power. Constitutions are designed to impose limits on the exercise of authority by the monarch or other holders of

power, and to formulate basic rights and freedoms and other fundamental values for the community. As Thomas Paine put it in *Rights of
Man*, the extensive pamphlet in which he subjected the British constitutional arrangements to withering criticism, '. . . government without
a constitution, is power without a right'.[3] In other words, government
under a constitution is the opposite of despotic government.

These considerations influenced the framers of the United States federal Constitution of 1787, although ten years or so after independence
from Britain, they had become more worried by the oppressive use of
power by state legislatures than the evils of absolute rule by a monarch.
Some of them justified their preoccupations in a collection of essays
known as the *Federalist Papers*, the most lucid analysis of fundamental
constitutional principles ever written in the English language. The
authors argued that in a liberal constitution power should be distributed
among three separate branches of government—the legislature, the executive (or government), and the judiciary—with the branches being able
to check each other. Only in this way could the danger of a concentration of power be averted.

The need for the powers of government to be limited by a constitution became a central theme of nineteenth-century history as authoritarian governments in France and in parts of the Austrian Empire were
replaced by more liberal parliamentary systems. Adherence to the principles of limited constitutional government is often referred to as *constitutionalism*, in much the same way as *liberalism* denotes support for
individual liberties and for minimal intervention with them by the state.
These two concepts are linked, but they do have different emphases.
The latter principle implies there are certain matters, for instance,
privacy and sexual freedom, which are no business of the state.
Constitutionalism is more concerned with the organization of political
structures to prevent the exercise of authoritarian power by any individual, group, or political party.

How influential have these ideas been in the evolution of the United
Kingdom constitution which, as already mentioned, has never been
incorporated in a single authoritative text? In an influential work on constitutional law written over 100 years ago, Dicey discussed the scope of
the subject and the contents of what he termed the 'English' constitution, but he seems never to have inquired what constitutions are for.[4]
Nor did he pay much attention to the idea of constitutionalism. Instead,

---

[3] (1791–2, Penguin edn., 1985), 185.   [4] Dicey, 23–35.

he enthusiastically put forward the principle of parliamentary sovereignty as the leading characteristic of the constitution. Under this principle, to be discussed at length in Chapter 5, the courts must accept and apply without reservation all legislation enacted by Parliament, just as in other countries their duty is to interpret and apply the constitution. Further, he argued that to impose binding restraints on Parliament would be incompatible with the English tradition of government by 'an absolute legislator'.[5]

It is not difficult to explain Dicey's omissions, unfortunately absolutely characteristic of English writing on constitutional law. No convention or constituent assembly has been convened, at least in the last 300 years, to contemplate what the 'constitution' should contain. Instead, constitutional arrangements have evolved gradually, so much so that the identity of particular rules as constitutional, and even of the very existence of the United Kingdom constitution, can be questioned. In the absence of the formal deliberations which preface the drafting of a documentary constitution, there has been little opportunity in United Kingdom history for reflection on the values, purposes, and structure of a liberal constitution.

Until the revival of interest in constitutional reform in the last decade, the only period when there has been sustained discussion in Britain of constitutional principles was the seventeenth century. To some extent the debate at that time developed themes which can be detected in earlier periods,[6] and in its turn it encouraged constitutional argument elsewhere, particularly in what were then the American colonies. One issue was the appropriate balance of power between the Stuart Kings and Parliament, another was the desirability of protecting individual liberties against both Crown and Parliament. In the Commonwealth period, 1649–60, there were even moves by the radical element among the Parliamentarians to formulate a written constitution which would have guaranteed some fundamental rights. Oliver Cromwell's *Instrument of Government* of 1653, which balanced the powers of Parliament and the Protector, was in all but name a codified constitution. Such steps were never repeated after the victory of Parliament over James II and the gradual formulation of the doctrine of parliamentary sovereignty, the rule identified by Dicey and most constitutional commentators as the principal feature of our constitutional law.

[5] Dicey, 68–9, n. 1, a note which repays careful attention.
[6] C. H. McIlwain, *Constitutionalism: Ancient and Modern*, (New York, 1947), esp. chs. V and VI.

Arguably, the doctrine of parliamentary sovereignty is incompatible with the principles of constitutionalism and of limited constitutional government. That is what Paine meant when he attacked the lack of a proper constitution in eighteenth-century Britain. We will see in the next chapter that it is more helpful to conclude that there is a constitution, although it is a deficient one. Its weaknesses are to some extent attributable to the failure to take seriously questions about the purpose and values of limited constitutional government. Until the last ten years or so, there has been relatively little interest in this country in the values of constitutionalism. The programme of constitutional reform introduced by the Labour government elected in 1997, prompted to some extent by the calls of Charter 88 and other organizations for a codified constitution, suggests that interest may finally have been awakened. Membership of the European Union has also contributed to this welcome development, largely because it is no longer possible to accept without qualification the absolutist doctrine of parliamentary supremacy. European Community law prevails over Acts of Parliament.[7] (However, neither the incorporation of the European Human Rights Convention nor devolution to Scotland will, in theory at least, affect the supremacy of the Westminster Parliament.[8])

It is important to distinguish liberal constitutions from the nominal or 'façade' constitutions of the kind that existed in the Soviet Union or even in Nazi Germany.[9] Nominal constitutions are indeed simply maps of political power, *describing* the powers of particular persons and institutions. Under these constitutions, as long as it observes the procedures set out in the text, a government (or Parliament) can never be said to act 'unconstitutionally'. On this perspective, Hitler and Stalin may have acted for the most part with perfect constitutional propriety. In contrast, adherence to constitutionalism means that the constitution must necessarily check absolute power; otherwise it does not deserve recognition as a proper, liberal constitution. Put another way, it can be said that there is little or no point to a constitution unless its structure and contents reflect the purposes of adopting one in place of despotic government. Otherwise the constitution is a façade to deceive the citizens, or foreigners, or both.

---

[7] See ch. 4, sect. 3.
[8] See ch. 2, sect. 5 and ch. 3, sect. 3.
[9] See the classic article by G. Sartori, 'Constitutionalism: A Preliminary Discussion' (1962) 56 *American Political Science Rev.* 853.

˙ This position received its classic formulation in Article 16 of the French Declaration of the Rights of Man of 1789:

Any society in which the safeguarding of rights is not assured, and the separation of powers is not established, has no constitution.

The separation of powers, discussed in the third section of this chapter, is a device, or set of principles, to check absolute power and thereby to foster constitutionalism. It is designed to prevent the concentration of power in the hands of one person or institution. All liberal constitutions attempt, admittedly in various ways, to balance or separate legislative, executive, and judicial powers. Secondly, most of them also guarantee some fundamental rights against infringement by the state and other public authorities. Under many constitutions, courts have jurisdiction to invalidate legislation which infringes these rights. This procedure is known as judicial review. In this respect, the United Kingdom constitutional arrangements are unusual; the courts have no authority to invalidate Acts of Parliament infringing a basic right, such as freedom of speech or the right to a fair trial, at least when it is clear that Parliament intended to infringe the right. (This position is not affected by the recent incorporation of the European Convention into United Kingdom law by the Human Rights Act 1998.) Thirdly, liberal constitutions sometimes divide legislative and governmental powers between federal and state authorities. This may be regarded as a vertical separation of powers, while the separation of power between legislature, executive, and the judiciary operates on a horizonal plane.

Something should be said about the variety of constitutions, before I discuss the separation of powers and the courts' power of judicial review, which is linked to the separation principle. This variety shows that a commitment to constitutional values does not entail adoption of a particular structure or form of government. There are more types of liberal constitution than there are of despotic or authoritarian regime. Particular attention will be paid to the constitutions of the United States, France, and Germany,[10] as these are the codified constitutions with which the United Kingdom uncodified arrangements are most frequently compared in this book.

---

[10] The text of these constitutions can be found in S. Finer, V. Bodganor, and B. Rudden, *Comparing Constitutions* (Oxford, 1995).

2. THE VARIETIES OF CONSTITUTION

Constitutions can be classified in a number of ways. Some of these are of little importance or are unhelpful. For instance, no attention need be paid now to the distinction between monarchical and republican constitutions. Two hundred years ago this was of interest during a period when many monarchs still exercised considerable power, but it is not of much significance at the end of the twentieth century. Another classification is that of written and unwritten constitutions. It has sometimes been said that the United Kingdom, in contrast to almost all other countries, has an unwritten rather than a written constitution, but it will be argued in Chapter 2 that it is better to say that it does not have a codified or documentary constitution. In any case, even codified constitutions, like those of the United States and France, may be supplemented to some extent by unformulated conventions or practices which have never been reduced to writing.

A classic distinction drawn by Bryce is that between flexible and rigid constitutions.[11] The constitution of the United Kingdom belongs to the former category, as did that of Ancient Rome. In a flexible constitution there is no difference between ordinary and constitutional laws. In terms of legal principle and procedures, the latter may be amended or repealed as easily as the former. For example, among the most fundamental constitutional statutes is the Act of Union with Scotland 1707 which, among other things, abolished the English Parliament and instituted a new British Parliament in Westminster. Yet provisions in this legislation have been amended by legislation passed by the Westminster Parliament in the normal way. Rigid constitutions, on the other hand, may only be amended by a particular procedure set out in the constitution itself, such as a referendum or the vote of a special majority, perhaps two-thirds, of the members of each house of the legislature. Article V of the US Constitution sets out a complex procedure, which broadly requires ratification of any amendment by three-quarters of the states. Moreover, some provisions in rigid constitutions are wholly unamendable. This is the case with a few of the most fundamental principles of the German Basic Law, including the federal principle, the separation of powers, and the guarantee of the right to human dignity.[12]

---

[11] J. Bryce, *Studies in History and Jurisprudence* (Oxford, 1901), Essay III.

[12] Art. 79(3). The 1949 German constitution has been known as the 'Basic Law', because it was considered provisional until re-unification. In fact, the term is still used to refer to the constitution of the united country.

There are two reasons why the distinction between flexible and rigid constitutions is now rather unhelpful. First, the group of flexible constitutions, those that can be amended by ordinary legislative procedure, is far too small: it may comprise now only the United Kingdom and New Zealand. Secondly, the distinction is misleading, in so far as it is taken to suggest that in practice rigid constitutions are necessarily impossible or very difficult to amend. In fact this varies considerably from one constitution to another. For instance, there have been only twenty-six Amendments to the US Constitution in over 200 years, while the much younger German Basic Law has been amended on nearly forty occasions.

Constitutions obviously vary considerably in their length and content. The United States Constitution is short, with only seven Articles. Even with its twenty-six Amendments, it only occupies barely a dozen or so pages of text. The German Basic Law in contrast has 146 Articles. But that is a thin document, compared to the constitution of India. Adopted in 1950 and frequently amended, it contains nearly 400 Articles with an additional ten Schedules. A draft constitution for the United Kingdom prepared by the Institute of Public Policy Research in 1991 has 136 pages. These differences are explicable in terms of both the range of topics covered and the degree of detail of their regulation. Some set out only the most important principles, leaving the legislature to implement them, while others attempt comprehensive regulation of a range of diverse matters such as the conduct of elections, parliamentary procedures, public finance, and the court structure. On the whole, short constitutions are preferable. They are easier to understand, and they are more likely on that account to enjoy widespread acceptance.[13]

As far as their content is concerned, there are substantial differences in the manner of guaranteeing fundamental rights. These may be stated without qualification, as in the First Amendment to the US Constitution: 'Congress shall make no law . . . abridging the freedom of speech'. Or the text may explicitly state that restrictions and conditions may be imposed on their exercise on a variety of grounds, for example, to protect public order or national security, or to safeguard public morality. Older constitutions tend to protect only the most fundamental political and human rights such as freedom of the person and property, speech, assembly, and association, while more modern constitutions protect additionally a range of social and economic rights. For

[13] See the classic judgment of Marshall CJ of the US Supreme Court in *McCulloch* v. *Maryland*, 4 Wheat (17 US) 316 (1819), and Wheare, n. 2 above, 32–4.

instance, the post-apartheid South African Constitution of 1996 naturally contains a comprehensive equality provision; it also protects rights to adequate housing, access to health care, basic education, and just administrative action.

Some constitutions spell out the courts' duty to intervene if the legislature or executive acts outside the powers conferred on it, while others are silent on this matter. A few take the opposite approach. They provide that certain principles are not enforceable by the courts, and that they are only intended to guide the government and the legislature. Part IV of the Indian Constitution contains 'Directive Principles of Social Policy' with this limited effect. Some Commonwealth countries refer to principles and rights in their Preamble, rather than in the text of the constitution itself, with the result that the courts cannot enforce them. (However, the French Constitutional Council has ruled that it can enforce the rights set out in the Declaration of the Rights of Man 1789, though they are only referred to in the Preamble of the Constitution of the Fifth French Republic.[14])

Two classifications of constitutions are particularly noteworthy. The first is the division between unitary and federal constitutions. Broadly, under federal constitutions such as those of the United States, Canada, Australia, and Germany, legislative and governmental competence is divided between the centre (or federation) on the one hand, and the states, or provinces as they may be termed, on the other. Neither the federation nor the states have exclusive legislative or executive power. The United Kingdom constitution is unitary, even though significant legislative powers will shortly be conferred on a Scottish Parliament. It is unitary, because the Westminster Parliament may, if it so wishes, withdraw these powers at any time. This complex topic is further discussed in Chapter 3. What should be emphasized at this point is that to some extent federal constitutions are framed to serve liberal constitutional values. In the first place, a federation brings together or integrates communities which historically and culturally may be very different in character. Equally, the division of powers between central and state (or provincial) authorities, each with its area of competence guaranteed by the constitution, is one way to prevent the exercise of total or arbitrary power.

A second striking distinction is that between parliamentary executive and presidential executive constitutions. In the former, the government

---

[14] See sect. 4 below.

is composed of members of the majority political party (or coalition of parties) represented in the parliament. Ministers, including the Prime Minister, sit in the legislature. Moreover, both individually and collectively they are responsible to it, so that in principle they should resign if they are defeated on a vote of no confidence taken in the principal legislative chamber, for example, the House of Commons. In contrast, in a presidential executive constitution, the President is separately elected, does not sit in the parliament or legislative assembly, and cannot be removed simply because a majority of its members loses confidence in his policies. Indeed, he may be a member of one political party or group, while the legislature is dominated by another party.

The United Kingdom, Germany, most other European states, and many long-standing members of the Commonwealth, such as Canada, Australia, New Zealand, and India have parliamentary executive constitutions. This aspect of the United Kingdom constitution will be discussed in later chapters, particularly Chapter 6. The German Basic Law specifically provides for the election of the Chancellor, the head of the government, by the Bundestag, the directly elected branch of the legislature.[15] In certain circumstances, the Bundestag may also remove a Chancellor with a vote of no confidence.[16] Unlike some Commonwealth constitutions, the Basic Law does not require ministers to be a member of the legislature, though they generally are in practice.

The leading example of a presidential executive constitution is that of the United States. This form of constitution is less popular than the parliamentary executive system, though it has provided a model for countries in South America. The text of the United States Constitution distinguishes the legislative powers of Congress from the executive powers of the President, spelling them out quite explicitly. (Judicial authority is vested in a Supreme Court and other courts which are established in legislation.) Congress is divided into two Houses, the House of Representatives and the Senate, composed of two Senators from each state. It has authority, for example, to impose and collect taxes, to regulate commerce abroad and between the states, to declare war, and to raise the armed forces.[17] The President is Commander in Chief of the armed forces; his powers under the Constitution are primarily those of treaty-making, appointing ambassadors, officers and judges, and ensuring the execution of the laws.[18] But the treaty-making and appointment

---

[15] Art. 63. Once elected, the Chancellor must be formally appointed by the Federal President, the Head of State.

[16] Ibid., Art. 67.   [17] US Constitution, Art. I, S. 8.   [18] Ibid., Art. II, Ss. 2 and 3.

power must be exercised with the consent of the Senate. The President may also decline to approve a Bill passed by Congress, but his veto may then be overridden by a two-thirds majority of both the House of Representatives and the Senate.

There are separate elections for Congress and the President. Indeed, in terms of strict constitutional law, the latter is chosen by an electoral college, composed of representatives of each state who are legally free to vote as they choose. The Constitution provides for the impeachment of the President by the House of Representatives, and trial by the Senate, for treason, bribery, and 'other high Crimes and Misdemeanors'.[19] The Articles of Impeachment adopted by the Judiciary Committee of the House of Representatives against President Nixon in 1974 referred to various abuses of power in connection with the Watergate cover-up. But whatever the precise scope of the impeachment power, it can only be invoked in unusual circumstances, and is quite different from the power of dismissal enjoyed by the legislature in a parliamentary executive constitution.

The Constitution of the Fifth French Republic, adopted in 1958, has a mixed character, showing features of both parliamentary and presidential executive constitutions. The government, and Prime Minister who directs its operations, are answerable to Parliament.[20] If the directly elected Chamber of Parliament, the National Assembly, passes a censure motion by a majority of all its members, or disapproves the government's programme, it must resign.[21] The effect is that the electorate chooses the government, as it does in a parliamentary system. But the Constitution has substantial elements of a presidential executive structure. In the first place, after a referendum called by President de Gaulle in 1962, the President is directly elected for seven years. He is guarantor of French independence and of respect for international treaties, as well as head of the army.[22] On this basis he has assumed general responsibility for the conduct of foreign affairs, though the exact demarcation of functions between President and Prime Minister in this context is far from clear. The President chooses the Prime Minister, and appoints and dismisses other ministers on the latter's recommendation. He is also entitled to dissolve the National Assembly to bring about a general election.[23] Like the US President, he is Head of State, but broadly, it seems, he is joint head of the executive with the Prime Minister. The arrangement may give rise to acute difficulties when they are members of

---

[19] US Constitution, Art. II, S. 4. [20] Art. 20. [21] Art. 50.
[22] Arts. 5 and 15. [23] Arts. 8–12.

different political parties, as happened twice when Mitterrand was President and is now the case with President Chirac.

The division of constitutions into parliamentary and presidential executive systems does oversimplify the infinite variety of possible arrangements. For instance, the South African Constitution of 1996 offers a variant of the parliamentary form: the President, in whom is vested the executive authority, must resign if the National Assembly passes a vote of no confidence in him. But he is also Head of State, must resign membership of the National Assembly once elected to office, and the Constitution grants him many powers which he may exercise independently.

Nevertheless, the classification is illuminating.[24] It brings out different constitutional techniques for regulating the relationship of the legislature (Parliament, Congress, or the National Assembly), on the one hand, and the executive (President, Prime Minister, and the government), on the other. This relationship is a major aspect of the separation of powers to be discussed in the next section. In a parliamentary system there is a fusion of the legislature and executive. The government is drawn from members of the Parliament or Assembly, almost invariably from the political party which controls it. It can, therefore, usually implement its policies by securing the passage of legislation through the parliament. Equally, the government is responsible to the legislature. Under a presidential system there is a strict separation between the composition of the legislative and executive branches; moreover, the constitution typically outlines the scope of their separate powers. They may therefore act to some extent independently of each other. However, a constitution may give one branch opportunities to participate, or intervene in, the distinctive functions of the other. The US Constitution, for instance, gives the President power to veto the legislation of Congress, while the Senate must approve his appointments of ambassadors, members of the Cabinet, and judges. At the risk of considerable oversimplification, it may be said that with the rise of modern political parties a constitution with a parliamentary executive system does less to counteract a concentration of power than a presidential constitution, where authority is divided between the President and the legislature who may come from different political parties.

---

[24] Contrast the view of de Smith and Brazier, 11–12.

3. CONSTITUTIONALISM AND THE SEPARATION OF POWERS

Constitutionalism is a belief in the imposition of restraints on government by means of a constitution. It advocates the adoption of a constitution which is more than a 'power-map'; its function is to organize political authority, so it cannot be used oppressively or arbitrarily. This is also the value underlying the classic principle of the separation of powers formulated by the French jurist, Montesquieu, in *L'Esprit des Lois*.[25] If the same person or body exercised both legislative and executive powers, he argued, society would fear tyranny through the ruthless enforcement of oppressive laws by the authority which had enacted them. For the same reason, the judiciary should be independent of the legislature and executive. The framers of the US Constitution similarly saw a division of powers between Congress, the President, and the judiciary as essential to prevent the concentration of power in the hands of particular parties, or factions, the term preferred by Madison, the leading author of *The Federalist Papers*. The strongest expression of the link between constitutionalism and the separation of powers principle was made in the French Declaration of the Rights of Man, where it was asserted that a society without the principle has no constitution.[26]

Montesquieu formulated the separation principle on the basis of his perception of the eighteenth-century British constitution. It was an odd interpretation. As will be explained in the next chapter, the United Kingdom constitutional arrangements did not then, and certainly do not now, observe the separation of powers as Montesquieu understood it. In this country, as in most parliamentary executive systems, there is no separation of *persons* between the legislature and the government. Cabinet and other Ministers sit in the House of Commons. Even, it may be said, the judiciary is not entirely independent, since its head, the Lord Chancellor, is both a member of the Cabinet and sits in the House of Lords.[27] Further, English writers on constitutional law tend to be dismissive of the separation of powers.[28] They point out that in this coun-

---

[25] *The Spirit of the Laws* (1748), with introd. by F. Neumann (New York, 1949), Book XI, sect. 6. For a study of the principle, see M. J. C. Vile, *Constitutionalism and the Separation of Powers* (Oxford, 1967).

[26] See p. 7 above.

[27] For discussion of his position, see Ch. 2, sect. 3, and Ch. 7, sect. 2.

[28] See, for example, I. Jennings, *The Law and the Constitution* (5th edn., London, 1959), ch. 1 and App. I, and G. Marshall, *Constitutional Theory* (Oxford, 1971), ch. V., T. R. S. Allan, *Law, Liberty and Justice* (Oxford, 1993) is more sympathetic to the principle.

try ministers and administrative bodies are frequently given authority by Act of Parliament to issue general rules, known as delegated legislation; in other words, the executive legislates. Moreover, statutes give local authorities and other bodies power, for instance, to decide applications for planning permission and to grant various types of licence; these decisions may be regarded as 'judicial' and so more appropriate for the courts. Similar developments have also taken place in the United States and elsewhere. Commentators therefore often conclude that the principle is of little value.

Certainly, these arguments reveal difficulties in what is often termed the *pure separation of powers* principle, that is, the theory that there are three clearly distinct functions of government—legislative, executive, and judicial—and that they should be allocated to different persons or bodies. It may be claimed, for example, that it makes no sense simply to characterize some type of decision as 'judicial' rather than 'executive' and then to allocate it automatically to judges rather than administrators. It may be better to allow an administrative authority or tribunal to decide some matters such as entitlement to welfare benefits, provided perhaps that there is some judicial control to see that procedural fairness is observed. Further, there may be good practical arguments, for instance, for enabling government departments or specialist agencies to issue delegated legislation, within the framework of powers conferred on them by the legislature. But these points miss the significance of the separation of powers principle.

The principle is concerned with the avoidance of concentrations of power. What it requires above all is that each branch of government—legislature, executive, and judiciary—is able to check the exercise of power by the others, either by participating in the functions conferred on them, or by subsequently reviewing the exercise of that power. As its framers intended,[29] the principle is reflected in the scheme of the US Constitution. The legislative power, for instance, is allocated to Congress, but the President may veto a Bill if he does not approve of it—though the veto may then be overridden by a two-thirds majority in both Houses of Congress. The Constitution also implicitly entitles the Supreme Court to invalidate legislation, or acts of the executive, which exceeds the powers conferred by it on Congress or the President. This version of the separation principle is often known as the *partial separation* theory, because unlike the *pure* version it does not require that only

[29] The classic exposition of this version of the separation principle is Madison's *Federalist Papers*, Nos. 47–51.

one institution exercises a particular function of government. More helpfully perhaps, it is also known as the system of *checks and balances*, since it sets up constitutional procedures under which institutions check or balance the exercise of power by other authorities.

The US Constitution therefore adopts this second version of the separation theory, as does to some extent any constitution under which the courts can review the constitutionality of acts of the legislature and the government. The German Basic Law, for instance, does so when it gives the Federal Constitutional Court competence to determine constitutional disputes between the federation and the states and between federal organs, such as the government and the Bundestag.[30] The separation of powers is a fundamental principle of the German constitutional order, clearly spelt out in Article 20 of the Basic Law. However, as in this country, there is no rigid separation of persons between legislature and executive; ministers sit in the Bundestag.

In the Nazi period the Reichstag delegated unlimited legislative power to Hitler and his ministers. Perhaps in reaction to this experience, the German Constitutional Court has held in a number of cases that the Bundestag itself must lay down the fundamental principles of any area of regulation, for instance, with regard to the environment or to the regulation of professional conduct.[31] In other words, the delegation of wide legislative power to the executive is unconstitutional. In these circumstances, the separation of powers principle, by its insistence on the active role of the legislature, reinforces democratic values; members of a parliament are directly responsible to the electorate, ministers and civil servants are not.

In contrast to the United States and now, to some extent, Germany, France has traditionally adopted the pure theory of the separation of powers in its constitutional law. This theory requires a rigid separation between the persons comprising the three branches of government— legislative, executive, and judicial—each of which must respect, and abstain from interference with, the exercise of the distinctive functions by the other branches. Under the 1958 Constitution, ministers may not sit in the National Assembly.[32] Judicial review of legislation has been regarded as inappropriate, because the courts would then be stepping into parliament's area of competence. Under previous constitutions, it

---

[30] Basic Law, Art. 93.
[31] For discussion of these cases, see D. P. Currie, *The Constitution of the Federal Republic of Germany* (Chicago, Ill., 1994), 125–34.
[32] Art. 23.

has been for the National Assembly itself to determine whether it is acting constitutionally. Further, the legality of executive action is not controlled by the ordinary courts, but by the Conseil d'État, an administrative council. Yet the pure theory is now compromised by the institution in the 1958 Constitution of a Constitutional Council (Conseil constitutionnel) which, among other functions, rules on the constitutionality of laws (*lois*) before they are promulgated.[33] The Council's rulings are binding, so that in effect it should be treated in the same way as a constitutional court. The French Constitution, therefore, now reflects the *checks and balances* aspect of the separation principle, more usually associated with the United States approach.

The separation of powers principle retains considerable vitality and effectiveness as a constitutional technique for guaranteeing limited government. It is more important than the federal principle, because it is desirable to observe it in all liberal constitutions, while federalism may be inappropriate for a small, homogeneous country. As I will explain shortly, the separation of powers provides an argument for the institution and practice of judicial review. It, therefore, sits uncomfortably with the fundamental principle of the United Kingdom constitution that Parliament is entitled to enact any legislation it likes, no matter what its impact is on fundamental rights. But that is an argument for discarding parliamentary sovereignty, rather than treating the separation of powers principle with undue scepticism.

4. JUDICIAL REVIEW

Judicial review is a feature of most modern liberal constitutions. It refers to the power of the courts to control the compatibility of legislation and executive acts with the terms of the constitution. Often this function is given to a special constitutional court; the ordinary courts must refer constitutional questions to it, if they arise during the course of litigation. That is the position, for instance, in Germany and Italy, where judicial review was introduced after the last war. But in other countries, notably the United States, any court is entitled to hold legislation invalid, subject, of course, to appeal to higher courts, eventually in the United States to the Supreme Court in Washington. A final introductory point is that decisions of the lower courts themselves, on a point of statutory or other law, for example, common law, may be reviewed if

---

[33] Arts. 61–2.

they fail to take account of relevant constitutional principles, in particular those guaranteeing the fundamental rights of individuals. In defamation cases, for example, the trial court must take account of rights to freedom of speech and of the press, and the right to dignity and to reputation which is also guaranteed in some constitutions.

Until its membership of the European Community, there has been no judicial review of this kind in the United Kingdom. Indeed, in this country the term is almost always used to refer to the courts' control of *administrative* action on the ground that it is outside the statutory powers conferred on, say, a local authority or government minister. Judicial review in that sense is a concern of administrative, rather than constitutional, law. Constitutional review of Acts of Parliament has not existed in the United Kingdom, largely because it conflicted with the principle of parliamentary supremacy. That does not now apply where an Act of Parliament conflicts with European Community law, a topic explored in Chapters 4 and 5. But United Kingdom courts may not invalidate an Act of Parliament on the ground that it violates human rights; the Human Rights Act 1998 does not alter this position.[34] For the most part, lawyers and politicians accept the argument, considered in the last section of this chapter, that judicial review of legislation is undemocratic, because it may lead to the invalidation by a few judges of a measure which had been enacted in Parliament by a democratically elected majority.

What then is the justification for judicial review of legislation? In some cases the answer is that the constitution itself explicitly provides for it, so that the courts would be in breach of their constitutional responsibility if they failed to annul legislation which infringed, say, a fundamental right to freedom of speech. The German Basic Law clearly provides for judicial review of legislation (as well as of executive acts) infringing fundamental rights; Article 1 states that the 'basic rights shall bind the legislature, the executive and the judiciary as directly enforceable law'. Other Articles lay down a procedure by which an individual can lodge a constitutional complaint directly to the Constitutional Court if one of his rights has been violated.[35] The Court is also given express power to resolve disputes between the federation and the states (*Länder*) and between the federal parliament and government. The South African Constitution of 1996 is even clearer, providing that a Constitutional Court 'makes the final decision whether an Act of Parliament, a provincial Act or conduct of the President is unconstitutional . . .'.[36]

---

[34] See Ch. 2, sect. 5.   [35] Basic Law, Art. 93(1), para. 4a.   [36] Art. 167(5).

However, the United States Constitution makes no provision for judicial review of federal legislation. The courts' power to invalidate legislation incompatible with the Constitution was instead formulated by the Supreme Court itself in *Marbury* v. *Madison*,[37] almost certainly the most seminal decision in the history of constitutional law. Its significance lies in the reasoning of Chief Justice Marshall to the effect that judicial review is integral to a written constitution. It makes a case for judicial review, irrespective of the terms of the Constitution's text, and is therefore of universal relevance. His argument went as follows. The purpose of a written constitution is to outline and limit the powers of the legislature and the other branches of government. Its principles are fundamental. But what would be the point of framing a constitution, if the legislature could exceed the limits of its powers? It is implicit in the very nature of a written constitution that legislation inconsistent with it is null and void. The second stage of Chief Justice Marshall's argument is that it is the duty of the courts to resolve a conflict between a constitutional provision and legislation challenged as repugnant to it. The court's duty, he concluded, is to apply the constitution as paramount law and to rule inconsistent legislation invalid.

This apparently logical argument is open to criticism. In particular, it assumed that the provisions in a constitution are to be treated as binding law enforceable by the courts, rather than regarded as a set of political principles to be interpreted and applied by the legislature.[38] This alternative is not just a hypothetical possibility. Until the post-war period only a few European constitutions, most notably the 1920 Austrian Constitution, recognized judicial review. It was not introduced in France until the institution of the Constitutional Council in the 1958 Constitution; moreover, it was only in 1971 that the Council began to hold laws unconstitutional for infringement of the Declaration of the Rights of Man of 1791.[39] Even today the Federal Tribunal in Switzerland may not review the constitutionality of federal legislation.

The conclusion in *Marbury* v. *Madison* was, therefore, not as inevitable as it appears on first reading. Moreover, Chief Justice Marshall ignored an important objection to judicial review, that it entails the court substituting its opinion for that of the legislature on a

---

[37] 1 Cranch 137 (1803).
[38] The Supremacy Clause (Art. VI, S. 2) does state that the Constitution is the supreme law of the land. But it is intended only to ensure the supremacy of federal over state law (see Ch. 3, sect. 2).
[39] Decision 71–44 DC of 16 July 1971, Rec. 25 (Favoreu and Philip, 275).

complex matter where the meaning of the constitutional provision may be far from clear. For very few cases of judicial review are clear-cut. For example, it is usual for a constitution to guarantee freedom of expression, but also to provide that exercise of this freedom may be restricted when this is necessary on one of a number of grounds, including the protection of morality. If the legislature enacts a statute to restrict or ban the dissemination of certain types of hard-core pornography, should the courts defer to its assessment that the measure was necessary to protect morality, or should the judges decide that question themselves?

Analogous problems arise when a court is asked to determine that the federal parliament has exceeded its powers by enacting legislation in an area which arguably belongs to the exclusive competence of the states, or conversely that a state has trespassed into an area of federal authority. For instance, constitutions typically give the federation specific power to regulate commerce or trade *between* the states (or provinces) rather than leave the matter to be regulated by each state independently. (Congress has this power in the US Constitution under what is known as the interstate commerce clause.) A constitutional court would almost certainly be right to uphold the constitutionality of federal regulation of transport charges between the states under a provision of this kind; but it is far from obvious whether it should also approve on this basis federal legislation banning goods produced by child labour from trade between the states. Finally, separation of powers questions are rarely straightforward. In one of the leading United States cases, the owners of steel factories challenged their seizure by an Executive Order of President Truman. He had issued it to avert a threatened strike at the factories during the Korean war crisis of 1952. The owners successfully argued that the President was exercising a legislative power, and so infringing the separation of powers.[40] Although generally regarded as correct, the decision was not unanimous. The lengthy dissenting judgment of Chief Justice Vinson urged that, in the absence of any Congressional statute prohibiting his action, the President was entitled to keep the steel factories operating during a national emergency.

These cases show just a few of the difficult constitutional judgments courts must reach if they are given, or claim, powers of judicial review. Quite apart from the argument that judicial review is undemocratic, a parliament, and certainly the executive government, may be better qualified than the judges to make the complex economic and political assess-

---

[40] *Youngstown Sheet and Tube Co.* v. *Sawyer*, 343 US 579 (1952).

ments necessary to reach a decision in these circumstances. Much of the argument in *Marbury* v. *Madison* assumed that once the texts of the con-stitution and the statute have been compared, it will be plain whether the legislature has exceeded its constitutional powers. But it is relatively uncommon for constitutional courts to be presented with simple cases that can be resolved in this way.

Despite these reservations, Chief Justice Marshall's argument is per-suasive. As we have seen, the main purpose of the United States Constitution, and indeed of all liberal constitutions, is the restraint of power. That is the justification for limiting the powers of each branch of government, including the legislature. The uncodified United Kingdom constitution may not impose such restraints, but that failure does disservice to the values of constitutionalism and that version of the separation of powers which emphasizes the importance of checks and balances. Moreover, the Supreme Court was right to treat the Constitution as law which must be interpreted and applied by the judges. Every constitutional text, or set of constitutional rules and prin-ciples, must be interpreted by the courts to determine whether the particular provision relevant to the case is legally enforceable or not. Indeed, we will see in Chapter 4 that the United Kingdom parliamen-tary supremacy principle is a rule of constitutional law fashioned and enforced by the courts. The question the Supreme Court asked itself in *Marbury* v. *Madison* was whether the Constitution should be interpreted to give it authority to review inconsistent legislation, or not to confer such authority. The Court answered the question in the right way. The alternative answer would have made less sense of the adoption of a writ-ten constitution which incorporated as its central feature the principle of the separation of powers.

5. CONSTITUTIONALISM AND DEMOCRACY

One issue brought to the US Supreme Court earlier this century was whether Congress was entitled to legislate to outlaw goods produced by child labour from trade between the states or whether the ban amounted to an unconstitutional interference in a matter which the states were entitled to decide themselves. In 1918 the Supreme Court, by a major-ity of five to four judges, held that in imposing the ban Congress had exceeded its power to regulate commerce between the states.[41] The

[41] *Hammer* v. *Dagenhart*, 247 US 251 (1918).

decision was widely unpopular and led to a proposal to amend the Constitution to give Congress power to regulate the employment of children. The amendment was ratified by a majority of the states, but not by enough of them to bring it into force. Eventually, after a change in the composition and attitudes of the Court, the Fair Labor Standards Act of 1938 was upheld; the Court reversed its earlier decision that the child labour legislation was unconstitutional.[42]

This history nicely brings out the central difficulty in accepting judicial review: how can it be justified when it leads to the frustration of the clear intentions of the legislature? A majority of the judges, who in the United States are appointed for life, thwarted Congress on a matter where the latter clearly represented majority opinion. In short, judicial review is undemocratic, or in the phrase of Alexander Bickel, a prominent constitutional scholar in the post-war period, the procedure is 'counter-majoritarian'.[43] It will not do to say that the Court does not have the last word, as the Constitution may be amended. The child labour episode shows it is not always possible to obtain the super-majority of three-quarters of the states to approve the necessary constitutional amendment.

The question posed at the beginning of the last paragraph must be considered by all who think seriously about constitutional law. For it is of practical significance to lawyers and judges, even in the context of constitutions like those of the United States and Germany, where judicial review is well established either by nearly two centuries of judicial precedents, as in the former country, or by the constitution itself, as in Germany, South Africa, India, and many other jurisdictions. In all these countries arguments may be, and frequently are, made to the constitutional court that it should not intervene, unless it is clear beyond doubt that the legislature has exceeded its powers. The courts should, it may be said, defer to the judgement of the democratically elected legislature or to that of the executive, at least when it is politically answerable to parliament. In this country the question is now of topical significance. The inconsistency of judicial review with democracy is the main argument against restraining the powers of Parliament by the incorporation of the European Human Rights Convention or through the adoption of a codified constitution. For that reason alone, it is right to pay attention to these arguments in this book.

---

[42] *United States* v. *Darby Lumber Co.*, 312 US 100 (1941).
[43] A. Bickel, *The Least Dangerous Branch* (Indianapolis, Ind., 1962), ch. 1.

Broadly, there are two principal types of argument to explain, or justify, the place of judicial review in a democracy. The first emphasizes the weaknesses of the democratic process, and draws attention to the dangers of exclusive reliance on a parliament for the effective protection of basic civil liberties. Essentially, these amount to practical or prudential arguments for judicial review. The legislature may be dominated by parties which represent only, say, 40 per cent of the electorate, while a particular statute may not reflect the view of the majority of the people. Alternatively, legislation may be rushed through parliament without consideration of its impact on the public.[44] Finally, majorities may be insensitive to individual rights or the interests of racial, religious, and other minorities.

Many of these points are persuasive, but they cannot alone carry the argument for judicial review. First, it must be admitted that, whatever the shortcomings of the electoral process, the legislature will always enjoy more democratic legitimacy than the courts; judges are appointed and are wholly unaccountable to the public. If the majority strongly dislikes a legislative measure, it can elect another parliament to repeal it. In contrast, the story of the child labour legislation in the United States shows how difficult it may be to reverse an unpopular judicial decision. But the shortcoming of the practical case for judicial review, as it was put in the previous paragraph, is that it does not address the arguments of moral and political principle.

One of these arguments is that judicial review fails to respect the equal *rights of participation* of all citizens to determine complex political and constitutional issues.[45] Respect for those rights would require parliament rather than the courts to have the last word on interpretation of the constitution. The point is that members of the legislature, unlike the judges in a constitutional court, are responsible to voters, who can seek to influence them in their determination of constitutional questions. Alternatively, it might be appropriate to institute procedures, such as referendums, in which members of the community can express their preferences. Against this, it can be said that the right to participate can also be exercised in the course of litigation before a constitutional court, in discussion of its decisions, and in campaigns for the reversal of a decision or a constitutional amendment.

---

[44] The Official Secrets Act 1911 and the Prevention of Terrorism (Temporary Provisions) Act 1974 were both enacted after a few hours of debate.

[45] J. Waldron, 'A Right-Based Critique of Constitutional Rights' (1993) 13 *Oxford Jo. Legal Stud.* 18, 36–45.

The second argument for judicial review is one of principle. Democracy surely means more than majority rule. It entails respect for fundamental rights, especially those which must be guaranteed for the democratic process to work effectively. Ronald Dworkin has argued we should reject the majoritarian premise, which holds that all fundamental political decisions, including decisions interpreting the constitution, must be taken in accordance with majority opinion.[46] Under this majoritarian model, rights, for example, to free speech and to freedom of association in political parties could be curtailed, because that is what the majority in the legislature wanted. Dworkin advocates a different model of democracy, which he terms 'constitutional' democracy. Commitment to this version of democracy entails the treatment of all members of the community with equal respect and concern and the recognition of fundamental rights, such as the right of free speech and to privacy. Courts may be more appropriate institutions to safeguard these rights than legislative bodies. They can do more justice to the arguments of the individual, examining them in the light of the facts of the particular case. Indeed, in Dworkin's view, judicial review of legislation can be justified as the most effective procedure for the protection of basic rights. As he puts it, 'democracy does not insist on judges having the last word, but it does not insist that they must not have it'.[47]

Whether in fact judicial review is the most appropriate procedure for safeguarding constitutional rights and values can only be determined by reference to the history and experience of particular societies. The constitutional history of Germany during this century would provide one answer. The Weimar Constitution made no provision for judicial review, while the Nazi regime of course did not tolerate an independent, let alone an interventionist, judiciary able to protect human rights. In contrast, the German Constitutional Court has effectively protected the fundamental rights guaranteed by the 1949 Basic Law, and has successfully upheld the division of powers between the federation and the states. Although they might dislike some particular decisions of the Court, it would be hard to persuade German commentators that judicial review is fundamentally incompatible with parliamentary democracy. The Constitutional Court is a respected, if sometimes controversial, institution.

---

[46] See his 'Introduction; The Moral Reading and the Majoritarian Premise' in *Freedom's Law* (Oxford, 1996). Also see S. H. Freeman, 'Constitutional Democracy and the Legitimacy of Judicial Review' (1990–1) 9 *Law and Phil.* 327.

[47] Dworkin, n. 46 above, 7.

In the United States, despite the decision of the Supreme Court in the first child labour case and other aberrations, most notably the *Dred Scott* ruling,[48] judicial review is generally regarded as the most appropriate procedure for the protection of fundamental rights. Hardly anyone argues that the courts should not enforce the separation of powers through judicial review. Brief reference may be made to two decisions to show the significance of judicial review in the modern United States Constitution; both decisions were controversial and involved the overruling of earlier precedents, yet they have now been accepted as legitimate exercises of judicial power. In *Brown* v. *Board of Education*,[49] the Court held unanimously that racial segregation in state schools violated the constitutional right to equal protection; the decision caused consternation in the southern states and encouraged the growth of the civil rights movement. Of equivalent importance in reshaping the political landscape was its decision in *Baker* v. *Carr*[50] that the constituencies for state legislatures should be of equal size; the decision put a halt to their domination by the rural population and gave fairer representation to city communities, including blacks and other minorities.

Perhaps neither the lessons of history nor the arguments of principle altogether succeed in reconciling judicial review with democracy. The boldest strategy might be to admit that it is incompatible with democracy, at least with the conventional majoritarian version. Adherents of constitutionalism, the belief in limited constitutional government, should be able to accept this position cheerfully. There is no reason, in their view, always to regard democracy as the supreme political value. The principle of the separation of powers, from which judicial review is derived, need not take second place to it. On the contrary, there is little point to framing a constitution, unless we are prepared to accept that power should be limited, even when it is exercised by a democratically elected legislature.

---

[48] *Dred Scott* v. *Sandford*, 60 US 353 (1857) invalidated a Congressional law outlawing slavery in the northern states, thereby precipitating the Civil War.
[49] 347 US 483 (1954).
[50] 369 US 186 (1962). See Ch. 7, sect. 4 for further discussion of this case.

2

The United Kingdom Constitution

1. DOES THE UNITED KINGDOM HAVE A CONSTITUTION?

THERE is no document in the United Kingdom equivalent, say, to the United States Constitution of 1787 or to the Constitution of the Fifth Republic in France approved in September 1958. Nor, for that matter, is there a set of statutes clearly indicated by their titles as 'Constitutional' or 'Basic laws'.[1] Yet judges, politicians, and commentators in the United Kingdom often refer in general terms to its constitution, and they describe various rules and principles as 'constitutional'. It is said, for example, that United Kingdom membership of the European Union has had a major impact on the constitution and that participation in the arrangements for a common European currency (Economic and Monetary Union) would have further implications for it.

Moreover, Law Lords and other judges sometimes state that cases raise issues of 'constitutional importance'; in one case Lords Diplock and Scarman specifically claimed that the constitution is based on the separation of powers.[2] Or, to take another topic, some commentators have argued that it is unconstitutional for a Prime Minister in effect to be elected by a vote of Members of Parliament from the majority party, as happened when John Major replaced Mrs Thatcher as leader of the Conservative Party, and hence as Prime Minister, in November 1990. In fact that step was perfectly proper, and certainly lawful, under present constitutional arrangements. What is interesting is that the constitutional propriety of the election procedure was even debated.

There is, therefore, a widespread assumption that the United Kingdom does have a constitution. But is that assumption justified? Towards the end of the eighteenth century Thomas Paine thought it was not. In his famous defence of the French Revolution, *Rights of Man*,

---

[1] New Zealand has a Constitution Act 1986, bringing together a number of earlier statutes, while the uncodified Israeli Constitution consists of a number of Basic Laws.

[2] *Duport Steels* v. *Sirs* [1980] 1 WLR 142, 157, 169.

he wrote that everything in England has a constitution except the nation itself. More polemically, he added that nobody would have dreamt of describing the arrangements for electing a Parliament which enjoyed unlimited powers as a constitution, 'if the cry of constitution had not been set up by the government'.[3] The implication was that it was disingenuous for the government of William Pitt to argue that the system of parliamentary democracy and legislative supremacy amounted to a genuine constitution. Fifty years later Alexis de Tocqueville was equally forthright. Since, he argued, Parliament is always free to repeal the most fundamental laws and introduce new legislation, the constitution in England may change continually. It would be better to say that there is no constitution at all.[4]

Both Paine and de Tocqueville apparently believed that it is appropriate to use the term 'constitution' only to refer to a higher set of rules, superior to ordinary laws. One characteristic of such higher rules is that they cannot be amended or repealed by the normal legislative process, so that a constitution is necessarily rigid.[5] Acceptance of that claim would certainly mean that the United Kingdom does not have one. Leaving aside conflicts between its enactments and some rules of European Community law,[6] the Westminster Parliament has been legally free to enact whatever legislation it chooses from one year to the next; it has not been limited in its freedom by any higher rules of law contained in an authoritative text. That is what is meant when it is said that Parliament is sovereign. (This position is not affected by the Human Rights Act 1998, discussed in the final section of this chapter.) As a result, although Magna Carta 1215 and the European Communities Act 1972 are in one sense fundamental laws, they can be as easily repealed as, say, the Animals Act 1971 or the Estate Agents Act 1979.

The view, implicit in the writing of Paine and de Tocqueville, that only a set of higher laws can qualify as a constitution is too restrictive. It is surely preferable to conclude that the United Kingdom does have a constitution, or at least some laws and arrangements which have that character. But in contrast to almost every other constitution it lacks any authoritative text or document. Moreover, it is flexible, in that it may be amended without recourse to any special procedure for the

---

[3] *Rights of Man* (1791–2, Penguin Classics ed., 1985), 193.
[4] *Democracy in America* (1835), i, ch. VI.
[5] For the distinction between rigid and flexible constitutions, see Ch. 1, sect. 2.
[6] The relationship of Acts of Parliament and European Community legislation is considered in Ch. 5, sect. 3.

introduction of constitutional laws. Granted that the United Kingdom rules and arrangements are extremely unusual, if not unique, it is better to explore the respects in which they differ from the documentary constitutions in, say, the United States, France, and Germany, than to exclude them from the category of constitutions altogether.[7] If we define the terms 'constitution' and 'constitutional law' too narrowly, we stifle debate over the respective merits of rigid and flexible constitutions and how far each type respects the values of constitutionalism discussed in Chapter 1. A broader use of the terms has an additional advantage. It enables sense to be made of their use in contemporary political and legal discourse; we would otherwise have to conclude that English judges are talking nonsense when they say that a case poses constitutional questions.

However, the lack of an authoritative constitutional text is significant. It may be difficult to decide what counts as constitutional law in the United Kingdom. In the United States and France, and indeed in virtually every other country, the principles of constitutional law are contained in the text of the document itself, as interpreted by the courts.[8] For example, the legislative powers of the United States Congress are set out in Article I of the 1787 Constitution. The exact scope of its powers, say, to impose taxes and to regulate trade between the states has been clarified in a number of rulings of the courts, particularly the Supreme Court. Further, in countries with a codified constitutional text, a rule has a constitutional character merely because it is contained in the document itself, irrespective of the importance of the provision. Thus, the rules in the German and Italian Constitutions prescribing the colours of the national flag are part of constitutional law, although they could be regarded as in substance rather trivial. The test for what counts as constitutional law is, therefore, largely formal: is the rule contained in the text, or does it emerge from judicial decisions interpreting that document?

There is no such simple criterion for what counts as constitutional law in the United Kingdom. Any test has to be substantive rather than formal. We must first formulate some ideas about what types of rule or principle should count as constitutional *in substance* before determining

---

[7] See T. C. Grey, 'Constitutionalism: An Analytic Framework' in *Constitutionalism*, in J. R. Pennock and J. W. Chapman (eds.), Nomos XX (New York, 1979), 189.

[8] Constitutions may also provide for the enactment of constitutional laws, in France known as organic laws, to supplement their provisions. These laws also form part of constitutional law.

whether a particular provision or court decision belongs to constitutional law rather than some other branch of law. In theory this should not be too difficult. Rules concerning the allocation of powers between Parliament, the government, and the judges, the manner and procedures by which these powers are exercised, and the relationship between these institutions, are clearly constitutional. They are more fundamental than other laws in that without them no other laws could be made or enforced, and no disputes could be decided. United Kingdom constitutional law is, in short, primarily concerned with the structure and powers of government. Equally, the protection of individual liberties and rights, such as freedom of speech and freedom of the person from arbitrary arrest and search, is generally considered an aspect of constitutional law. This may be because these fundamental rights express certain basic values of the society, or it may be because they are closely connected with its constitutional structure. Freedom of speech, for instance, is closely linked to the right to vote for a democratically elected legislature. The guarantee of these individual rights is also an essential aspect of constitutionalism, the belief that the powers of government should be limited.

Whether other aspects of the law should be classified as constitutional is much more doubtful. Social rights, for example, rights to education, to adequate housing, and to a healthy environment, are not regarded as of constitutional importance in the United Kingdom.[9] Equally, it is unclear whether all of the Crown's residuary discretionary powers, known as prerogative powers, should really be regarded as aspects of the constitution.[10] Textbooks on constitutional law have generally mentioned the Crown's prerogative right to treasure trove, that is gold or silver for which no owner can be traced,[11] and the right to print, or authorize the printing of, copies of the Authorized Version of the Bible and the Book of Common Prayer. But it has been hard to regard these rights as constitutionally significant.

Moreover, there are some notorious grey areas: for example, how far should the membership and financing of political parties, the allocation of election broadcasts, and the treatment of politics and current affairs by the media be regarded as matters which might be regulated appropriately

[9] The South Africa Constitution 1996 is unusual in protecting a wide range of social rights.

[10] For the prerogative powers, see Ch. 6, sect. 2.

[11] The Treasure Act 1996 has replaced the Crown's prerogative right with statutory rights.

by constitutional law? These topics have a constitutional dimension, as they are closely connected with the election of Members of Parliament and the scrutiny of government. However, the political parties, particularly the Conservative Party, have generally argued that, as they are essentially private bodies, it would be wrong for the law to regulate their activities. The media are, to some extent, regulated by special statutes, which are rarely considered in the United Kingdom to be of constitutional importance.

Uncertainty about the contours of the constitution does not, however, affect only the contents of constitutional law books. It also affects the tone of public debate. Opponents of a particular Bill or other development often argue that it is of constitutional significance. Such claims may have the effect of raising the temperature of the debate; constitutional disputes tend to become particularly heated. The extension of the right to vote and the introduction of the secret ballot were controversial 100 years ago for this reason; conservatives resisting change argued that these developments altered the constitution. Now opponents of devolution to Scotland and Wales, and of United Kingdom participation in Economic and Monetary Union, make the same argument. The point is that in the absence of an authoritative text (or of a constitutional court with final authority to rule on its interpretation) it is often difficult to substantiate or repudiate claims that a development has constitutional significance, let alone to resolve its merits.

Conversely, in the absence of a codified constitution, it is very difficult for judges in the United Kingdom to rule plainly that government conduct is unconstitutional. Of course, under the fundamental principle of parliamentary sovereignty or legislative supremacy, discussed at length in Chapter 5, they have not been able to rule that an Act of Parliament is invalid. On the other hand, courts are prepared to hold executive action unlawful, if it is outside the powers conferred on the minister, government agency, or other administrative body by the relevant legislation. But in these circumstances, a court simply rules that the action is unlawful or unauthorized. It is unusual for judges to state that such conduct is unconstitutional. This reluctance may be attributable to a fear that use of the term would make the ruling more controversial. The effect of this reluctance is to make it more difficult in the United Kingdom than in other countries to see what are the principles of the constitution.

Even in those cases when there is a clear constitutional issue, judges prefer to minimize its significance. When, for instance, there was a challenge to the constitutionality of accession to the European Community in 1971, the Court of Appeal rejected it on the ground that it was no business of the courts to question how the Crown, in effect the government, exercised its prerogative power to enter into treaties, in this case the Treaty of Rome.[12] The decision was correct on traditional principles;[13] the point is, however, that the judges refused to consider the argument that accession to the Community entailed the surrender of parliamentary sovereignty. In a later case, involving an unsuccessful attempt to question the legality of ratification of the Maastricht Treaty, on the ground that it involved the transfer of power over foreign policy, the court considered the constitutional arguments exaggerated.[14] In the absence of a codified constitutional text, it was difficult for the English courts in these cases to do full justice to constitutional arguments about loss of sovereignty. In comparison, both the French Constitutional Council and the German Constitutional Court have reviewed at length the constitutionality of accession to the Maastricht Treaty.

Another example may be given of the judges' preference for avoiding constitutional issues when they can base their decision on other grounds. Towards the end of 1993, the Home Secretary announced that he would not exercise his power under the Criminal Justice Act 1988 to bring into effect the provisions of that legislation putting the scheme for compensating the victims of criminal injuries on a statutory basis; instead he introduced a cheaper scheme, acting under the authority of the Crown's non-statutory, common law or prerogative powers. In effect, by not implementing the statute and by introducing the alternative scheme, the executive was claiming a power to legislate, a breach of the principle of the separation of powers discussed in section 3 of this chapter. But the majority of the House of Lords preferred to decide the case on the basis of a well-established principle of administrative law that a minister should not abandon a discretionary power conferred on him by parliamentary enactment, in this case his power to bring into effect the more generous statutory scheme.[15]

The absence of a constitutional text is in short very significant. Political arguments may become exaggerated, while courts may be

---

[12] *Blackburn* v. *Attorney-General* [1971] 1 WLR 1047.   [13] See Ch. 7, sect. 4.
[14] *R* v. *Secretary of State for Foreign and Commonwealth Affairs, ex parte Rees-Mogg* [1994] QB 552. For the Treaty of Maastricht, see Ch. 4.
[15] *R* v. *Secretary of State for the Home Department, ex parte Fire Brigades Union* [1995] 2 AC 513. For further discussion, see Ch. 6, sect. 2(iv).

unable, or reluctant, to do justice to arguments of a genuinely constitutional character. In particular, they are understandably inclined to avoid these issues when they can decide the case on the basis of the interpretation of a statute or on the basis of the principles of administrative law. However understandable this caution may be, it makes it hard to formulate the principles of constitutional law in the United Kingdom. Certainly, it is more difficult than it is in other countries where the courts are required to give meaning to the provisions and principles set out in the text.

2. THE CHARACTER OF THE UNITED KINGDOM CONSTITUTION

According to Dicey, the United Kingdom has an unwritten, or partly unwritten, constitution.[16] That proposition is acceptable inasmuch as it is another way of stating that there is no single authoritative text. But it is quite inaccurate if it is taken to mean that there is no *written* constitutional law. For much of the constitution, and certainly all constitutional *law*, is written. There are in the first place many important statutes. They include the Bill of Rights 1689, enacted after the Glorious Revolution; it established the illegality of levying taxation without the consent of Parliament and curtailed other powers of the Crown. Other important statutes are the Act of Settlement 1701 which regulates the succession to the throne and guarantees the independence of the judiciary, the Parliament Acts 1911–49 which limit the legislative power of the House of Lords, and the European Communities Act 1972 which gives effect in the United Kingdom to Community law and which establishes its supremacy over domestic law. To this list should now be added the Human Rights Act 1998 and the enactments devolving power to Scotland and to Wales.

Secondly, of course, court decisions are written. There are for instance the great cases of the eighteenth century establishing that the Crown cannot issue general search warrants,[17] the recent ruling of the House of Lords to the effect that ministers may be in contempt of court if they do not comply with court orders,[18] and rulings on the scope of the Crown's non-statutory or prerogative powers.[19] Indeed, the funda-

---

[16] Dicey, 32.
[17] e.g., *Entick* v. *Carrington* (1765) 19 St. Tr. 1030; *Wilkes* v. *Wood* (1763) 19 St. Tr. 1153.
[18] *M* v. *Home Office* [1994] 1 AC 377.
[19] See Ch. 6, sect. 2(ii).

mental constitutional principle of parliamentary legislative supremacy has been gradually formulated and refined in judgments of the courts.

Perhaps the only unwritten parts of the constitution are conventions, that is the non-legal rules, for instance, obliging the Monarch to assent to Bills which have passed Parliament and requiring her in almost all circumstances to act on the advice of the government. (Constitutional conventions are discussed in section 4 of this chapter.) Even conventions may be expressed in writing, perhaps in the letters page of *The Times*. That happened in 1950 when there was a long correspondence, including a letter from George VI's Private Secretary, concerning the King's right to refuse a request from the Prime Minister to dissolve Parliament for a general election. But it is rare for conventions to be formulated clearly in a single authoritative text, equivalent to a statute or the judgment of a court.

The constitution is therefore very largely a written one. The point is that it is *uncodified*. It is a jumble of diffuse statutes and court rulings, supplemented by extra-legal conventions and practices. It has also been described as a *common law* constitution.[20] There is a connection between these two descriptions. The common law consists of court rulings, modified or partly replaced by statutory rules, which must then be interpreted by the courts. Under the common law constitution of the United Kingdom it is the courts, rather than a constitutional text, which lay down its fundamental principles, although these may in their turn be reformulated by statutes. This general statement is best exemplified by reference to the most fundamental of these principles, that of parliamentary legislative supremacy. This is a common law principle, as is evidenced by the number of court decisions upholding the unlimited right of Parliament to enact any legislation it likes. But what counts as parliamentary legislation has been modified by the Parliament Acts 1911–49 reducing the powers of the House of Lords. Further, the principle of legislative supremacy has been compromised by another statute, the European Communities Act 1972. According to the courts, that legislation indicates that European Community law should in some circumstances prevail over inconsistent statutes. It is appropriate to describe the uncodified arrangements in the United Kingdom as a common law constitution, because it is the courts which have hitherto permitted Parliament to legislate without restraint. The authority of Parliament rests on case law, rather than on any codified constitution.

[20] O. Dixon, 'The Common Law as an Ultimate Constitutional Foundation' (1957) 31 *Aust. LJ* 240; T. R. S. Allan, *Law, Liberty, and Justice* (Oxford, 1993), esp. ch. 1.

We saw in Chapter 1 how the constitution evolved from the political struggles of the seventeenth century between Crown and Commons which were resolved at the end of the century in favour of Parliament. The Bill of Rights of 1689 declared that the consent of Parliament was necessary to levy taxation and to keep an army during peace-time. Moreover, the Monarch lost his prerogative powers to suspend the application of parliamentary laws and to dispense individuals from obedience to them. This history explains in part why the constitution may also be described as *political*.[21] It emerged from a political conflict and represented a triumph for one side in that conflict. The role of politicians in determining the scope and application of the conventions of the constitution, crucial to its modern operation, adds credibility to this description. Finally, there is the obvious point that governments are almost invariably now drawn from the leading members of a single political party which, in normal circumstances, controls the passage of legislation through Parliament.

The constitution is therefore uncodified, common law, and political in character. It is also flexible, in the sense that even the most important laws can be amended or repealed by the ordinary legislative process. Finally, its *unitary* character should be mentioned. There is no legally binding division in the United Kingdom between the powers of a central federal parliament and government, and those of corresponding bodies with powers in, say, Scotland, Wales, and discrete English regions. The distinction between unitary and federal constitutions and the characteristics of devolution are considered further in Chapter 3, as is the constitutional position of local government. The rest of this chapter is devoted to three important features of the United Kingdom constitution: the fusion of powers, the role of constitutional conventions, and the residual character of civil liberties.

3. THE FUSION OF POWERS

As we saw in Chapter 1, Montesquieu based his famous doctrine of the separation of powers on his understanding of the contemporary eighteenth-century constitution in this country. He was also influenced by the writings of John Locke, and by Henry St John Bolingbroke, the Tory politician whom he had met when he visited London in 1729. But the separation of powers, at least as formulated by Montesquieu, has

[21] See V. Bogdanor, 'The Political Constitution' in his collected essays, *Politics and the Constitution* (Aldershot, 1996).

never really been taken seriously in the United Kingdom. Instead, one of the principal characteristics of the constitution is said to be the fusion of powers. Walter Bagehot wrote in a much quoted remark: 'the efficient secret of the English [*sic*] Constitution may be described as the close union, the nearly complete fusion, of the executive and legislative powers.'[22] What he meant was that the government, or executive, is drawn from members of the legislative body, mostly the House of Commons, to which it is responsible. Equally, the executive is able to secure the passage of its legislation in normal circumstances by the threat of its head, the Prime Minister, to dissolve Parliament and call a general election.

Certainly, the United Kingdom constitution does not recognize the pure theory of the separation of powers as it has traditionally been understood in France. Nor does it reflect the system of checks and balances incorporated in the Constitution of the United States, with, for example, Senate control of some executive and judicial appointments, and judicial review of legislation by the courts. In particular, as Bagehot emphasized, there is no separation of membership of the legislative and executive organs, as there is in both the United States and France. A provision in the Act of Settlement 1701 would have prevented persons holding offices under the Crown from sitting as Members of Parliament, and thereby have protected the House of Commons from Crown influence, but it was never implemented. During the eighteenth century the distinction was drawn between ministers who have been permitted to sit in the House and civil servants and other officers, e.g. of the armed forces, who are not. The current law is contained in the House of Commons Disqualification Act 1975 and the Ministerial and other Salaries Act 1975. A key provision of the former statute allows no more than ninety-five ministers to sit in the Commons. That is still about 15 per cent of its total membership; a significant proportion of Members of Parliament are also members of the executive.

On the other hand, there is a sharper separation of the judicial power. No full-time judge, whether High Court, circuit court, or stipendiary magistrate, may sit in the House of Commons, though the principle is compromised so far as the House of Lords is concerned. Law Lords may speak and vote on legislative measures, though under a strong constitutional convention no lay peer is entitled to sit with them when they consider appeals as the Appellate Committee of the House of Lords, in

---

[22] Bagehot, 65.

effect the supreme court of the United Kingdom. Perhaps of more significance is the role of the Lord Chancellor, who is Speaker of the House of Lords, a member of the Cabinet, and entitled to sit in the Appellate Committee of the Lords as a judge. He, therefore, participates in all three functions of government. His position constitutes a clear violation of that aspect of the separation of powers, requiring each function of government to be discharged by a distinct person or institution.

However, the apparently anomalous position of the Lord Chancellor is more comprehensible if it is seen as a legacy of a traditional understanding of the constitution popular in the seventeenth and eighteenth centuries.[23] Under the theory of balanced government, each part of government, at the time drawn from a distinct social class, was able to share in the performance of several functions. It was not confined to the performance of one of them. The most important illustration of this principle was that the Commons, Lords, and King all participated in the enactment of legislation. Equally the House of Lords enjoyed legislative and judicial power, as in certain contexts did the Commons. At the same time the King's executive powers, in particular to raise money or keep a standing army, needed the consent of the Houses of Parliament under the Bill of Rights 1689. The balance of the constitution, and the avoidance of arbitrary government, were under this theory ensured by the checks that each class, or branch, could impose on the others when they jointly exercised the same function. It was in a sense a forerunner of the formal separation of powers found in many modern constitutions, a separation which is legally enforceable by the courts with powers of constitutional judicial review.[24]

What has happened over the last century in the United Kingdom has been a growing imbalance between the branches of government, largely attributable to the rise of the mass political party system. First, neither the House of Lords nor the Monarch can be regarded as an effective check on the House of Commons. As will be explained in Chapter 5, the House of Lords has lost a significant part of its legislative power. The Crown's prerogative power to refuse assent to legislation enacted by Commons and Lords has been limited by the clear convention that Royal Assent must be given to a Bill which has passed through Parliament; the Monarch's power to exercise other important prerogatives may now be very limited.[25] During the eighteenth and nineteenth centuries there was a rough balance between the legislature and execu-

---

[23] See M. J. C. Vile, *Constitutionalism and the Separation of Powers* (Oxford, 1967).
[24] See Ch. 1, sects. 3 and 4.   [25] See Ch. 6, sects. 2 and 3.

tive, which gradually freed itself during these centuries from the King's control. The formation and survival of the executive (or government) depended increasingly on the support of the House of Commons rather than of the Monarch. In the middle of the nineteenth century in particular, governments often resigned because they were unable to command the shifting loyalties of Members of Parliament.

With increasing party discipline and the perception that the electorate votes for a party and its programme, the executive is normally able to control the legislature through the threat to dissolve Parliament and therefore hold a General Election. If the government is defeated on an important legislative measure, it can in effect reverse the defeat by tabling a vote of confidence in the House of Commons. That happened in July 1993 when the Conservative government lost its motion to bring the legislation incorporating the Maastricht European Union Treaty into effect. A number of Conservative dissidents hostile to the Maastricht Treaty voted with the Opposition. The Prime Minister, John Major, immediately tabled a vote of confidence which the government won comfortably, because the rebels were unwilling to precipitate an election at which many of them would almost certainly have lost their seats. The episode nicely illustrates the ability of the executive to control Parliament, even over matters of great political and constitutional controversy. The United Kingdom not only lacks a clear separation of legislative and executive institutions, but has lost the balance of powers which characterized the traditional constitution of the eighteenth and nineteenth centuries.

Apart from the judicial branch, there is therefore no strict separation of institutions in the United Kingdom. But there is to a limited extent a separation between the three *functions* of government. The government is not sharply separated from the legislature, and is now able normally to control it, but it must nevertheless use Parliament to enact general rules. The origins of this principle can be traced back to the early seventeenth century when, in the *Case of Proclamations*,[26] it was held that the King was not entitled to change the law by proclamation. (At much the same time it was also decided he could not sit in the courts.[27]) It would have infringed the separation of powers if the Monarch, then the effective head of the executive power, was able to legislate without recourse to Parliament. The provisions in the Bill of Rights 1689 which, among other things, outlawed the power of the Crown to impose

[26] (1611) 12 Co. Rep. 74.   [27] *Prohibitions del Roy* (1607) 12 Co. Rep. 63.

taxation without the consent of Parliament and its power to suspend legislation also illustrate the separation of functions. Any attempt by the executive to exercise these powers would amount to a trespass on the functions of the legislature.

The requirement that general rules be made by the legislature is an important one, even though the government controls the Parliamentary timetable, can secure the passage of its own measures, and may block any attempt by a back-bencher to introduce a Bill. The parliamentary process subjects legislation to public debate and scrutiny, and it affords the possibility of amendment under pressure from concerned individuals and interest groups. In this respect, the separation of powers principle reinforces an aspect of parliamentary legislative supremacy: the Crown cannot set itself up as a body with rival legislative powers.

However, the principle of the separation of functions is not always followed rigorously in the United Kingdom, or for that matter in other countries. Acts of Parliament and of, say, the United States Congress frequently delegate broad rule-making powers to the executive. Exceptionally wide powers are delegated in war-time and other emergency periods.[28] But even in normal circumstances ministers and executive agencies are given delegated legislative powers to supplement or fill in the details of statutes. Parliament may even give ministers power to make regulations which amend Acts of Parliament; these provisions are sometimes known as 'Henry VIII clauses' after the autocratic Tudor monarch.[29] Delegated legislation contravenes the strict separation of legislative and executive functions, but there are many practical arguments in favour of it: the difficulty of finding adequate Parliamentary time for the enactment of legislation, the need to avoid excessively detailed and complex legislation, and the flexibility which comes from the power of ministers to amend statutes. What is important is that there is provision for scrutiny of delegated legislation by Parliament. Regulations made by ministers are usually issued subject to annulment by resolution of either House of Parliament, but on occasion must be approved by affirmative resolutions of both. Further, the courts may review regulations to ensure that the executive has not exceeded its power to make delegated legislation.

The separation of functions is also blurred when judicial functions are given to administrative tribunals or authorities. For instance, decisions

---

[28] Ch. 9, sect. 2.
[29] For delegated legislation, see H. W. R. Wade and C. F. Forsyth, *Administrative Law* (7th edn., Oxford, 1994), ch. 22, and P. P. Craig, *Administrative Law* (3rd edn., London, 1994), ch. 7.

on entitlement to social security benefits are taken by specialist adjudication officers with appeal to a tribunal, while many decisions concerning immigrants are appealable to independent adjudicators and then to an Immigration Appeal Tribunal. Arguably these are judicial functions which belong to the courts, but there are practical arguments for assigning them to administrative tribunals. Such bodies generally adopt a more informal procedure than the ordinary courts; perhaps as a result, they are relatively inexpensive to both tax-payers and litigants. They develop an expertise within their particular area of competence. We will see in Chapter 7, however, that the judges are normally anxious to preserve their jurisdiction in civil liberties cases and to protect the right of individuals to challenge administrative decisions in the courts. They rightly consider it important to prevent the total usurpation of the judicial function by the executive, for that would be a significant step in the direction of arbitrary or totalitarian government.

The high-water mark of this aspect of the separation of powers principle came in a decision of the Privy Council, *Liyanage* v. *The Queen*,[30] discussed more fully in Chapter 7. After an unsuccessful coup the parliament of Ceylon (now Sri Lanka) enacted legislation specifically to deal with the chief participants; among other things it retrospectively created new offences, instituted a special tribunal to try them, and altered the normal rules of evidence. The Privy Council held these provisions violated the separation of powers principle, which was implicit in the structure of the constitution of Ceylon. *Liyanage* was a Privy Council decision, and so it is not binding on the English and Scottish courts when they decide a point of constitutional law. Strict application of the principle of parliamentary legislative supremacy would probably require an English court to enforce the most monstrous retrospective legislation, including a measure akin to that struck down in *Liyanage*.[31]

It is in fact hard to reconcile the legislative supremacy of Parliament with any strong commitment to the separation of powers principle. For that reason it is difficult to take too seriously Lord Diplock's view that the constitution is based on it.[32] At most it is a principle which has influenced aspects of the United Kingdom constitution, in particular the independence of the judiciary. In contrast to other countries, notably the

---

[30] [1967] AC 259.
[31] See Allan, n. 20 above, ch. 3, for the view that English courts should disallow legislation which usurps the judicial power.
[32] *Duport Steels* v. *Sirs* [1980] 1 WLR 142. Sir John Donaldson has described the principle as a constitutional convention: *R* v. *HM Treasury, ex parte Smedley* [1985] QB 657.

United States, it would be hard to conclude that the separation principle has exercised a decisive influence on the development of the constitution in general or on the treatment of major constitutional cases. If, as was argued in Chapter 1, the separation of powers is a fundamental principle of a liberal constitution, its weak status in the United Kingdom brings out much of what is inadequate in the present arrangements—their failure to impose significant checks on the conduct of government.

4. CONSTITUTIONAL CONVENTIONS

One prominent characteristic of the United Kingdom constitution is the role played by conventions. These rules, sometimes known as 'rules of constitutional morality', create powers and impose obligations which are not legally enforceable, but which are regarded as binding. It is improper, in a sense unconstitutional, to violate a convention, though it is not illegal. The most important conventions in the United Kingdom limit the legal powers of the Monarch and regulate the relationship of the government to Parliament; they are crucial to the modern constitution.

Conventions may be found in other constitutions. For example, under Article II of the US Constitution the President and Vice-President are chosen by a college, comprising Electors from each state; the number of these Electors reflect each state's size. By convention, however, the President and Vice-President are elected by popular vote, the Electors automatically casting their vote in the electoral college for the candidates who win the election in that state. Another important convention forbade a President from serving more than two terms of four years each, but after its breach by Roosevelt in 1940 the rule became law by a formal Amendment to the Constitution. Similarly there are some important conventions in France, particularly concerning the division of authority between the President of the Republic and the Prime Minister when they come from different political parties. The text of the Constitution of 1958 does not make plain, for example, whether it is for the President or the Prime Minister to determine foreign policy. But it was agreed in 1986-8 during the period of 'cohabitation', as it was termed, between President Mitterrand (nominally) a Socialist, and Chirac, his Gaullist Prime Minister, that the President had responsibility for the broad direction of foreign policy; Mitterrand was therefore able to veto the appointment of a Foreign Minister, although the

Constitution provides that the President appoints ministers on the recommendation of the Prime Minister.[33]

Dicey went so far as to claim that conventions were as important to the United States Constitution as they were to the English.[34] Whatever its merits at the end of the nineteenth century, that view is quite implausible now. A student conversant with the text of the United States Constitution, and the decisions of the Supreme Court in Washington interpreting it, would have a reasonable, if incomplete, idea of how it works in practice. This is even more true of the German Constitution, where the notion of constitutional conventions is virtually unknown. All constitutional questions are in principle questions of law for resolution by the Constitutional Court. In both these systems there is some correspondence between the scope of constitutional law and the operation of the constitution in daily life.

In contrast, an equally knowledgeable observer of United Kingdom constitutional *law*, but ignorant of its conventions, would be totally at sea. He would, for instance, believe that the Queen has unfettered discretionary power to give or refuse Royal Assent to legislation after its passage through Parliament, and also that she has a free choice in deciding whom to invite to form a government. Nor would he know anything about the significance of a vote by the House of Commons of no confidence in the government (a matter covered by the text of both the French and German Constitutions[35]). In terms of strict constitutional law the Monarch does have discretion to refuse Royal Assent and choose the Prime Minister, while the law says nothing about the responsibility of government and ministers to the House of Commons.

But all these matters are to a greater or lesser extent regulated by constitutional conventions, which, to use Sir Ivor Jennings's graphic description, 'provide the flesh which clothes the dry bones of the law'.[36] Some of them are as well-established and as clear as any rule of law. For instance, the convention requiring the Crown to assent to measures passed by both Houses of Parliament has evolved over the last 200 or 300 years since the Assent was last refused by Queen Anne in 1707. Others are less firmly established. For instance, there is now in most circumstances a clear convention requiring the Monarch to appoint as Prime Minister the person chosen by the majority party as its leader under its current rules. It is, however, of recent origin; also it is unclear

---

[33] Art. 8. See Bell, 58–62.   [34] Dicey, 28–9. Also see Wheare, ch. 8.
[35] Constitution of 1958, Arts. 49–50; German Basic Law, Arts. 67–8.
[36] *The Law and the Constitution* (5th edn., London, 1959), 81.

how it would apply in the unusual circumstances of a hung Parliament where no party had a clear majority. Further, there is real controversy about the scope of the convention requiring the Crown to dissolve Parliament at the request of the Prime Minister.[37]

What then are constitutional conventions and what is their relationship to constitutional law? And to pose a less familiar question: is it good that they play such an important role in the constitution? Monographs on constitutional law offer a variety of definitions, but broadly they can be described as non-legal rules stating the powers and obligations of the branches of government, in particular the executive, and their relations with each other. Thus, a number of conventions impose obligations on the Monarch, for example, as already mentioned, to assent to legislation, to choose the leader of the majority party in the Commons as her Prime Minister (at least in most circumstances), and generally to act on his and other ministers' advice.

Other conventions are concerned with the working of the Cabinet, but these are now less clear. The principles of collective Cabinet responsibility, under which all its members must observe the confidentiality of Cabinet discussions and support its decisions, are regarded as constitutional conventions. But Prime Ministers now claim a power to dispense with the requirement of Cabinet solidarity in certain circumstances, and this may have reformulated the convention. This power was illustrated by the Labour Cabinet's agreement to disagree in 1975 over the question whether it was right to stay in the European Community; Harold Wilson gave Cabinet ministers freedom to campaign in the referendum for withdrawal from the Community against the majority decision. The new convention, if that is what it is, was formulated by James Callaghan in 1977 when, as Prime Minister, he tolerated similar dissent with regard to passage of the European Assembly Elections Bill: the doctrine of collective responsibility applied 'except in cases where I announce that it does not'.

According to the Supreme Court of Canada, the purpose of conventions is 'to ensure that the legal framework of the Constitution will be operated in accordance with the prevailing constitutional values or principles of the period', in particular the democratic principle of responsible government.[38] For many of the legal rules of the constitution, particularly those concerned with the fundamental discretionary powers

---

[37] For further discussion of these important political conventions, see Ch. 6, sects. 2 and 3.
[38] *Reference re Amendment of the Constitution of Canada* (1982) 125 DLR (3d.) 1, 84.

still in law exercisable by the Monarch personally, have been fossilized since the constitutional settlement of 1689. United Kingdom constitutional law says very little about the Prime Minister and Cabinet. A crucial role of constitutional conventions is, therefore, to limit the vast powers of the Monarch; they also recognize the status of the Prime Minister and other ministers when they impose an obligation on the Monarch to exercise these powers on their advice. This general obligation to act on ministerial advice constitutes perhaps the most important constitutional convention. The conventions of collective and individual ministerial responsibility enforce the accountability of government to the elected legislature, a central principle of a liberal democracy.[39]

In other countries conventions provide an informal method of constitutional amendment. This is important where it is difficult to amend, because it is necessary, say, to obtain the approval of the people by referendum, or in a federal constitution the consent of a large majority of the states. That may partly explain why the development of conventions has not occurred in Germany; the Basic Law is relatively easy to alter and amendments have been made frequently. Conversely, though the United Kingdom constitutional arrangements are flexible in theory, the basic legal structure has rarely been amended by statute over the last 300 years. (Only two or three statutes, the Parliament Acts 1911 and 1949 and the European Communities Act 1972, have brought about radical constitutional reform, though the measure devolving legislative and executive power to Scotland may prove to be equally significant.) The gradual change effected by the constitutional conventions mentioned in the previous paragraphs has been much more important in altering the balance of power between Crown, ministers, and legislature.

There is a lot of argument about how conventions are created or arise. Unlike rules of law they are not instituted by the legislature or the courts. A practice of compliance with the rule is often important, as it creates a series of precedents on which reliance can be placed. If a convention has been observed, and accepted as binding, over a long period, it is hard to dispute its existence. The reason we can speak with confidence of the constitutional duty of the Crown to assent to Bills is that the Royal Assent has not been refused since 1707; in normal circumstances everyone accepts it as a rule of the constitution.[40] But precedent is neither necessary nor sufficient. It is unnecessary, because conventions may arise simply from the agreement of those affected by the rule.

---

[39] See Ch. 6, sect. 4.   [40] But see Ch. 6, sect. 2(ii).

This is illustrated by the Balfour Declaration of 1926, which established the convention that the Westminster Parliament could not legislate for Canada, Australia, and the other Dominions of the Empire without their consent. (The convention was subsequently incorporated in the Statute of Westminster 1931.) More importantly, practice alone is not enough. A convention arises only when its content is accepted as a binding rule by the institution affected, for example, the Monarch or members of the Cabinet or government. This point is fundamental. Conventions must be distinguished from mere practices or usages which are only adopted out of habit. Finally, Sir Ivor Jennings argued that a convention must be supported by reason, in the rather limited sense that it must accord with contemporary political philosophy.[41] That perhaps was rather a posh way of making the point that a convention which does not fit contemporary attitudes is unlikely to be accepted as a binding standard. Like other legal rules, the terms of a constitution may survive in force even when they no longer enjoy public support; in contrast, a convention which becomes outdated can no longer be regarded as part of the constitution.

Much the most interesting question for a constitutional lawyer is the relationship of conventions to law. Dicey sharply distinguished them. Constitutional conventions are not laws, because the courts can not enforce them. This view is broadly right.[42] It has been supported by the Canadian Supreme Court.[43] It is inconceivable, for example, that the courts would issue an order to enforce the Monarch's duty to assent to Bills or a government's obligation to resign after defeat on a confidence motion. Conventions are enforceable politically, either by Parliament or by public opinion. For instance, if the Monarch persistently failed to take her ministers' advice and insisted on exercising her legal powers, steps would be taken to curtail them by statute.

Though not directly enforceable, conventions may have some legal significance. The courts may use them as a foundation for a principle of common law. That was what happened in the *Crossman Diaries* case,[44] when Lord Widgery CJ considered whether to grant an injunction to restrain publication of a former Cabinet Minister's diaries. He held that the remedy would be appropriate when publication amounted to a breach of confidence. The relationships of confidence between members

---

[41] N. 36 above, 136.
[42] C. R. Munro, 'Law and Conventions Distinguished' (1975) 91 *LQR* 218.
[43] *Reference re Amendment of the Constitution of Canada* (1982) 125 DLR (3d.) 1, 87.
[44] *Att.-Gen.* v. *Jonathan Cape Ltd.* [1976] QB 752.

of the Cabinet arose under the convention of collective Cabinet respon-sibility. The courts are also competent to determine whether a conven-tion exists, at least when this jurisdiction is expressly conferred by statute. On that basis a majority of the Canadian Supreme Court held that there was a convention requiring the consent of the Provinces before the federal parliament presented proposals to the United Kingdom Parliament to amend the British North America Act 1867, then the Canadian Constitution. This ruling was more significant than the Court's decision that the consent of the Provinces was not required as a matter of constitutional law; in the light of this decision, the Canadian government accepted an obligation to seek the Provinces' approval before proceeding with its constitutional reform.

Does it matter that conventions play such an enormous part in the working of the United Kingdom constitution? Commentators such as Sir Ivor Jennings have tended to emphasize their role in bringing the constitution up to date with contemporary political values. Against the background of fossilized legal rules their role is wholly beneficial. But it is also sensible to ask whether there are disadvantages to reliance on con-ventions, compared to the adoption of a codified constitution and its periodic amendment. One point is that they are frequently vague. This is particularly true of the major conventions of collective and individual ministerial responsibility.[45] As will be argued in Chapter 6, they have become so unclear that it is hard to determine how far they really exist in any significant sense. The weakness of these conventions, if not of those regulating the Monarch's discretionary powers, is that they are not enforceable. Nor are the courts generally able to determine their scope or their application to a particular set of circumstances; the *Crossman Diaries* case was exceptional in this respect. Instead, these questions are decided by politicians and political parties, as James Callaghan cheer-fully claimed when, as Prime Minister, he reformulated the principle of collective responsibility.

The central part played by conventions in the constitutional arrange-ments of the United Kingdom indicates a preference for self-regulation by governments and politicians over a system of legal checks and balances enforceable by the courts, which is much more characteristic of modern codified liberal constitutions. That conventions are so important to the working of the constitution in the United Kingdom should occasion no surprise. They are an integral aspect of the 'political' constitution.

[45] G. Marshall, *Constitutional Conventions* (Oxford, 1984), 211–12.

5. CIVIL LIBERTIES AND THE CONSTITUTION

A prominent characteristic of liberal constitutions, already mentioned in Chapter 1, is that they recognize that individuals have basic rights which the state must respect. In some constitutions courts are explicitly required to hold legislation and executive decisions and acts invalid if they infringe these rights.[46] In contrast, in the United States judicial review to protect fundamental rights has been developed by the Supreme Court without a clear mandate to do this in the text of the Constitution. Its decisions striking down legislation for violation of the Bill of Rights have sometimes been criticized on the ground that it is undemocratic for judges to interfere with the will of the elected legislature.

The constitutional position in the United Kingdom has been completely different. As we will see towards the end of the chapter, it is now changing with the incorporation into its law of the European Convention on Human Rights (ECHR) by the Human Rights Act 1998. Hitherto the rights of individuals have not been set out in any code or Bill of Rights, let alone a full codified constitution. Some rights against sexual and racial discrimination are admittedly protected by statutes: the Equal Pay Act 1970, the Sex Discrimination Act 1975, and the Race Relations Act 1976. But the vast majority of the fundamental rights normally found in a constitution (or international human rights treaty) have never been explicitly guaranteed in English or Scots law until the enactment of the Human Rights Act 1998. People have been simply free to do those things which have not been prohibited or restricted by the law, whether statute or common law. For example, freedom of speech is the right to say or write anything not forbidden by the common law of libel, blasphemy, and other rules, or by legislation such as the Official Secrets Act 1989 and the Obscene Publications Act 1959. No law proclaims a right of personal freedom from arbitrary arrest or a right not to have one's property searched and taken without good reason. These freedoms exist only because the Police and Criminal Evidence Act 1984 and other statutes have not granted the police unlimited powers of arrest and search and impose certain conditions and restrictions on what they may do in the investigation of crime.

That is why civil liberties in the United Kingdom have been described as 'residual', the rights left over for individuals to enjoy when

---

[46] German Basic Law, Art. 1(3).

statute and common law no longer apply. In the absence of a constitutional or statutory code, civil liberties are at best formulated by judges when they decide, say, a case on the scope of the police powers of arrest or a prosecution under the Obscene Publications legislation; but the legal argument will be about the scope of the statutory or common law power limiting the liberty, rather than about what the liberty should cover. But courts do now sometimes refer to freedom of speech, the freedom of public protest, and other freedoms as valuable rights which should not be restricted, unless at least it is clear that is what the statute means.[47]

Until the last twenty years or so there has been general satisfaction with this position. Dicey even thought it was much better to protect freedom by the common law rather than trust to the guarantees afforded by written constitutions. While the latter could always be suspended during an emergency,[48] English judges, he claimed, could be relied on to protect freedom by effective remedies.[49] It was for the courts to rule on the meaning of Acts of Parliament, so they could ensure that legislation did not interfere inappropriately with personal freedom.

However, it has been the case that the courts may not question legislation which clearly restricts, or authorizes the restriction of, civil liberties. Under the principle of parliamentary supremacy, they may not accept an argument that legislation should not be applied, or is invalid, because it infringes a fundamental right. There is, in short, no constitutional judicial review in the United Kingdom, comparable to the powers exercised, say, by the United States Supreme Court or the German Constitutional Court. Instead of a legal check on Parliament, reliance is placed on political argument and public opinion to act as restraints on any temptation felt by ministers and Members of Parliament to enact oppressive legislation. This is another aspect of the political character of the United Kingdom constitution, to which attention has frequently been drawn in this chapter.

We discussed in Chapter 1 whether judicial review to protect fundamental rights could be reconciled with majoritarian democracy or whether it was better to conclude that democracy should give way to the values of liberal constitutionalism. But even leaving aside this question, the view of civil liberties as essentially residual suffers from some

---

[47] One notable example is the decision of the Lords in *Cozens* v. *Brutus* [1973] AC 854, giving a narrow interpretation to the word 'insulting' in the public order legislation in order to preserve the right to peaceful protest.
[48] See Ch. 9.   [49] Dicey, 195–203.

weaknesses. If everyone is free to do whatever the law does not prohibit, it means that, in the absence of any legislation on a matter, the government may be free to do whatever it likes irrespective of the impact on individuals.[50] The implications of this position emerged in *Malone* v. *Metropolitan Police Commissioner*, where the plaintiff claimed an injunction to stop telephone tapping on the warrant of the Home Secretary.[51] As there is no common law right to privacy, and at that time no statute regulating telephone tapping, the judge was unable to stop the practice. (The gap in the law was subsequently remedied by the Interception of Communications Act 1985, enacted after the European Court of Human Rights had found the United Kingdom in breach of Article 8 of the ECHR for interfering with the plaintiff's right to respect for his private life.[52])

A more important point is that, as civil liberties are merely residual, courts in the United Kingdom have not been able to use them to redress government or parliamentary inaction. For instance, no English court could compel Parliament to enact non-discrimination legislation, or to strengthen it, with a decision that the existing common law or statutory provisions failed to comply with the constitution's provision of a right to equality or its prohibition of discrimination. Courts can take this step only where the constitution sets out basic rights, for example, to freedom of speech or to equal protection of the laws. Under these constitutions judicial decisions may act as a spur to legislation or executive action, as well as checking it when it violates civil liberties. That happened in the United States, when the Supreme Court ruled that school segregation violated the rights of blacks to equal protection, and that the southern states should take steps to achieve racial integration in their schools;[53] this and other Court decisions prompted the introduction of modern civil rights legislation. A ruling of this sort is possible only when rights are guaranteed by the constitution itself; it cannot be taken on the common law approach to civil liberties.

Much of this may now change with the incorporation into the United Kingdom constitution of the European Human Rights Convention by the Human Rights Act 1998. The ECHR is a treaty of the Council of Europe, under which states undertake to respect the rights and freedoms

---

[50] This proposition is not true of local authorities and other statutory bodies, which may only exercise those powers Parliament has conferred on them: see A. Le Sueur and M. Sunkin, *Public Law* (London, 1997), 169–71.

[51] [1979] Ch. 344.   [52] *Malone* v. *United Kingdom* (1985) 7 EHRR 14.

[53] *Brown* v. *Board of Education*, 347 US 483 (1954).

set out in the Convention. What is most distinctive about it is that individuals are entitled to bring an application against a state before the Human Rights Commission in Strasbourg if they consider that, say, the United Kingdom legislation or a court decision violates their rights under the Convention. The case may be referred to the European Court of Human Rights. (The Commission and Court will soon be merged, so that it will be possible for an application to be made directly to the Court.) A finding by the Human Rights Court of a violation of a right under the Convention places the state concerned under a duty to amend its law. For example, after a ruling of the Strasbourg judges that the English rules of contempt of court unnecessarily restricted press freedom, guaranteed by Article 10 of the ECHR,[54] the Contempt of Court Act 1981 relaxed the constraints previously imposed on the media by those rules.

What has been unsatisfactory is that individuals have been able to have their rights protected by the European Court of Human Rights, in circumstances where judges in the United Kingdom have been unable to help them because they are constitutionally required under the principle of parliamentary supremacy to apply legislation which curtails them. If judicial review by constitutional courts is wrong in principle, then it would have been logical to withdraw from the Convention altogether. It made no sense at all to deny English judges the power of judicial review to protect human rights, but then to permit the disappointed individual to apply to Strasbourg, a process which was time-consuming and expensive.

The Labour government elected in 1997 decided to incorporate the ECHR into United Kingdom law, so that the courts in this country could more effectively protect the rights guaranteed in it. Under the Human Rights Act 1998 it is unlawful for any public authority to act incompatibly with the Convention rights. Legislation must be interpreted, so far as possible, to be compatible with the ECHR. But the government decided against giving the courts authority to declare legislation (whether past or future) invalid or inapplicable because it violates the Convention. That full power of judicial review would be inconsistent with parliamentary sovereignty.[55] The courts are only entitled formally to declare that a legislative provision is incompatible with the Convention, and it is then for the government to make an Order amending

---

[54] *Sunday Times* v. *United Kingdom* (1979) 2 EHRR 245.
[55] White Paper, *Rights brought Home: The Human Rights Bill* (1997) Cm 3782, paras. 2.9–2.15.

the legislation to bring it into line with the Convention. It is odd, incidentally, that a government so committed to parliamentary supremacy should introduce legislation giving it (and its successors) power to amend legislation impinging on human rights by ministerial Order.

This reform certainly represents an improvement on the previous position. Some litigants will be spared the need to go to Strasbourg to secure human rights. But the result of the compromise outlined in the previous paragraph is that legislation violating human rights may remain in force, unless the government is prepared to take steps to put the matter right by making an amending Order. One may expect this to be done speedily in the vast majority of cases, but that forecast might prove too optimistic. If a court ruling holds that legislation violates the Convention rights of, say, political radicals, religious or sexual minorities, or prisoners, government may be in no hurry to amend it, and there will be little public pressure on it to do so. The reliance on government to put things right shows again the political character of the United Kingdom constitution. Politicians rather than courts have the last word on human rights questions.

3

Federalism and Devolution

1. INTRODUCTION

THE United Kingdom has a unitary, rather than a federal, constitution. Since the Act of Union with Scotland 1707, legislative and executive authority has been concentrated in the Westminster Parliament and the government in London. That has remained the position until the introduction of the devolution measures by the Labour government elected in 1997. Considerable legislative power is now to be devolved to the Scottish Parliament, while an Assembly for Wales is to take over the executive responsibilities hitherto discharged by the Secretary of State. Devolution measures were enacted in 1998. Radical though these changes are, they do not in theory affect the unitary character of the constitution. As a matter of constitutional law, the Westminster Parliament remains free to repeal the legislation setting up Scotland's Parliament or to enact a measure which falls within the latter's area of competence.[1]

Local authorities in England and Wales, Scotland, and Northern Ireland enjoy a wide range of powers, including the authority to make by-laws, a type of subordinate legislation, but these powers are conferred by statutes of the Westminster Parliament and can easily be removed by it. Indeed, as we will see in section 4 of this chapter, local authorities themselves have been abolished by statute. In other words, they enjoy no independent constitutional status in the United Kingdom. That was also true of the Northern Ireland Parliament (the Stormont Parliament), which from 1920 until 1972 enjoyed substantial delegated powers to enact laws for Northern Ireland. Following the onset of civil unrest the Westminster Parliament suspended that authority in 1972; since then Ulster has been governed almost continuously by direct rule through the Secretary of State for Northern Ireland.

These arrangements should be contrasted with federal constitutions, which distribute power between central (or federal) legislatures and

[1] For further discussion of these points, see sect. 3.

governments on the one hand, and state (or provincial) authorities on the other. Neither the federal nor a state authority may trespass into the legislative or executive competence of the other; moreover, unlike the Westminster Parliament, a federal or central Parliament is not free unilaterally to strip the states of their powers under the constitution. The following section of this chapter outlines the main features of federal constitutions, and discusses their advantages and disadvantages. Few people in the United Kingdom, in particular in England, know much about federalism, let alone have any enthusiasm for it. But we should be aware of its principal characteristics, partly so we are in a position to evaluate properly the claim that the European Union already has, or is moving inexorably towards, a federal constitution.[2] A greater awareness of the principal features and merits of federalism might perhaps lessen the anxiety felt about such constitutional developments in Europe. Moreover, an appreciation of these characteristics should increase understanding of the constitutional implications of the devolution of power to Scotland and Wales. Devolution bears some resemblance to federalism, but from a legal point of view the differences are significant.

2. FEDERALISM

The best known federal constitution is that of the United States of America, so a short exposition of its origins and some of its principal features makes a good introduction to the topic. After the War of Independence, the newly independent states adopted the Articles of Confederation, the first American constitution, in force from 1781 to 1788. It made no provision for a central government or judiciary; the Continental Congress, consisting of delegates from the states such as Massachusetts and Virginia, had some legislative power over the states, but no authority to impose taxes or to regulate commerce between the states. Moreover, it had no legislative authority over individuals in the states. Article II declared that each state kept its sovereignty and independence. Moreover, changes to the Articles of Confederation had to be approved by all thirteen state legislatures.

The Continental Congress was too weak to resolve conflicts over boundaries, trade, and tariffs. Many states printed their own currency. There were even occasional military skirmishes. Eventually, at the

---

[2] See Ch. 4, sect. 4.

prompting of James Madison and Alexander Hamilton,[3] a convention was gathered of delegates from all the states to consider reform of these unsatisfactory arrangements. The Constitutional Congress in Philadelphia drafted the Federal Constitution, which under its own terms (Article VII) came into force when it had been ratified by conventions held in nine states. The principal object of the new Constitution was to strengthen power at the centre, principally by the establishment of a federal Congress with broad legislative powers, including the power to tax and impose other obligations on individuals, and to regulate inter-state commerce. It also provided for the election of a President with significant executive powers, and the institution of the United States Supreme Court.

Two provisions of the new Constitution are of particular importance. Article VI, known as the Supremacy Clause, establishes the supremacy of the Constitution, laws, and treaties of the United States over state constitutions and laws. State judges are expressly required by the Clause to apply the federal Constitution and laws in their courts, whatever the state constitution and laws provide. When, therefore, an Act of Congress grants rights or imposes duties directly on the citizens of the states, the Supremacy Clause requires judges in the states to enforce it, notwithstanding any inconsistent provision in state law. (There is now a similar principle in the constitutional law of the European Community; some rules of Community law have supremacy over inconsistent national law.[4]) In the United States the institution of federal courts, with a right of appeal to the Supreme Court established by Article III of the Constitution, further helped to secure the effective supremacy of federal law.

Secondly, Article V provides for amendments to the Constitution to come into force when proposals have been ratified by three-quarters of the states. The only qualification is that each state may veto an amendment to deprive it of its equal representation in the Senate, the branch of Congress which represents the states. Constitutional amendment is therefore difficult. But it may be achieved without the unanimous consent of the states, a significant difference from the requirement in the Articles of Confederation.

The US Constitution was drafted to bring closer together the 'People of the United States'.[5] Integration is often a function of federations

---

[3] They are, with John Jay, the authors of the *Federalist Papers*, an explanation and defence of the draft federalist constitution.

[4] See Ch. 4, sect. 3, and Ch. 5, sect. 3.

[5] Preamble to the Constitution. By contrast, the Treaties of Rome and Maastricht refer to the 'Peoples [plural] of Europe', while the European Parliament consists of

where some degree of union, rather than complete political and legal unity, is desired: the federal Swiss Constitution and the German Constitution of 1871 provide other examples. These constitutions strengthened the powers of the central or federal Parliament and government at the expense of previously more powerful bodies in the Cantons or states. Equally, in the other direction, federal constitutions (or constitutions with some federal characteristics) may be adopted to loosen the grip of central power in countries which have previously had unitary constitutions. That has recently happened in Belgium and Spain, where a measure of constitutional autonomy has been granted to particular communities (Flemish, Walloon, Basque, Catalan) without the dissolution of those countries into separate independent states. Clearly, any eventual European Union federal constitution would belong to the first group of integrating constitutions, while a federal constitution of the second type might conceivably result from the devolution of power to Scotland and Wales.

What is common to both types of federal constitution is the distribution of legal power between central or federal authorities and a number of state (or regional) institutions. Put simply, the intention is to avoid a concentration of power. Before developing this idea, it would be useful to mention some standard aspects of federal constitutions, almost all of which are found in the United States Constitution.[6] The Constitution divides legislative authority between the federation and the states (or provinces or regions). Neither federation nor states are legally supreme or sovereign, as the Westminster Parliament is in the United Kingdom. It is quite impossible to locate legal supremacy anywhere, for both federal and state institutions must act in accordance with the constitution. The term 'sovereign' is indeed not to be found in the text of the US Constitution; it belongs perhaps to the people of the United States who established it in the conventions held in the states to ratify the Philadelphia draft.[7]

Normally a federal constitution prescribes the powers given to the federation, while the states retain all residual powers. For example, the German Basic Law provides that the *Länder* (states) such as Bavaria and Hesse have the right to legislate in so far as it does not confer legisla-

---

'representatives of the peoples of the States brought together in the Community . . .': Art. 137 of the Treaty of Rome.

[6] See G. Sawyer, *Modern Federalism* (Carlton, Vic., 1976) for a comprehensive treatment of this topic.

[7] See A. R. Amar, 'Of Sovereignty and Federalism', 96 *Yale LJ* 1425 (1987).

tive power on the Federation.[8] The Canadian Constitution Act 1867 (formerly known as the British North America Act) is much less typical in that it gives general law-making power to the Federal Parliament, assigning competence to legislate only on specified matters to the Provinces.[9] It is standard for some important powers to be reserved for the federal authorities, in particular the conduct of defence and foreign affairs, the raising of income and other taxes, the regulation of inter-state commerce, and the printing of currency. It would be usual now to add environmental protection, transport, and immigration control to this list. The interests of the states or regions are often protected politically by their representation in a Second Chamber or Senate. This is the case, for instance, in the USA, Australia, and Germany. In the first two countries, each state, whatever its populaion, is represented in the Senate by an equal number of directly elected representatives. In contrast, the German Federal Council (Bundesrat) is composed of members of the states' (*Länder*) governments; the more populous states have more votes in the Council than those with fewer inhabitants.[10]

Another common feature is that disputes between the central and regional institutions about their respective legislative and other competences are resolved by a supreme or constitutional court. Judicial review of the constitutionality of legislation may also be a feature of those unitary constitutions such as those of France or Italy, where a court may intervene to adjudicate separation of powers disputes between the legislature and the executive or to protect fundamental rights. But judicial review is not essential for the effective working of a unitary constitution; further, as we saw in Chapter 1, the practice may be considered wrong in principle, on the ground that it is counter to majoritarian democracy. In a federal constitution, on the other hand, courts must be able to strike down *state* legislation for infringing the competence of the central government; otherwise federal law would apply in some states, but not in those others where inconsistent state legislation had been enacted. In a famous aphorism, Oliver Holmes, one of the greatest American judges, wrote:[11]

---

[8] Art. 70(1). Also see Art. 30: '[t]he exercise of governmental powers and the discharge of governmental functions shall be incumbent on the *Länder* in so far as this Basic Law does not otherwise prescribe or permit.'

[9] Ss. 91-2.

[10] Basic Law, Art. 51. The delegates of each *Land* must vote as a block (see Art. 51(3)), which means that the Bundesrat will be in opposition to the Bundestag if the governments of a majority of the, or of the more populous, *Länder* have a different political composition from that of the federal government.

[11] *Collected Legal Papers* (London, 1920), 295.

I do not think the United States would come to an end if we lost our power to declare an Act of Congress void. I do think the Union would be imperiled if we could not make that declaration as to the laws of the several States.

As we have seen, the Supremacy Clause of Article VI provides a firm basis in the Constitution for the supremacy of federal over state law; the courts must hold the latter invalid when it conflicts with the federal rule.[12]

However, judicial review of *federal* legislation on the ground that it infringes the competence of the states or regions may not be so essential. The Swiss Federal Tribunal reviews the constitutionality of Cantonal, but not federal, legislation. In the last twenty years, the United States Supreme Court has sometimes been reluctant to entertain challenges to Congressional statutes on federalism grounds. In one case the Court, by a majority of five to four judges, rejected a challenge by a state public transit authority to the application to its employees of a federal statute regulating minimum wages and other work conditions.[13] The main ground for the Court's decision was that the States should protect their interests through the political process, in particular their representatives in the Senate. However, recently the Court has invalidated an Act of Congress which made it an offence to possess a gun within 1,000 feet of school premises. The measure bore no relation to the power of Congress to regulate inter-state commerce; moreover, it interfered with the traditional responsibility of the states over education and schools.[14] While the United States Supreme Court has fluctuated in its approach to the review of federal laws, the German Constitutional Court has generally had little hesitation in striking them down when they exceed the powers conferred by the Basic Law on the Bundestag.[15]

Federal constitutions in fact vary considerably. They differ in their allocation of particular powers to the federation and the states, and in the extent to which the courts are prepared to control federal laws. Moreover, it would be wrong to conclude that they establish a rigid boundary between the fields of competence belonging to federal and state authorities, the system sometimes termed 'dual federalism' to refer to a strict division of powers. The position is almost always much more flexible than that. Under the United States Constitution, for example,

---

[12] German Basic Law, Art. 31 provides for the supremacy of federal law.
[13] *Garcia* v. *San Antonio Metropolitan Authority*, 469 US 528 (1985).
[14] *United States* v. *Lopez*, 115 S Ct. 1624 (1995).
[15] e.g. the Court struck down a federal order instituting a national television channel, since cultural matters are reserved for the *Länder*: 12 BVerfGE 205 (1961).

the states may be free to legislate even in an area where Congress has power, unless this is specifically forbidden by the terms of the Constitution or unless state legislation would affect inter-state commerce.[16] Under the German Basic Law, the federation and the *Länder* have concurrent authority to legislate on a vast range of matters; the entitlement of the states lapses only when, and to the extent that, the Bundestag has exercised its right to legislate on the matter.[17] In both these countries, and in other federations, the system is broadly one of 'co-operative federalism' under which the federal government may in some circumstances allow the states to act on their own, or may authorize them to act on the federal government's behalf to implement a national policy. In the course of this century the trend has been for the effective power and influence of the centre to expand, largely because of its greater financial resources. But this process has not been even or uniform.

The capacity of federal constitutions to evolve in response to different political and social needs is one of their merits.[18] Moreover, they enable variety and diversity to flourish, while the Bill of Rights guarantees the uniform enjoyment of some basic rights throughout the federation and the central government ensures that the states provide a minimum standard of welfare. In that event the constitution provides a degree of uniformity, while tolerating greater differences than have usually been allowed in a unitary system like that of the United Kingdom. It is difficult to improve on the conclusion of a leading American scholar: '[f]ederalism seeks to maintain political decentralization and social diversity while simultaneously promoting national measures to meet national needs and prevent localized oppression.'[19]

At the same time more traditional arguments for federalism, classically formulated in the *Federalist Papers*, should not be ignored. Madison and Hamilton were worried by the growth of what they termed 'factions', that is, sectional groups which had dominated the conduct of state legislatures under the Confederation. The formation of a strong central government was intended to limit their influence.[20] Nowadays there is probably more anxiety about the growth of central power under unitary constitutions where local authorities are entirely subordinate to

[16] See M. H. Redish, *The Constitution as Political Structure* (New York, 1995), chs. 2–3.
[17] See Basic Law, Arts. 72 and 74.
[18] See Sawyer, n. 6 above, who refers to the 'stages of federalism' in *Modern Federalism*, ch. 8.
[19] R. B. Stewart, 'Federalism and Rights', 19 *Georgia L Rev.* 917 (1985).
[20] See especially Papers 9, 10, 28, 51.

central government. In this context one merit of a federal constitution is that it safeguards the interests of regional communities; state or provincial assemblies are more likely to take account of their needs than a remote central Parliament which may be dominated by the representatives of other geographical areas or of national groups.

In short, a federal constitution, like the separation of powers principle, reduces the risk of a concentration of power and the danger of arbitrary government. The former distributes authority vertically between the centre and the states or regions, while the separation principle operates on the horizontal level to allocate powers between different institutions or organs of government. Both therefore serve the value of constitutionalism in similar ways.

Nevertheless, there is a case against federal constitutions. For small, homogeneous societies they would be too complex and cumbersome. Dicey was very critical of them, albeit largely in the context of the argument for a federal constitution for the British Empire which was sometimes made at the end of the nineteenth century. In his view, federal government was always weak government.[21] Moreover, 'federalism means legalism'; judges determine the balance of power between the federation and the states. That of course explains why federal constitutions are unpopular with politicians accustomed to working with the laxer constraints of a unitary one. The charge that federal government is weak can hardly be taken too seriously in the light of the experience of the United States and modern Germany, while federalism works well in other countries as diverse as Austria and Australia.

However, federalism is not a popular or easily comprehensible form of government. Whatever the merits of his other points, Dicey rightly concluded in 1915 (in his Introduction to the eighth edition of *Law of the Constitution*[22]) that there was little desire for it in England. His observation is as accurate now as it was at that time. It is a far less exciting cause or value than, say, human rights or political equality. Until recently, it has not been easy to envisage circumstances in which a unitary constitution with a long tradition, such as that of the United Kingdom or France, would transform itself into a federation. Nevertheless, the devolution of legislative powers to a Parliament in Scotland may mean that this development is not now as inconceivable as it has been. The difference, as we will see, between federalism and legislative devolution may be greater in theory than it turns out to be in practice.

---

21 Dicey, 171–5, but see the criticism of his analysis by Sawyer, n. 6 above, 124–5.
22 Reprinted in Indianapolis (1995), cii–cvi.

3. DEVOLUTION

A state with a unitary constitution may decide for a number of reasons to devolve powers to regional assemblies. One common motive is the desire to decentralize political authority so that it is more responsive to the needs of local communities. Alternatively, devolution may primarily be a response to political pressure from nationalist groups and parties. Either full legislative and executive powers may be transferred to the region, or only the latter. This second alternative has been adopted for Welsh devolution in the Government of Wales Act 1998; it may eventually extend to those English regions which request a transfer of power. In contrast, devolution to Scotland has involved the removal from Westminster of broad legislative power to a Scottish parliament, sitting in Edinburgh, with only specified powers being reserved for the United Kingdom Parliament. There will also be a Scottish Executive, presided over by a First Minister, responsible to the Edinburgh parliament.

In principle there is a clear difference between a federal constitution and a constitution which grants, or allows the grant of, substantial legislative (and other) powers to the regions. Under a federal constitution, there is a distribution of legal powers between national and state (or provincial) authorities which can only be altered by constitutional amendment. Moreover, normally both the centre and the states have the right to participate in the amendment process, so neither can alter the distribution of powers unilaterally. (On the other hand, it is unusual for a single state to be able to block a proposed amendment.) In contrast, under devolution arrangements, the central legislature can generally regain some or all of the devolved powers, usually by the enactment of ordinary legislation repealing or amending the measure which had transferred them to the regional bodies. That is what is intended in the arrangements for devolution to Scotland; the Westminster Parliament retains its sovereignty,[23] so in theory it will be free to regain some of the powers transferred to Edinburgh or even repeal the entire devolution legislation.

It may sometimes be difficult to determine whether a constitution is federal or unitary with substantial devolved powers. The Spanish Constitution of 1978 is particularly hard to characterize. The Regions enjoy wide legislative and administrative authority, though some areas of competence are reserved by the Constitution for the centre. Their

---

[23] White Paper, *Scotland's Parliament* (1997) Cm 3658, para. 4.2.

powers were conferred by statutes of autonomy formally enacted by the central Spanish Parliament, rather than by the Constitution itself. A few regions, notably Catalonia, Galicia, and the Basque region, enjoy wider powers than the others. At first glance this looks like a unitary decentralized constitution. But the statutes of autonomy may only be amended by agreement of the region concerned and the centre; it is for the former to take the initiative and draft the law. In practice, the scheme is very similar to a federal constitution.[24] On the other hand, the post-war Italian Constitution of 1948 is almost certainly not federal, though the text itself grants the regions, described as 'autonomous institutions', significant legislative, administrative, and financial powers.[25]

But even if it is possible to distinguish between federal and devolved constitutions in theory, in practice there may be no great difference between them. Once powers have been devolved, it may be politically impractical for the central legislature and executive to attempt to regain or assert authority over the transferred matters, even if in terms of strict constitutional law it would be permissible for it to do that. Alternatively, the central legislature may lose all interest in the area to which powers have been transferred. In these circumstances there is effectively a *de facto* federation. Something like this happened in the United Kingdom, when the Government of Ireland Act 1920 transferred legislative power to Stormont 'to make laws for the peace, order and good government of Northern Ireland . . .'. Section 75 provided that this did not affect the authority of the Westminster Parliament. But in practice London took little interest in Ulster affairs until civil unrest persuaded it to intervene and assume direct legislative and executive power, as in terms of constitutional law it had always been free to do. The point is that for nearly fifty years Stormont had been left free to regulate the internal affairs of the Province. During this period the London government was much less concerned about civil rights matters than, say, the United States federal government has been since 1954 over the enforcement in the states of equal educational facilities for whites and blacks.[26] This contrast shows that there may be no great difference between the operation in practice of federal and devolved systems; it would certainly be wrong to suggest

---

[24] See J. J. Solozabál, 'Spain: A Federation in the Making?' in J. J. Hesse and V. Wright (eds.), *Federalizing Europe?* (Oxford, 1996), 240.

[25] Arts. 115–19.

[26] The federal government became involved in this question after *Brown* v. *Board of Education*, 347 US 483 (1954), when the Supreme Court required states to integrate their schools.

that the latter necessarily leads to constant 'interference' by central government.

Despite this argument, there is no doubt that devolution is in legal terms a more adaptable arrangement than a federal structure. One point is that it allows for different types of devolution to the various regions, whereas a federal constitution usually treats all the states or provinces equally. (Canada is an obvious exception, with a number of special arrangements for Quebec.) The devolution arrangements for Scotland and Wales are quite different, and it may be that a third pattern will emerge, if eventually power is to be transferred to some of the English regions. Secondly, these arrangements do not legally preclude action by the central government, if regional authorities abuse or fail to exercise their devolved powers. In short, there is a flexibility which is always useful, and which may be imperative during war or in an economic crisis. In contrast, the effective working of a federal constitution may depend on the courts' willingness to take a sympathetic view of central legislation or action which on a strict reading of the constitution would infringe the competence of the regions. In the last fifty years, the United States Supreme Court has usually taken a broad view of the legislative powers of Congress, particularly to regulate commerce between the states,[27] in that way increasing the authority of the centre with regard to the states.

Some of the fundamental questions raised when power is devolved are similar to those which arise under federal constitutions. One issue is whether the devolution measure should confer specific powers on the regional assemblies, or whether, as the Government of Ireland Act 1920 did, it should transfer a general power, leaving enumerated reserve powers for the United Kingdom Parliament and government. The Scotland Act 1998, devolving powers to the Edinburgh Parliament, follows the 1920 legislation in listing reserved matters for Westminster. Amendments may be made to this list by Order in Council, which must be approved by both the United Kingdom and the Scottish Parliaments. One of the difficulties in earlier devolution Bills introduced by the Labour government in the 1970s was that they devolved specific powers to the Scottish and Welsh Assemblies; this meant that civil servants and lawyers had to go through the statute book in detail to determine which powers it was appropriate to transfer. The option chosen by the Labour government elected in 1997 is preferable, since it is less likely

---

[27] See Ch. 1, sect. 5.

to lead to legal doubts about the entitlement of the Scottish parliament to enact legislation. Interestingly, it is in line with the more usual approach to the allocation of power in federal constitutions.[28]

Other fundamental issues are whether the regional assembly should have tax-raising power, and how to resolve disputes between the central and regional assemblies and executives. Again, similar questions are raised in the context of federal arrangements. There are detailed provisions in the German Basic Law concerning the power of the Federation and the states to tax and their rights to have revenues assigned to them.[29] The Federation has the exclusive power to impose customs duties and a concurrent power to impose taxation, the revenue from which accrues to it wholly or in part. As the Federation shares the revenue from income and corporation taxes equally with the states (as a group), it is entitled to impose these taxes.[30] On the other hand, the revenue from inheritance, motor, and beer taxes accrues to the *Länder*, so they are entitled to levy them. Without some ability to raise its own revenue, a regional assembly will constantly complain that it is unable to discharge its functions owing to the meanness of central government in allocating revenues. In fact, the Scotland Act 1998 grants the Edinburgh parliament power to increase or decrease the basic rate of income tax set by the United Kingdom Parliament by up to 3p.; authority to control local authority taxation and expenditure within Scotland has also been devolved.

In a federal constitution, the courts have the responsibility of umpiring disputes between the federation and the states about their respective competences. As mentioned, in some countries (though not always in the United States) they have been willing to strike down federal as well as state legislation. The Scotland Act 1998 is different in this respect. Explicit provision is made for disputes about the validity of legislation of the Scottish Parliament to be referred to the Judicial Committee of the Privy Council, in effect the House of Lords, before the measure is sent for Royal Assent. The ordinary courts may also rule on the validity of Acts of the Scottish Parliament in litigation subsequent to enactment, with an appeal to the Privy Council. There will, therefore, be legal checks to ensure that the Scottish parliament does not trespass on

---

[28] See the discussion of the US and German Constitutions in sect. 2.

[29] Basic Law, Arts. 105–6.

[30] In effect the states can only tax when the Federation has not exercised its concurrent power: see Art. 72(1), providing that the *Länder* may exercise concurrent powers only in so far as the Federation has not exercised them.

the powers reserved for Westminster. But the latter Parliament remains free as a mater of constitutional law to legislate over non-reserved matters.[31] Naturally, over time something like a constitutional convention may develop that it is wrong for the United Kingdom Parliament to trespass into a non-reserved area, at least without the consent of the Scottish parliament and Executive.

One of the most intractable of all the constitutional problems associated with devolution is known as the 'West Lothian Question', so named because it was first raised by the Member of Parliament for West Lothian, Tam Dalyell, in the 1970s: should Scottish Members of Parliament be free to vote in the Westminster Parliament on matters which have been devolved to Scotland? (The same question can, of course, be asked about Welsh Members, but it is much less urgent, since only executive powers are devolved to Wales.) Scotland should, of course, continue to be represented in the Westminster Parliament for non-devolved matters such as foreign affairs and defence, but it would be anomalous for its Members to continue to vote on questions, say, of education, health, and housing affecting only England. Their votes might well overturn the clear majority of English Members of Parliament on an English Bill.

There are practical objections to attempting to resolve the difficulty by limiting the voting rights of Scottish Members; a Cabinet then might have majority support in the House on those matters where Scottish Members were entitled to vote, but not on others. The solution contemplated by the Scotland Act 1998 is to reduce Scottish representation at Westminster, as used to be the position with Northern Ireland until the imposition of direct rule. This is really a compromise. It is worth pointing out that this difficulty does not arise under federal constitutions. Under those systems there are two separate legislative bodies with distinct areas of competence. Representatives from, say, California may not cast a (perhaps decisive) vote on a matter affecting New York or Pennsylvania, which California, but not New York or Pennsylvania, is entitled to decide for itself.

The 'West Lothian Question' brings out one of the weaknesses of devolution arrangements: they may not provide a sufficiently firm framework for the resolution of acute political tensions. It is hard to imagine that English politicians will long tolerate a system which allows Scottish Members to vote on matters solely affecting England, when

[31] This power was expressly spelt out in cl. 1 of the Scotland and Wales Bill 1976, and in the Government of Ireland Act 1920, s. 75.

they have no corresponding voice on similar Scottish questions. With goodwill and tolerance these arrangements might survive for a period. The point is that they provide no constitutional obstacle to their amendment, in particular to an attempt by the majority in England to regain its full legislative powers. A federal constitution, in contrast, does prevent a majority at the centre from expanding its powers at the expense of the regions. Legislation which infringes the competence of the regions may be stopped politically (in the Senate or Upper House) or, if enacted, may be challenged in the courts. Further, the federation acting on its own has no authority to amend the constitution without the support of a majority of the states. Devolution arrangements, a compromise between unitary and federal constitutions, may prove too fragile in the long term to guarantee constitutional stability.

4. LOCAL GOVERNMENT

Before the institution of the Scottish Parliament and the Welsh Assembly, local authorities were the only bodies outside central government to enjoy general powers, including the legislative power to make by-laws. It is this multi-purpose role which is one of their characteristics, distinguishing them from authorities such as health authorities which have only a single function. Other significant features of local authorities are that they are elected, may raise revenue, and have a degree of discretion in allocating priorities and determining expenditure.[32] For these reasons they have provided the only balance, certainly the only democratic balance, to the power of central government in the United Kingdom constitution.

The present system dates back to the end of the nineteenth century, when county councils took over most of the administrative functions previously performed by justices of the peace. Its legal basis in England and Wales is now provided by the Local Government Act 1972, which established a uniform two-tier system of county and district councils. (There is a third tier of parish councils with minor functions.) But the structure was altered in 1985 when the Conservative government abolished the Greater London Council and six metropolitan county councils outside London, largely because it disliked the focus they provided for opposition to its social policies. Further changes were made in England

---

[32] See M. Loughlin, 'The Restructuring of Central-Local Government Relations' in J. Jowell and D. Oliver (eds.), *The Changing Constitution* (3rd edn., Oxford, 1994), 261, 263–5.

in 1996, with the abolition of long-established county authorities like Berkshire, while in Wales the two-tier system has already been replaced with unitary authorities. The Labour government elected in 1997 has put forward proposals for the re-establishment of an elected authority for London, and, more radically, for a directly elected mayor with executive powers.

The rapid and constant change in the structure of local government has, if anything, been outpaced by developments in central government control over its expenditure and revenue-raising powers. Local authorities are statutory bodies and can only incur expenditure for those purposes which have been authorized by Parliamentary legislation. If they exceed these powers, they act *ultra vires* and the expenditure can be stopped; councillors responsible for unauthorized expenditure may be personally liable. The Secretary of State for the Environment has effective control over the capital expenditure of local authorities. Moreover, central government grants may be reduced if annual expenditure exceeds the level prescribed by Whitehall. Most radically, the government has taken power to limit the amounts an authority may raise itself by local taxation; this used to take the form of rates, in effect a property tax, but they were replaced by the much-hated poll tax, officially known as the 'community charge'. The council tax took its place at the beginning of 1993. Finally, the discretionary powers of local authorities have been transferred or curtailed in a number of contexts. For example, the Education Reform Act 1988 enables the Secretary of State to prescribe the national curriculum for local authority schools. Other legislation requires authorities to sell council housing to tenants who wish to buy, and to put out services, such as refuse collection and office cleaning, to competitive tender by private contractors.

Much of the work of local authorities, for instance, the allocation of council housing and the grant of planning permission, is essentially administrative. Detailed consideration of such functions belongs to books on administrative law, as does the treatment of the principles of judicial review over the exercise of these powers. But an exposition of the constitutional position of local government is important because strong local authorities might provide a balance or counterweight to central power. In fact its position is weak. As we have seen, Parliament can freely alter its structure and abolish particular councils. Central government is free to take over the functions traditionally discharged at the local level and may compel authorities to privatize services. Since Parliament enjoys legislative supremacy, it may constitutionally strip local government of all its discretionary or revenue-raising powers, or even abolish it altogether.

It is unlikely that such extreme steps could be taken in Germany where the Basic Law gives local government a degree of protection against both federal and state government. Article 28(2) provides:

The communes [*Gemeinden*] must be guaranteed the right to regulate on their own responsibility all the affairs of the local community within the limits set by law.

The communes have standing to complain to the Constitutional Court if they consider a law violates their right to self-government. The Court has ruled that a state must not strip communes of a particular responsibility unless it is clear they cannot properly discharge the task. There is a presumption in favour of local responsibility, and the *Land* parliament should give more weight to the close links of citizen and local authority than it does to considerations of cost. Laws removing powers from the communes should be carefully reviewed by the courts.[33] In practice, however, the Court has been reluctant to intervene when a state has transferred functions from individual communes to their associations or other bodies, or has reorganized local government.

English courts have, if anything, been unsympathetic to the claims of local authorities to preserve their discretionary powers, particularly against curtailment by Parliamentary legislation. It is crucial to remember that they have only those powers which Parliament has conferred on them. Unlike the Crown, they have no general power of action under the common law, and therefore they are unable to formulate or apply their own political policies in the absence of statutory permission. This is strikingly illustrated by two cases from different periods. In *Roberts* v. *Hopwood* in 1925[34] the House of Lords held Poplar Borough Council had no power to pay men and women equally or to set a generous minimum wage for its employees. It was outside its powers to pursue what were then regarded, at least by the judges, as eccentric egalitarian policies. Recently, the Court of Appeal decided that a local authority could not ban fox hunting over land it had acquired for amenity purposes.[35] A local authority has, therefore, less power to control the use of its land than a private landowner or a body such as the National Trust, because it must point to a statutory provision authorizing a policy of this type. In the absence of such a provision, it was improper for a council to take

---

[33] 79 BVerfGE 127, 143–55 (1988).   [34] [1925] AC 578.
[35] *R* v. *Somerset CC, ex parte Fewings* [1995] 1 WLR 1037.

this step over 'a sensitive national issue' which in the view of the Court of Appeal should be resolved by Parliament.

Nor have local authorities succeeded when they have challenged the Secretary of State for the Environment's control of their expenditure and revenue-raising powers. In two leading cases,[36] the House of Lords has expressed great reluctance to question decisions of the Secretary of State involving the formation and implementation of national economic policy, at least when the ground of challenge was that his decision had been 'irrational' or 'unreasonable'. One factor influencing this reluctance was that in both cases, at various stages, the initial policy or implementing decisions had been approved by a vote of the House of Commons. The implication was that it is for the Commons, and not the courts, to control central government in this context. The result was that the Secretary was able to impose limits on local authority expenditure, in the later *Hammersmith* case by 'capping' the community charges levied by the councils. The striking constitutional point to emerge from these cases is that the courts did not approach them with any predisposition in favour of local government autonomy, as perhaps they might have done if its position were constitutionally guaranteed as it is in Germany. Instead, they preferred merely to check whether the Secretary of State had acted within the terms of the legislation in implementing a policy of national economic importance.

Therefore, there are no legal constraints on the ability of Parliament and central government to control local authorities. It has been argued, however, that there have been some constitutional conventions governing the relationship of central and local government, designed to ensure the latter a degree of independence.[37] On the other hand, Westminster politicians have at times hinted at the existence of a convention requiring local authorities to abide by the spending limits fixed by central government. On that view, the statutory controls conferred on central government during the 1980s merely put the convention on a legal footing. These conflicting views suggest at least that the conventions have been unclear, and probably that there have been none at all. In any case, we saw in the previous chapter how hopeless it is to place reliance on conventions as a check on the exercise of power.

[36] *R* v. *Secretary of State for the Environment, ex parte Nottinghamshire CC* [1986] AC 240; *R* v. *Secretary of State for the Environment, ex parte Hammersmith and Fulham LBC* [1991] AC 521.
[37] Loughlin, n. 32 above, 262–5; V. Bogdanor, *Politics and the Constitution* (Aldershot, 1996), ch. 9.

What is to be done about this? A Council of Europe Charter of Local Self-Government calls on member states of the Council to recognize the principle of local self-government, if possible constitutionally, and to provide it with general competence. These standards have been recognized, for example, by Article 28(2) of the German Basic Law. The United Kingdom has recently signed the Charter and should now consider how its principles should be implemented in our constitutional arrangements. The devolution of legislative power to the Scottish Parliament provides a good opportunity to establish local government north of the border on a firm constitutional footing. (Some tension between the Scottish government and outlying local communities has been anticipated, since the interests of the latter may be subordinated to those of Glasgow and Edinburgh.) One possible step would be to incorporate a principle of local self-government in the devolution legislation, in that way fettering the freedom of the Scottish Parliament to curtail the powers of local authorities. Another approach would be for an agreement or Concordat to be reached by the government in Edinburgh and local authorities to ensure respect for the interests of the latter. That would have the effect of establishing a Scottish constitutional convention in this context.[38]

The United Kingdom constitutional arrangements have too long ignored local government. Few major politicians in London, unlike, say, those in Paris, have had much experience of work as a mayor or councillor. The powers of local government have been consistently reduced over the last twenty years. One consequence is that turn-out at local elections is low. A second is that local government rarely attracts the services of able and ambitious people. (The election of a mayor for London, and perhaps later for other cities, would counteract this trend.) Local government would surely be more effective, and enjoy more respect, if it had wider powers. Moreover, if its position were guaranteed in a codified constitution, it could provide a valuable check to the authority of central government, a check which is particularly necessary in the context of a unitary constitution.

[38] Constitution Unit, *Scotland's Parliament*, paras. 476–8.

4

The Constitution of the European Union

1. INTRODUCTION

THE European Union, and the rules of Community law, now exercise an enormous influence on the United Kingdom, including its constitutional law. We will see in the next chapter that the House of Lords has ruled that parliamentary legislation should not be applied when it conflicts with a rule of Community law. In effect, it has modified the principle of parliamentary legislative supremacy which the courts had consistently upheld for the last 300 years. A constitutional question more frequently asked now, particularly in the context of possible membership of Economic and Monetary Union, is whether the European Union is developing into a confederation or perhaps a full federation. The implication of the latter is that the United Kingdom might be about to lose its national sovereignty, since in effect it would become a state of a federation, in the same way that California is a state of the USA or Bavaria one of the *Länder* of Germany. This question can only be answered when we have examined the legal character of the Union and the European Communities on which the Union is based.

At first sight the title of this chapter might appear baffling. Whatever its legal character, the European Union is not a state. Nor is it founded on any single document labelled as a 'constitution'. Rather, it was established by the Treaty of Maastricht 1992, which built on and amended earlier treaties, notably the Treaty of Rome 1957 founding the European Economic Community. But it would be wrong to think that the Union cannot have a constitution, just because it is not a state for the purposes of international law. Lots of institutions draft constitutions for much the same reasons that states adopt them. Clubs, political parties, trades unions, and other organizations generally draw up a document which sets out their aims and values, allocates responsibilities to particular officers and committees, and provides for annual general and other meetings of their membership. It is immaterial how these documents are described; they perform the same role for that institution as, for instance, the United States Constitution or the German Basic Law does for those countries. In effect they are constitutions. Equally, the United Nations Charter could have been termed the 'Constitution of the United Nations'. There is no doubt, therefore, that the European Union, and the European Communities on which it is based, could have a constitution. It is another matter whether they do in fact have one.

This issue bears some resemblance to the question, discussed in Chapter 2, whether it is appropriate to describe the hotch-potch of statutes, case law, and conventions concerning government in the United Kingdom as amounting to a constitution. In the absence of a codified text and of statutes which have an explicit constitutional status, we asked whether these rules have in *substance* a constitutional character. Do they perform the same functions as the provisions usually found in a constitutional text? Are these rules concerned to allocate powers to various political and governmental institutions and to impose constraints on the exercise of these powers? The answer is that there is a relatively clear body of rules which we can safely describe as amounting to a constitution, though its contours may be much less precise than those of a constitutional text.[1]

The same approach can be taken when the question is raised in the context of the European Union. A full answer would involve a detailed examination of the treaties setting up the Union and the Communities on which it is based. It would also need to take account of the rulings of the European Court of Justice (ECJ), which was established for the very purpose of providing authoritative interpretations of the treaties and Community legislation. In fact, that Court has described the Treaty of Rome 1957 (which established the European Economic Community and Euratom) as 'the constitutional charter of a Community based on the rule of law'.[2] As we will see, that view is right. The treaties allocate competence between different institutions and provide legal and other means of checking those institutions when they exceed their powers. But the constitutional order of the European Union is a complex and flawed one.

The next section of this chapter briefly outlines the structure of the Treaty of Maastricht and the functions of the Community institutions which were established by earlier treaties, and which now serve the European Union. Section 3 brings out some of the leading constitutional

---

[1] Ch. 2, sect. 1.
[2] Opinion 1/91 on the European Economic Area Agreement [1991] ECR I‑6000, 6102.

principles formulated by the European Court of Justice, which has played the same creative and controversial role in developing a European constitution as the United States Supreme Court did for the USA, particularly in the early years of the nineteenth century. Finally, in section 4 I answer the question which troubles so many politicians and others in the United Kingdom: is the European Union already a federation, or must it inevitably become one?

2. THE STRUCTURE AND INSTITUTIONS OF THE UNION

The establishment of the European Union by the Maastricht Treaty 1992, known formally as the Treaty on European Union (TEU), marked a further stage in the process of European integration which was initiated after the Second World War. Two earlier treaties founded the three European Communities on which the Union is based: the Treaty of Paris 1951 established the European Coal and Steel Community, and the Treaty of Rome 1957 established the European Economic Community, now known simply as the European Community (EC), and the European Atomic Energy Community. Rather confusingly, both the terms 'European Union' and 'European Community' are still used in the texts. The confusion has regrettably not been clarified by the recent Treaty of Amsterdam 1997 which amends both the Maastricht Treaty and the earlier Community Treaties. Broadly, the term 'Union' is used in the provisions introduced by the Maastricht Treaty, in particular those concerned with a common foreign and security policy (CFSP) and those relating to police and judicial co-operation in criminal matters. The term 'Community' refers to the Union when it acts under the provisions of the older treaties, most importantly the Treaty of Rome. It is usual to refer to 'Community law', since that term has been current since 1957 and is used by the Court when it has developed constitutional principles and the rules of substantive EC law. In other political contexts, however, it is now standard to refer to the European Union. The terminology employed in this chapter follows this distinction.

The Union is served by the institutions which had been created by the earlier Treaties. They comprise the European Parliament (EP), the Council of Ministers, the Commission, and the Court of Justice (ECJ), to which is attached the Court of First Instance. Under the Treaty of Rome, the Council of Ministers has power to issue regulations and directives, the two types of Community legislation. Regulations automatically become part of the legal system of each Member State, while directives impose binding objectives on the states, though they have discretion how they are implemented in national law.[3] Though a Community (and now Union) institution, the Council is composed of representatives of each Member State. Each Member State takes its turn to assume the Presidency of the Council for a six-month period. The President is responsible for convening and chairing meetings, and additionally may use his position to propose new initiatives. Negotiations in the Council of Ministers are often protracted, as each state attempts to safeguard its interests before agreeing to a compromise. It meets in secret, which is contrary to the ethos and practice of proper legislative bodies. Sometimes the Council is entitled under the treaties to enact measures by simple majority, but more usually they require it to act by a 'qualified majority'. This is a procedure under which each state is allocated a number of votes proportionate to its size; for instance, the four largest states (France, Germany, Italy, the United Kingdom) each have ten votes, while the smallest, Luxembourg, only has two. By requiring sixty-two votes in favour of a legislative proposal, the procedure enables a significant minority of states to block its enactment. Some important decisions must be taken unanimously.

Legislation must be formally proposed by the Brussels Commission, which also acts as a permanent executive and has the responsibility of securing the enforcement of Community law, if necessary by initiating proceedings before the Court of Justice. It also enjoys some legislative power, which is either directly conferred on it by the EC Treaty or delegated by the Council of Ministers. In contrast to the latter, the Commission is genuinely supra-national in its character. Though its members are nominated by agreement between the Member States, they must be wholly independent and are forbidden to seek or take instructions from a government or other body.

Since 1979 Members of the Parliament have been directly elected by the people in the various states; the United Kingdom has always resisted, until recently, the adoption of a uniform voting procedure, a step required by the Treaty of Rome. The EP is not a legislature in the conventional sense, let alone a sovereign body with general powers.[4] However, like the Council, it may request the Commission to submit proposals for a regulation or directive. It also has participation rights in

---

[3] EC Treaty, Art. 189, renumbered Art. 249 by the Treaty of Amsterdam.
[4] See French Constitutional Council Decision 92–308 of 9 Apr. 1992, RJC I–496, para. 34 (Favoreu and Philip, 781, 788).

the legislative process, which vary according to the subject-matter of the legislation. At the minimum, it usually has a right to be consulted, but in some instances enjoys significantly greater powers. Under the co-decision procedure introduced by the Treaty on European Union it may in effect veto the passage of legislation on various matters prescribed by the treaties. But the Parliament is never able to insist on the passage of its own amendments against the opposition of the Council.[5] The Maastricht and Amsterdam Treaties have further strengthened the EP by giving it the power to approve or reject the nomination of the President of the Commission by the governments of the Members States; it then has the power to approve the body of twenty Commissioners chosen by the governments in consultation with the President.[6] The Parliament has always enjoyed the power to compel the resignation of the whole Commission (but not individual Commissioners) by a two-thirds majority of the votes cast. Finally, the EP acts as a forum for open debate and for scrutiny of the executive, two of the traditional roles of a legislative body.[7]

The major institutional development of the TEU is the prominent place given to the European Council, which 'shall provide the Union with the necessary impetus for its development and shall define the general political guidelines thereof'.[8] In fact it had developed from meetings of Prime Ministers of the Member States since 1974 and was first recognized formally by the Single European Act of 1986 amending the Treaty of Rome. The Council meets at least twice a year, and is composed of the Heads of State (in the case of France) or Government and the President of the Commission, assisted by the Ministers of Foreign Affairs and a second member of the Commission.

The TEU amended the Treaty of Rome in many significant respects, for instance, expanding the powers of the European Parliament and giving the Community for the first time some competence in the fields of culture, health, and consumer protection. It also established citizenship of the Union; every national of a Member State is also a citizen of the Union, with an entitlement, among other rights, to vote and stand as a candidate for local and European elections in a state in which he resides under the same conditions as the nationals of that state.[9] The Treaty

---

[5] Under Art. 189b (renumbered Art. 251 by the Amsterdam Treaty), if the Council approves EP amendments, it may adopt the amended measure by qualified majority. If it does not, a Conciliation Committee attempts to resolve the disagreement.
[6] Art. 158, renumbered Art. 214 by the Amsterdam Treaty.
[7] For discussion of these functions, see Ch. 5, sect. 4.
[8] TEU, Art. D (Art. 4 of the Amsterdam Treaty).
[9] EC Treaty, Arts. 8–8e (Arts. 17–22 of the Amsterdam Treaty).

also provided the legal basis for the eventual introduction of Economic and Monetary Union (EMU).

But of more general constitutional interest is the fact that the Treaty on European Union instituted two inter-governmental procedures, one for the development of a common foreign and defence policy, the other for co-operation in the fields of justice and home affairs (under the Amsterdam Treaty, common action in the fields of police and judicial co-operation in criminal matters). In contrast to the legislative process in the earlier EC Treaty, there is little room in these two procedures for the involvement of the Commission and European Parliament, while the Council of Ministers of the Member States is usually required to act unanimously. (However, in an attempt to strengthen European foreign policy, the Treaty of Amsterdam has given the Council of Ministers authority to take some action in this area by qualified majority, when it implements a common strategy agreed by the European Council.[10]) Most importantly from a legal point of view, the Court of Justice has little jurisdiction in these two highly political areas, though the Amsterdam Treaty will give it authority to rule on the validity and interpretation of measures under the provisions relating to police and judicial co-operation.[11]

Consequently the Union established by the Maastricht Treaty rests, it is said, on three separate pillars: the first, the European Community, concerned with such subjects as the single market, agriculture, transport, and other economic and social matters; the other two, the CFSP and the provisions relating to police and judicial co-operation. From a constitutional perspective, the legal principles for these pillars are quite different. Community law, as we will see, has developed a set of clear constitutional principles, which make it possible to describe the Community as a federation, albeit a rather peculiar one. On the other hand, the provisions of the CFSP, and those concerned with the police and judicial co-operation, bear much more resemblance at present, even after the Treaty of Amsterdam, to a loose international treaty, establishing only a framework for co-operative action. (The states are not bound to any particular course of conduct, although they must ensure that their policies conform to the common positions adopted by the Council of Ministers with regard to foreign and security policy.) Moreover, the provisions of the TEU, which are concerned with the two non-Community pillars, have little, if any, direct impact on individuals;

---

[10] TEU, Art. J.13, renumbered Art. 23 by the Treaty of Amsterdam.
[11] TEU, Art. K.7, renumbered Art. 39 by the Amsterdam Treaty.

in particular, they do not give the citizens of the Member States rights which they can enforce before their own national courts.[12] In other words, in contrast to the Community treaties, their provisions do not create 'directly effective' rights of the kind discussed in the next section of this chapter.

3. CONSTITUTIONAL PRINCIPLES

In what sense is it appropriate to describe these treaties as the *constitution* of the Community, or now the Union? As already mentioned, the European Court of Justice has referred to the Treaty of Rome as 'the constitutional charter of a Community based on the rule of law'. It is a constitution in the sense that it sets out the objectives and competence of the Community, and of its political institutions. For instance, the Community lacks any explicit authority under the treaties to enact rules of criminal law or to lay down standards of education or housing; implicitly these, and many other, matters are for the Member States to decide without Community interference.[13] However, there is no provision expressly reserving for the states those powers not explicitly transferred to the Community. In this respect, the treaties differ from federal constitutions, which usually provide for the states or provinces to exercise powers not conferred on the central authorities.[14]

The Treaty of Rome also allocates powers between the various political branches: the Council of Ministers, the Commission, and the EP. Perhaps most significantly it instituted a court, the ECJ, with final power to rule on its interpretation, and on the validity and meaning of Community legal measures such as Council regulations and directives. The courts of the Member States may, and in the case of final courts must, refer questions on the validity and interpretation of Community law to the ECJ. These provisions have enabled that Court to play a decisive role in the development of Community law, whether constitutional law or particular substantive areas such as competition and internal market law.

However, the Treaty of Rome is not the constitution of a state, but of a Community, 'a new legal order for the benefit of which the States

---

[12] See pp. 76–7, 96–7

[13] Recently, the ECJ has held that the Community lacks competence to accede to the European Human Rights Convention: *Opinion 2/94 on the Accession of the Community to the European Human Rights Convention* [1996] 2 CMLR 265.

[14] See Ch. 3, sect. 2.

have limited their sovereign rights . . .'.[15] Similarly, the Treaty of Maastricht provides a constitution for the Union, albeit an unduly complex one. Arguably, as we have seen in the preceding section, the provisions of the Treaty concerned with foreign affairs and law enforcement, the second and third pillars, bear as much resemblance to an international agreement as they do to a constitution. At all events, these provisions are not so clearly based on the rule of law as those of the Treaty of Rome, in view of the limited role of the ECJ in interpreting their meaning. Indeed, the ECJ has no jurisdiction at all with regard to the CFSP pillar.

The character of the Community constitution has only gradually emerged over the last forty years. The Court of Justice has formulated the basic principles of this constitution. Perhaps the most important of them is that provisions of the Treaties may create directly effective rights, which individuals are entitled to enforce before their national courts.[16] Subsequently the principle of 'direct effect' has been extended to regulations and, more controversially, to directives issued by the Council of Ministers. Whether any particular Treaty provision, regulation, or directive is directly effective is a matter for the ECJ itself to determine when the question has been referred to it by a national court such as the Court of Appeal or House of Lords.

The principle can be illustrated by reference to the *Van Duyn* case.[17] Yvonne van Duyn, a Dutch national, was refused entry into the United Kingdom because she intended to take an offer of work with the Church of Scientology, regarded in this country as a harmful, although not illegal, institution. She argued that the refusal interfered with her right to free movement (including the right to enter the country to take up work) which was conferred by Article 48 of the Treaty of Rome and governed by Community legislation. The ECJ ruled that Article 48 and the key provision of the relevant directive were directly effective and could be enforced in national courts. It reached this conclusion, despite the provision in the Treaty enabling Member States to restrict the right of free movement on the basis of public policy. Under Directive 64/221, however, they could only refuse entry on the ground of public policy if the decision was based on the personal conduct of the individual concerned. The national courts were perfectly capable of applying these rules, for example, by determining whether Van Duyn was an active member of

[15] Case 294/83, *'Les Verts'* v. *European Parliament* [1986] ECR 1339, 1365.
[16] The principle was first formulated in Case 26/82, *Van Gend en Loos* [1963] ECR 1.
[17] Case 41/74, *Van Duyn* v. *Home Office* [1974] ECR 1137.

the Church, so that her personal conduct was involved. If she was not, she would have a right to enter under Community law, which the English courts must enforce.

The doctrine of direct effect is crucial, for it means it is no longer tenable to argue that the European Community is merely an association of states or international organization, such as the United Nations, governed solely by the principles of international law. Moreover, from the principle of direct effect flows the principle of Community supremacy over national law, which was stated by the ECJ in its famous *Costa* v. *ENEL* ruling.[18] It would be nonsense, say, for individuals in Germany to be able to protect their directly effective rights under Community law to equal pay or to free movement to take up work, when individuals in France could not. That situation might result, if the German courts were willing to apply Community law, but the French judges were not because they took the view that national law must prevail over Community rules. The principle of Community supremacy precludes that possibility. Further, the ECJ has ruled that Community law prevails over inconsistent national law, even when the latter is enacted subsequent to the EC regulation or directive; it is the duty of the national courts to apply the Community rule in these circumstances.[19] We will see in the next chapter that the House of Lords has accepted this principle of Community supremacy; it has declined to apply Acts of Parliament, even if they were enacted after the passage of the inconsistent Community legal provisions.[20]

These principles of direct effect and of Community supremacy are certainly not the only constitutional principles formulated by the European Court of Justice. First, it emphasized, in an early case under the Coal and Steel Community Treaty, the importance of the balance of powers between Community institutions.[21] The ability of each institution to check the others prevents any of them from abusing its powers and so safeguards indirectly the rights and interests of people affected by Community law. This is not only a political principle, but may be enforced by the ECJ. Article 173 of the Treaty of Rome[22] requires the Court to review the legality of binding measures adopted jointly by the Parliament and Council, by the Council, Commission, and the European Central Bank. The Court even allowed the Parliament to bring proceedings to enforce its rights to participate in the legislative process,

---

[18] Case 6/64, [1964] ECR 585.   [19] Case 106/77, *Simmenthal* [1978] ECR 629.
[20] Ch. 5, sect. 3.   [21] Case 9/56, *Meroni* v. *High Authority* [1958] ECR 139, 152.
[22] Art. 230 of the Treaty of Amsterdam.

when the text of Article 173 at that time did not allow it to bring such an action.[23] It is admittedly difficult to analyse the Community constitution in terms of the separation of powers principle.[24] The Council, Commission, and EP all participate in the legislative process, while the executive powers generally belong to the Commission, subject to scrutiny by the Parliament. What emerges is a complex system of institutional balances, rather than a rigid separation of functions under which one institution performs only one of the three functions of government.

Secondly, the Court is concerned to protect the rights of Parliament in order to enhance democracy within the Community.[25] The Treaty of Rome normally requires the EP, at least, to be consulted on the merits of legislation drafted by the Commission, although in many cases it now enjoys fuller rights in the legislative process. The Court takes the EP's right to participate in the process seriously. It is prepared to hold invalid a regulation which the Parliament has not had an opportunity to comment on.[26] Moreover, it is unacceptable for the Council to base a directive on an Article of the Treaty, under which the EP only enjoys consultation rights, when it could also have based it on Article 100a, which gives the Parliament the right to legislate jointly with the Council under the co-decision procedure. That level of participation 'reflects a fundamental democratic principle that the peoples should take part in the exercise of power through the intermediary of a representative assembly'.[27] These decisions indicate the Court's concern to reduce so far as possible what is often termed 'the democratic deficit' in the Community by strengthening the position of the only institution elected by the people.

Another feature has been the development of fundamental rights within the Community legal order. In a line of cases the Court has held that it will not uphold Community measures which conflict with fundamental rights such as freedom of speech and the right to property.[28]

---

[23] Case 70/88, *EP* v. *Council* [1990] ECR I–2041, 2072–4. The right of the Parliament to bring such an action has subsequently been incorporated by an amendment to the Treaty of Rome.

[24] See K. Lenaerts, 'Some Reflections on the Separation of Powers in the European Community' (1991) 28 *Common Market L Rev.* 11.

[25] G. F. Mancini and D. T. Keeling, 'Democracy and the European Court of Justice' (1994) 57 *MLR* 175.

[26] Case 139/79, *Roquette Frères* v. *Council* [1980] ECR 3333.

[27] Case 300/89, *Commission* v. *Council* [1991] ECR I–2867.

[28] e.g., see Cases 11/70, *Internationale Handelsgesellschaft* [1970] ECR 1125, and 4/73, *Nold* [1974] ECR 491.

The Treaty of Rome in fact makes no explicit mention of human rights, except perhaps for the prohibition of discrimination on the basis of nationality and the right of men and women to equal pay for equal work. Nevertheless, the ECJ requires Community institutions to respect the fundamental rights guaranteed by the constitutions of the Member States and by international treaties to which they are parties, in particular the European Convention on Human Rights. The Court's approach has been recognized by the TEU, which requires the Union to respect these rights.[29]

One contrast with United Kingdom constitutional arrangements is the relatively small part played by extra-legal conventions. Probably the most important instance of a convention in the Community are the Luxembourg Accords of 1966. This compromise registered acceptance of the French view that, where 'very important interests' of a Member State are at stake, the Council should only decide matters unanimously, and not as the Treaty often specifies by majority vote. In recent years much less use has been made of the Accords and their current standing is far from clear. In any case there is little doubt that the Council may disregard them and take decisions by a qualified majority vote when the Treaties permit this course. In fact, under the Maastricht and Amsterdam Treaties, qualified majority voting has frequently replaced previous requirements for unanimity. There may be a few other conventions under the EC constitution. The ECJ has, for instance, referred to a principle of the collective responsibility of the Commissioners 'on the political level',[30] one implication being that it would be improper for a Commissioner to speak in public against decisions taken by the body. But broadly, the Community constitution is similar, say, to the German Basic Law in failing to afford conventions a significant role. In principle, every constitutional question is a matter for the Court of Justice; Member States are not free to waive or suspend Treaty provisions by an informal agreement whenever it suits them.

4. A FEDERAL EUROPE?

Much the most controversial constitutional question, discussed with great passion by some politicians in the United Kingdom, is whether the Union is moving towards a federal state, perhaps a United States of Europe. The next stage of development is Economic and Monetary

---

[29] Art. F (Amsterdam Treaty, Art. 6).
[30] Case 5/85, *AKZO Chemie* v. *Commission* [1986] ECR 2585, 2614.

Union, when participating states will share a common currency, with monetary policy determined by the European Central Bank. Some argue that this step will lead inexorably to full political union, with further powers being granted to the European Parliament. The European Union will, therefore, be in essence a federation, whether it assumes the name or not. As the powers of the European institutions, particularly the Parliament, increase, it will be impossible to take the notion of national sovereignty seriously. The United Kingdom will have become a Member State of a European federation.

It is in fact arguable that this transformation has already occurred, and that the European Union should already be characterized as some sort of federation. Without doubt the Community established by the Treaty of Rome is a distinct legal system. It has its own political and legal institutions, and may, like national governments, initiate or defend legal proceedings.[31] (Confusingly, the Union does not have legal personality, so could not strictly participate in legal proceedings.) The Treaty of Rome is, as we have seen, a constitutional charter for the Community. Moreover, the ECJ has repeatedly stated that the states have transferred their sovereignty, albeit within the limited fields specified by the Treaty. Within those fields Community law prevails over inconsistent national law, and the courts of the Member States must apply directly effective rules of the former.

For these reasons alone the European Union bears some resemblance to a federation, at least so far as the first pillar is concerned, where in effect it acts as the Community under the constitutional principles formulated by the Court of Justice in the last forty years. The related principles of direct effect and Community supremacy clearly indicate it is more than a league or alliance of states. Loose associations of this kind cannot issue rules binding the individual citizens of the participating states, any more than international organizations such as the United Nations are able to do. Even the US Articles of Confederation of 1781 did not institute any direct legal relationship between the Congress and the citizens of the states. Acts of Congress bound only the states. The transformation to a true federation was brought about by Article VI of the 1787 Constitution, the Supremacy Clause, which provides that state courts must give effect to the federal Constitution and laws of the federal Congress, no matter what state law itself says on the matter.[32] The related principles of directly effective rights and the supremacy of

---

[31] Arts. 210–11, renumbered Arts. 281–2 by the Treaty of Amsterdam.
[32] For fuller discussion, see Ch. 3, sect. 2.

Community law indicate that the Union has constitutionally more in common with the United States federation than with its earlier confederal arrangements.

Another resemblance to the US Constitution appears in the complex Community law principle of 'pre-emption' developed by the ECJ in a number of cases. Under the doctrine a Member State may not legislate or act in a field reserved by the Treaty of Rome for legislation by the Community. In these areas the Community enjoys exclusive competence. The doctrine clearly applies when the Community has already legislated;[33] some decisions suggest it may also apply where the Community has not yet taken steps to implement its powers.[34] At most a state may take necessary measures in the common interest with Commission approval. This principle is strikingly similar to the approach taken by the US Supreme Court to interpretation of the Interstate Commerce Clause: Article I, Section 8. Even where Congress has not exercised its power under the Clause to regulate an aspect of interstate commerce, the states are conceded only a limited freedom to regulate that matter; the Court has, therefore, curtailed the powers of the states, although the Constitution does not explicitly forbid state action in this context. It is inconceivable that a pre-emption principle would be formulated under a loose confederal constitution.

Recently Member States, particularly the United Kingdom, have been anxious to reduce the volume of Community legislation, and thereby restrict what they consider to be unnecessary interference with the freedom of national legislatures. To this end, the Maastricht Treaty introduced the principle of subsidiarity, while the Amsterdam Treaty has added a Protocol to flesh out the principle. The Community must respect the principle, as defined in the amended Treaty of Rome:[35]

In areas which do not fall within its exclusive competence, the Community shall take action, in accordance with the principle of subsidiarity, only if and in so far as the objectives of the proposed action cannot sufficiently be achieved by the Member States and can therefore, by reason of the scale or effects of the proposed action, be better achieved by the Community.

---

[33] See Case 60/86, *Commission* v. *United Kingdom* [1988] ECR 3921, where the Court ruled that cars sold in the UK could not be required to carry 'dim-dip' devices, since the requirement was not imposed by the relevant EC directive.

[34] e.g. Case 804/79, *Commission* v. *United Kingdom* [1981] ECR 1045.

[35] Art. 3b, renumbered Art. 5 under the Amsterdam Treaty. The Union is required to implement its objectives in conformity with the Community subsidiarity principle: TEU, Art. B, renumbered Art. 2.

There is considerable controversy whether the subsidiarity principle is justiciable in view of the difficulties any court, even the ECJ, would have in determining whether a state acting alone can achieve an objective sufficiently or whether, if not, the Community could accomplish it more effectively. Moreover, the principle may be of limited application, in view of the pre-emption principle which seems to concede exclusive competence to the Community in areas reserved to it, at least when it has exercised its powers. Perhaps it would be more appropriate to see the principle primarily as one of political, rather than legal, significance. But what is constitutionally significant is that the subsidiarity principle reveals the 'federal' character of the Community. Subsidiarity is designed to redress the balance of authority between the Community and the states or, to put it another way, to counteract the inevitable tendency in federations for powers to gravitate to the centre.[36] Indeed, it is likely that the subsidiarity principle was partly modelled on Article 72(2) of the German Basic Law. That states that the Federation is entitled to legislate on matters on which it enjoys concurrent powers with the *Länder* (states), when the subject cannot be effectively regulated by the individual states.

Indeed, there would be no occasion for a subsidiarity rule if the Community were only a loose confederation. In that situation states would always be free, at least legally, to renegotiate the terms of the confederation and the powers transferred to the centre; moreover, the scope of these powers would not be determined by a federal court. It is only because the EC is already more than a confederation that the subsidiarity principle could be considered necessary. There is, finally, the irony that the supporters of a strong subsidiarity rule favour its enforcement by the ECJ; they would also prefer that court to rule as often as possible in favour of exclusive state competence. But for the Court of Justice to police the subsidiarity principle would reinforce the federal nature of the Union. It is characteristic of federations, and of no other constitutional arrangement, that a central court determines the limits of federal and of state powers.

So from the perspective of *constitutional law* the Community—on which the European Union is largely based—resembles a federation. At the *political* level, however, another view is plausible; this alternative perspective is particularly relevant to the Union, in so far as it rests on its two other pillars concerning foreign policy and judicial co-operation. The heads of government of the Member States meeting in the European Council determine the direction of the Union, while their

---

[36] See Ch. 3, sect. 2.

ministers are ultimately responsible in the Council for the passage of Community legislation. The political development of the Union, therefore, depends on the states, not on a federal government, as would be the case with a true federation. Moreover, even though its powers have been extended by the Treaties of Maastricht and Amsterdam, the Parliament is not yet a full legislative body. It consists of 'representatives of the peoples of the States brought together in the Community', not the people of the Union as a separate political entity.[37] As yet, there are no genuinely European political parties, though national parties combine to form groups to work together in the EP, and their role was acknowledged by the Treaty of Maastricht. Another institutional difference from federations such as the USA and Germany is that there is no system of federal courts sitting at regional or state level. There are only the ECJ and, attached to it, the Court of First Instance with a limited jurisdiction. The Community legal system depends on co-operation between national courts sitting in each state and the ECJ.

With regard to its substantive powers, the Union differs in at least two major respects from the typical federation. First, it has only recently acquired a role in the conduct of foreign and security policy. In this area it acts under guidelines from the European Council, and neither the Commission nor Parliament participates in the formation of policy. In practice, therefore, the system continues to be one largely of co-operation between the states, whereas foreign and defence matters are quintessentially matters for the centre in federal systems. Secondly, the Community has no independent taxing power over individuals and corporations. A system of the Community's 'own resources' has been instituted under which it is entitled to receive a proportion of the VAT levied throughout the Community, as well as customs duties and other levies paid in respect of trade with non-member states. Although the Community has established Regional Development and Social Funds to redistribute money to poorer areas, these constitute a tiny fraction of the total states' budgets and are far removed from the funds available, say, to the federal governments in Washington and Bonn/Berlin to influence the social policies of the constituent states.

At the political level, therefore, the Community has more in common with a confederation than a true federation.[38] While the Court, and so far as they are able the Commission and Parliament, exercise a federalizing influence, the Member States control the pace of development.

[37] Treaty of Rome, Art. 137, renumbered Art. 189.
[38] See J. J. Weiler, 'The Transformation of Europe', 100 *Yale LJ* 2403 (1991).

Formally this is done within the European Council, an institution of the Union. In practice, development is dependent on a continuous process of debate between the heads of government (and the President of France), a debate which has been dominated for much of the last forty years by France and Germany. Among the states, there is naturally a wide range of attitudes, with some of them sympathetic to the federalist perspective and others, notably the United Kingdom, largely hostile.

The fullest legal analysis of the constitutional character of the Union is to be found in the decision of the German Constitutional Court of October 1993 on the challenge to German ratification of the Maastricht Treaty.[39] It was argued that the transfer of powers to the Union and Community institutions entailed by the Treaty infringed the rights of German voters to participate effectively in free democratic elections; as pointed out earlier in this chapter, the Community legislative power lies with the Council of Ministers, rather than the elected European Parliament. The Court rejected the challenge, largely on the ground that the nation states retained their sovereign powers and that it was for them, subject to control by their own parliaments, to determine the future development of the Union.[40] The German Court does not regard the European Union as a state, but as a *Staatenverbund*, a concept previously unknown in German constitutional history. It can roughly be translated as a 'confederation of states'. It is, the Court added, for the states, not the Union itself, to determine whether further steps are taken towards full European integration and a federal system. That is correct. Amendments to the Maastricht and Rome Treaties can only be made by agreement of the states and must be ratified by all of them in accordance with their own constitutional requirements.[41] The Court also emphasized the absence of European political parties and of common newspapers and broadcasting, the development of which would be necessary for the foundation of a democratic European state.

It is at the moment unclear how far the Union will evolve in that direction. Though the Amsterdam Treaty of June 1997 has increased the powers of Parliament and strengthened the inter-governmental foreign and defence pillar of the Union, it does not mark any decisive step

[39] 89 BVerfGE 155 (1994), reported in English as *Brunner* [1994] 1 CMLR 57.
[40] In Decision 92–312 of 2 Sept. 1992, RJC I–505, para. 45 (Favoreu and Philip, 781, 795), the *Conseil constitutionnel* refused to decide whether the transfer of powers to the Union under the TEU contravened the French constitutional principle that national sovereignty belongs to the people: Constitution of 1958, Art. 3.
[41] TEU, Art. R, as amended by the Treaty of Amsterdam, and now renumbered Art. 52; EC Treaty, Art. 247, renumbered Art. 313.

towards a federation. However, Economic and Monetary Union will involve the institution of further supra-national institutions, the European System of Central Banks and the European Central Bank, with power to determine monetary policy and to control the issue of the common currency. It is uncertain whether the states will remain free in practice to pursue wholly independent economic and taxation policies after EMU. At all events, it involves a further transfer of sovereignty, in the sense of effective political and economic power, to European institutions in Brussels and Frankfurt, the seat of the European Central Bank. Interestingly, the French Constitutional Council ruled in 1992 that EMU would deprive Member States of their powers over matters concerned with national sovereignty.[42]

It is clear that the Union is not a federation in the same sense as, say, the United States, Germany, and Australia. In all those countries, there is a division of powers between identifiable federal governments and parliaments on the one hand, and state governments and legislatures on the other. Although there is a similar division of legal power between Brussels and Westminster, there is no European government nor a proper European Parliament with full legislative powers. Furthermore, even if the Community, or now the Union, may be regarded as in some sense a federation, it is not a federal *state*. The Union does not even have legal personality; neither it, nor the Community, is represented in the United Nations or other international organizations.

On the other hand, from a constitutional perspective, the Union is much more than a loose confederation. Perhaps it is unhelpful to try to characterize the Union as either a federation or a confederation; it has significant elements of both constitutional structures.[43] Both the political sovereignty and the legislative supremacy of national parliaments have already been largely surrendered. But the states have not given up their power to determine the future development of the Union. In that sense, it is right to conclude that they have retained a degree of sovereignty, not enjoyed by, say, California or Bavaria. The European Union, therefore, resists clear classification. We have seen in earlier chapters that it is sometimes hard to characterize a national constitution;[44] it is, therefore, hardly surprising that similar difficulties arise for constitutional analysis in the context of the continuing process of European integration.

---

[42] Decision 92–308 of 9 Apr. 1992, RJC I–496, paras. 43–4 (Favoreu and Philip, 781, 789).
[43] See the discussion in the *27th Report of the House of Lords European Communities Committee*, (1990) HL 88, paras. 20–2.
[44] See Ch. 1, sect. 2, and Ch. 3, sect. 2.

5

Parliament and Legislative Power

1. PARLIAMENTARY SUPREMACY

ONE striking consequence of the absence of a codified constitution in the United Kingdom is that the legislative powers of Parliament have never been set out in any definitive form. The Bill of Rights 1689, still the most important statute on the powers of Parliament, was primarily concerned to protect its rights against interference by the Monarch; among other things, it declared that it was illegal for the Crown to levy taxes without Parliamentary consent and to suspend the application of Parliamentary enactments. Other significant legislation, the Parliament Acts 1911–49, as we will see later in this chapter, removed the requirement that the House of Lords consent to legislation. But these statutes assume that Parliament is entitled to enact legislation, that is, rules of general application. They do not establish its right to legislate.

In contrast, codified constitutional texts spell out the powers of the legislature quite explicitly, as well as its composition and methods for its election. For instance Article I, Section 1 of the US Constitution states clearly that '[a]ll Legislative Powers herein granted shall be vested in a Congress of the United States, which shall consist of a Senate and House of Representatives'. Other Sections of the Article prescribe the composition of the Senate and House and the procedure for enacting legislation, as well as enumerating a number of specific legislative and other powers, such as the power to 'lay and collect Taxes' and the power to regulate inter-state commerce. Similarly, Article 34 of the Constitution of the Fifth French Republic spells out the legislative powers of Parliament, while Article 77 of the German Basic Law states that Bills must be adopted by the Bundestag if they are to become federal laws.

(i) The Source and Scope of Parliamentary Supremacy

What is the source of the United Kingdom Parliament's legislative authority and what is the scope of that power? The short answer is that the source of its legislative authority is the common law, the uncodified rules of law formulated by judges when they decide particular cases. Further, it is for the courts to determine the scope of that authority. They must decide, for instance, whether Parliamentary legislative authority prevails over or gives way to inconsistent rules of European Community law, a complex question discussed in section 3 of this chapter. It is largely for this reason the United Kingdom constitution can be described, among other things, as a common law constitution.[1] The law reports are full of statements to the effect that it is the duty of the courts to give effect to enactments of Parliament, or that they cannot be challenged for infringing some fundamental right or the rules of international law. For example, a court easily rejected the argument that it was unconstitutional for Parliament to introduce the offence of incitement to racial hatred, because the law limited the fundamental right to freedom of speech.[2] Judges have emphasized that the United Kingdom Parliament has unlimited legislative supremacy, or that it is sovereign.

It is therefore the courts, rather than Parliament itself, which have formulated the principle which is the corner-stone of the uncodified constitution of the United Kingdom. Naturally, Parliament could declare by an Act of Parliament that it is legally sovereign and that it has unlimited entitlement to enact any legislation it likes.[3] But such a declaratory statute would not add anything to its legislative capacity. Parliament can hardly confer constitutional authority on itself by its own enactment.

There was a time when the judges were unclear whether there are limits to the scope of parliamentary legislative supremacy. Early in the seventeenth century Coke CJ wrote that Acts of Parliament contrary to common right and reason should be regarded as of no effect.[4] But it is very rare to find anyone saying that after the Glorious Revolution of 1688. Judges gradually accepted Parliamentary rule, and during the course of the eighteenth century the principle of its legislative supremacy became firmly established. Naturally, it has generally been welcomed by politicians and ministers, for they can employ it to secure compliance with their policies, at least when they control Parliament. Significant reservations have, however, been expressed by some Scottish

---

[1] Ch. 2, sect. 2.   [2] *R* v. *Jordan* [1967] Crim. L Rev. 483.
[3] There is a precedent for such a statute, since the Bill of Rights 1689 is a measure *declaring* the rights and liberties of Parliament against the 'pretended' powers of the Monarch.
[4] *Dr Bonham's case* (1610) 8 Co. Rep. 114, 118.

judges;[5] legislative supremacy was not an established feature of the
Scottish Parliament before it was merged with the English Parliament
under the Act of Union in 1707. But their doubts have rarely, if ever,
been shared by English judges.[6]

As the courts have formulated the principle of parliamentary
supremacy, it is also for them to decide what amounts to an Act of
Parliament. The common law rule is that Parliament consists of the
House of Commons, the House of Lords, and the Crown. Together they
constitute the Queen in Parliament. Subject to the changes made by the
Parliament Acts 1911–49, each House sitting separately and the
Monarch must assent to a Bill for it to become a statute. As a matter of
constitutional law, legislative supremacy means the supremacy of the
Queen in Parliament, not just the House of Commons. A resolution of
the House of Commons may be binding on Members of Parliament, but
it cannot change the law of the land.[7]

As with other aspects of constitutional law the formulation of the
principle of parliamentary supremacy has largely been left to writers on
the constitution. The doctrine of parliamentary supremacy is particularly associated with the greatest of these scholars, Dicey. For him it was
the dominant legal principle of the constitution. Indeed, it does play
much the same role in United Kingdom constitutional law as the codified constitutional text does in other countries: it lies at the root of most,
if not all, other important aspects of the constitution. It is, of course, in
isolation not as comprehensive as, say, the United States or French
Constitution. But the principle is as fundamental as a codified constitution. Because Parliament enjoys legislative supremacy, it is entitled, for
instance, to alter the powers of the Crown or to establish new courts. In
other countries, the powers of these institutions would be derived from
the constitution itself.

Dicey and other writers on the constitution have generally referred to
Parliament's legislative supremacy as 'Parliamentary Sovereignty'. This
is a rather confusing description, and it is better to avoid it. It is confusing because the concept of 'sovereignty' is more often used in political discourse either to refer to the ultimate sovereign power of the
electorate or alternatively to the sovereignty, that is the independence,

---

[5] *MacCormick* v. *Lord Advocate*, 1953 SC 396, 411–13.

[6] But see the views of Lord Woolf, 'Droit Public-English Style' [1995] *Pub. Law* 57,
69, and Sir John Laws, 'Law and Democracy' [1996] *Pub. Law* 72, 84–8.

[7] See *Stockdale* v. *Hansard* (1839) 9 Ad. & E 1 which held that a Resolution of the
House could not protect Hansard from a libel action in respect of his reports of
Parliamentary proceedings.

of the nation state. Parliament may be *legally* sovereign, but it is misleading to use a word which can be understood to suggest it also enjoys ultimate political control. It certainly does not carry that implication. First, voters elect the Members of Parliament and, therefore, in a sense choose the government every few years. Secondly, as a matter of political reality, in normal circumstances the government controls Parliament through the ability of the Prime Minister to dissolve Parliament, if the government is not supported by members of the majority political party. As a matter of constitutional law, the legislative supremacy of Parliament means simply that the Queen in Parliament has unlimited capacity to enact laws. Parliamentary legislative supremacy means no more than that.

(ii) Parliamentary Supremacy and Political Reality

Taken to its logical limits, the supremacy of Parliament appears to have absurd implications. The Westminster Parliament, it has been said, could as a matter of law make it a crime for French citizens to smoke on the streets of Paris. Strictly, English courts would have to apply such a rule and could fine a Frenchman who is arrested and charged with the offence while resident or on holiday in this country. The law can depart from reality in circumstances of this sort.

Such problems were, however, far from hypothetical at the time when Dicey formulated his theory. At the end of the nineteenth century and in the first three decades of this, it was unclear whether the Westminster Parliament was still entitled to legislate for the Dominions, for example, Canada, Australia, New Zealand, and South Africa. Legislation such as the British North America Act 1867 (the first Canadian Constitution) had given the local parliaments freedom to enact laws, provided their provisions were not incompatible with United Kingdom statutes. It followed that the Westminster Parliament was still entitled to legislate for the Dominions, as it had at least in theory been for the American colonies before the United States became independent. This possibility was only removed as a matter of law in 1931 when the Statute of Westminster enacted the convention that the United Kingdom Parliament could not legislate for a Dominion without the request and consent of that country.[8]

The relationship of the principle of parliamentary legislative supremacy to political reality is perhaps best illustrated now by the 1969

----

[8] Statute of Westminster 1931, s. 4.

ruling of the Privy Council in *Madzimbamuto* v. *Lardner-Burke.*[9]
Immediately after the Unilateral Declaration of Independence (UDI) by
the minority White regime in Southern Rhodesia, the UK Parliament
enacted the Southern Rhodesia Act 1965. This repealed an earlier enactment which had given full authority to the Rhodesian Parliament; it also
empowered the Crown to introduce Orders in Council to regulate that
country. The Privy Council decided that Parliament's legislative power
was not limited by the established convention that it should not legislate for Rhodesia without its consent. Lord Reid added:

> It is often said that it would be unconstitutional for the United Kingdom
> Parliament to do certain things, meaning that the moral, political and other rea-
> sons against doing them are so strong that most people would regard it as highly
> improper if Parliament did these things. But that does not mean that it is beyond
> the power of Parliament to do such things.

In other words, the legislative supremacy of Parliament and political
reality may part company. That had not happened in the Rhodesia case
because at the time of the Privy Council judgment a few years after
UDI, it was unclear whether the attempts of the London government
to exercise effective control were doomed to failure. But constitutional
law would depart from reality if Parliament were to enact legislation
which purported to amend United States criminal law or to proscribe
smoking on the streets of Paris.

(iii) Can Parliament bind its Successors?

The relationship to political reality of constitutional law in general, and
the principle of parliamentary supremacy in particular, is usually of only
theoretical interest. Of potentially more practical significance is the
question whether it is possible for Parliament to enact legislation which
effectively binds its successors, that is, later Parliaments. The answer
might be important, because it would determine whether Parliament
could enact, for example, a Bill of Rights or a measure devolving power
to a Scottish Parliament, and effectively preclude the repeal of these
measures by a later Parliament. The question is generally put in this
way: is it possible for Parliament to *entrench* legislation against repeal, or
amendment, by a subsequent enactment passed in the traditional way?
Dicey denied that Parliament could do this, though his reasons are very
unpersuasive.[10] All they amount to is the dogmatic assertion that
Parliament must as a matter of logic always retain its sovereign capacity

---

[9] [1969] 1 AC 645.   [10] Dicey, 64–70.

to repeal its earlier laws and (less attractively) that England has always been ruled by an absolute legislator, at one time the King and now Parliament.

Admittedly, some cases do establish that Parliament cannot fetter itself simply by stating that a legislative provision is to endure 'for ever' or that a section in a subsequent Act should not have any effect if inconsistent with it.[11] In these circumstances there are no strong reasons for applying the provisions in the earlier statute in preference to those in the later one. It is reasonable for the courts to apply the later statute which is taken impliedly to repeal the inconsistent provisions of the earlier one. But it would be wrong for them to reach the same conclusion, if Parliament were to provide, say, in a Bill of Rights statute that any future legislation infringing these fundamental rights, or repealing the Bill of Rights itself, must secure a two-thirds majority in the House of Commons or be approved by a referendum. It would be dogmatic in these circumstances to insist that the Bill of Rights could be repealed (or any right set out in it infringed) by the traditional simple majority procedure. For there are obviously good reasons why Parliament might intend fundamental human rights to be guaranteed against interference in a Bill only approved by a simple majority of a subsequent Parliament. The requirement of a two-thirds majority or approval at a referendum provides some safeguard against a government decision, approved by its supporters in the Commons, to restrict the exercise of fundamental rights. In the absence of powerful counter arguments, one would expect the courts to respect that guarantee.

Yet defenders of Dicey's views argue that entrenchment of a Bill of Rights or other fundamental legislation in this way is constitutionally impossible.[12] Their case is that the principle of parliamentary legislative supremacy necessarily means that the Houses of Parliament (or more specifically the House of Commons) must be able to pass laws by simple majority and that the Parliament cannot change this rule, even for the enactment of certain types of important legislation. The rule is said to be quite different from any other rule of the common law, in that it alone cannot be modified by statute. Any amendment to that rule, it is claimed rather fancifully, would amount to a legal revolution. The argument is very unconvincing. For a start the common law rule does not require Parliament to enact legislation by simple majority. The Houses

---

[11] *Ellen Street Estates* v. *Minister of Health* [1934] 1 KB 590.
[12] The classic exposition of this case is by H. W. R. Wade, 'The Basis of Legal Sovereignty' [1955] *Cambridge LJ* 172.

happen to use that procedure, but there is no reason to believe that the practice is sacrosanct or could not be changed by an Act of Parliament. Secondly, as we will see shortly, Parliament has changed the rules for the enactment of legislation in the Parliament Acts 1911–49 by reducing the powers of the House of Lords. If there is no difficulty in accepting a change in the composition of Parliament which strengthens the prerogatives of the House of Commons, there should not be any problem in accepting a change in the manner of enacting legislation which reduces those prerogatives—either by the introduction of the requirements of a two-thirds majority or by requiring certain legislation to be approved at a referendum. Some cases from other countries show that legislation can be entrenched in these ways.[13]

One bizarre implication of the traditional Diceyan perspective is that the United Kingdom constitutional arrangements would have to be regarded as rigid in practice. For its defenders claim that the common law rule of parliamentary supremacy is so fundamental that it cannot be modified. As a result, it would be impossible to amend the present constitutional arrangements by entrenching a Bill of Rights, let alone introduce a federal or confederal constitution. In contrast, the vast majority of codified constitutions, generally characterized as more rigid than the flexible constitution of the United Kingdom, can be amended by a procedure set out in the text.[14] It is hard to accept that the United Kingdom Constitution is so rigid that the principle of parliamentary supremacy can never be modified without a legal revolution.

What is clear is that the judiciary is as much the guardian of the United Kingdom constitution as it usually is of codified constitutions. It would be for the courts to determine whether Parliament can bind its successors by making radical amendments to the procedure for enacting legislation, just as they have decided, as we will see, that Parliament is free to bind itself not to enact legislation contrary to European Community law.[15] As a matter of prediction, it is uncertain whether they would accept that Parliament can entrench, say, a Bill of Rights in preference to the traditional Diceyan view. But there can be no doubt that they should uphold the entrenchment of a Bill of Rights or of a

---

[13] See in particular *Harris* v. *Minister of the Interior* (1952), (2) SA 429 (AD), and *Bribery Commissioners* v. *Ranasinghe* [1965] AC 172 (Privy Council appeal from Sri Lanka). Recently, the Israeli Supreme Court has held that when the Knesset, a sovereign legislature, enacts Basic Laws on human rights, it binds itself not to enact ordinary legislation which infringes those rights.

[14] For the amendment of rigid constitutions, see Ch. 1, sect. 2.

[15] See sect. 3 below.

measure devolving power to Scotland or other parts of the United Kingdom. Such an approach would better promote the values of liberal constitutionalism, discussed in Chapter 1, than continued adherence to the traditional view. Parliamentary legislative supremacy allows governments in effect to use a simple majority in the House of Commons to do what they like without constitutional restraint.

2. THE HOUSE OF COMMONS AND THE HOUSE OF LORDS

Like many other countries the United Kingdom has a bi-cameral legislature, that is, there are two Houses of Parliament, the House of Commons and the House of Lords. Until about the end of the eighteenth century the House of Lords, frequently referred to as the Upper Chamber to denote its seniority, was at least an equal partner to the Commons in the 'balanced constitution'.[16] But with the gradual extension during the nineteenth century of the right to vote and the advent of democratic politics, its legitimacy has increasingly been called into question. At first by constitutional convention, and now by law under the Parliament Acts 1911-49, its legislative role has been significantly limited. In effect, the Lords must assent to a Bill certified by the Speaker of the House of Commons as a Money Bill within a month after it has been sent to the Upper Chamber, while, with one exception, they can only delay other Public Bills for one year.[17] This reduction in the Lords' powers does not apply to a Bill to extend the life of a Parliament, or, to put it another way, to postpone a General Election, beyond the five-year period established in 1911 for the duration of Parliaments. However, even in this context the legislative power of the Lords is not entrenched, for the House could only delay for a year a Bill to remove this last vestige of the 'veto power'.

The Parliament Acts 1911-49 have established the dominance of the House of Commons. There were unsuccessful attempts during the passage of the 1911 measure to exempt Bills dealing with 'constitutional issues' from the new procedure, so retaining the Lords' right to veto major changes to the existing arrangements.[18] Not surprisingly there

---

[16] See Ch. 2, sect. 3.

[17] Under the 1911 Act it could delay Public Bills for two years, but this was reduced to one year by the 1949 measure, itself enacted under the 1911 Act procedure.

[18] See J. Jaconelli, 'The Parliament Bill 1910-1911: The Mechanics of Constitutional Protection' (1991) 10 *Parliamentary History* 277.

was little agreement over which measures should be given constitutional status for this purpose, while the Liberal government was anxious to exclude the courts from any jurisdiction to determine these matters. The supremacy of the Commons is ensured by giving the last word on the question of what amounts to a Money Bill and other issues arising under the Parliament Acts to the Speaker of the House of Commons, hardly a neutral umpire if there were a serious disagreement between the two Houses.

What is the significance of this reform, one of the most important amendments made to the uncodified constitution in the course of this century? In the first place it gave legal expression to the gradual alteration in the balance of powers between the Commons and Lords which had occurred over the previous century. Parliamentary legislative supremacy now clearly means the supremacy of the elected House of Commons, a development which alarmed its great apostle, Dicey. It even prompted him in his later writings to urge use of the referendum to act as a constraint on the Commons' potentially dictatorial powers. Whatever the weaknesses of the House of Lords, at least in theory it could check abuses of power by the stronger branch of the legislature. The constitutional value of checks and balances was sacrificed in 1911–49 to the interests of democracy.

The second point, already made in section 1, is that the Parliament Acts have altered the common law rule which provides the basis of the informal UK constitution. When the Speaker certifies that a Bill is a Money Bill or that it satisfies other requirements of the Parliament Acts, the courts must apply it even if the consent of the House of Lords to the measure had not been obtained. Acceptance of legislation enacted under the procedure prescribed by the Parliament Acts 1911–49 shows that there is nothing immutable or sacrosanct in the common law formulation of the principle of Parliamentary supremacy.

It is now taken for granted that the abolition of the peers' veto power was a reasonable step in the context of their obstruction of Lloyd George's 'People's Budget' in 1909 and of the illegitimacy of the composition of the Upper Chamber. At that time the House was composed more or less entirely of hereditary peers, the only other members being some Bishops of the Church of England and the Law Lords, given life peerages to sit as Lords of Appeal in Ordinary. Now about a third of the House are life peers, appointed by the Prime Minister, albeit sometimes on the nomination of Opposition parties. But that has done little to enhance its legitimacy. In effect, recent Crown appointees have been added to the more substantial numbers of hereditary peers, themselves the heirs of dukes and other nobles given their titles in previous centuries.

The Preamble to the Parliament Act 1911 refers to the desirability of replacing the hereditary House with a Second Chamber constituted on a popular basis, that is, by election. But nothing has been done to bring this about. Reform of the composition of the House of Lords remains one of the most intractable problems of constitutional reform.[19] The central difficulty is that it would be difficult to establish an elected Second Chamber without undermining the democratic legitimacy of the Commons. One possibility would be for the members of the Second Chamber to be elected to represent Scotland, Wales, and separate English regions; that would be a sensible step if the United Kingdom were eventually to adopt something like a federal constitution. In this context it is important to note that the most influential Upper Houses are to be found in federal constitutions; the United States and Australian Senates and the German Bundesrat are good examples. If successful reform of the Upper Chamber's composition could be achieved, it might also be appropriate to consider strengthening its functions, for example, by restoring its power to veto certain types of Bill, such as those affecting fundamental rights or amending the constitution.

The positions of the House of Lords and its members have been further weakened by constitutional conventions. Though there is no legal bar to a peer becoming Prime Minister or Chancellor of the Exchequer, such an appointment is almost certainly precluded by convention. Even if George V's appointment of Baldwin as Prime Minister in preference to Lord Curzon in 1923 does not afford a wholly persuasive precedent for the existence of the convention,[20] the fact that Sir Alec Douglas-Home renounced his peerage on the invitation to succeed MacMillan as Prime Minister in 1964 indicates that a rule of this kind is now generally accepted. The possibility that a political party (or its Members of Parliament) would elect a Peer as its leader can safely be discounted.

There is also arguably a convention to the effect that, except in extreme cases, the House of Lords should not exercise its legal power to delay the passage of legislation, at least when an intention to introduce the measure has been stated in the governing party's manifesto. Whether this is so or not, only one Bill has been delayed by the House

---

[19] For a valuable recent contribution to the debate, see the Constitutional Unit's report, *Reform of the House of Lords* (1996).

[20] See V. Bogdanor, *The Monarchy and the Constitution* (Oxford, 1995), 89–93.

since 1949; that was the War Crimes Bill, a non-party measure conferring jurisdiction on United Kingdom courts to try certain Second World War crimes, even when committed outside the country. In practice, whatever the political colour of the government, the House is extremely reluctant to assert its view against that of the Commons. The key point is that with its present composition, and with its weak legal authority further restricted by convention, the Upper Chamber is not an effective check on the legislative supremacy of the House of Commons.

3. EUROPEAN COMMUNITY LAW AND PARLIAMENTARY SUPREMACY

(i) The Principle of Community Supremacy

One straightforward aspect of the principle of parliamentary legislative supremacy is that the courts must apply the legislation of Parliament in preference to other types of law, such as the by-laws of a local authority or Orders made by the Crown in the exercise of its prerogative powers. But the position is not nearly so simple when there is a conflict between an Act of Parliament and the rules of European Community law. As was explained in the previous chapter, under European Community law, as developed by the European Court of Justice (ECJ) in Luxembourg, some provisions of the Treaty of Rome and of Community legislation confer rights on individuals which national courts must protect. These provisions have 'direct effect' in the legal systems of the Member States; they must be automatically applied by national courts. Further, national courts must enforce directly effective rights, notwithstanding any incompatible provisions in the law of that state. For instance, many provisions in the Community Equal Pay and Equal Treatment Directives create directly effective rights; they must, therefore, under Community law be given priority over any inconsistent national rules which may be found, for example, in the United Kingdom Equal Pay Act 1970 and the Sex Discrimination Act 1975.

The European Court of Justice has held that directly effective Community provisions must be applied, even over incompatible national law which has been enacted after the introduction of the Community legislation.[21] The statutes and other laws of the Member States must give way to these Community provisions. This is a crucial aspect of the principle of the supremacy of the Community law, formulated by the European Court of Justice in a number of landmark rulings.[22]

[21] *Simmenthal* [1978] ECR 629.   [22] See Ch. 4, sect. 3.

In theory, it would be possible for the ECJ to state the principles of direct effect and Community supremacy, but for the courts of the United Kingdom (and of France, Germany, and other Member States) to give priority to national law. However, a moment's reflection shows that this divergence of approach would be quite impracticable. It would undermine the development of a distinct Community legal order. The application of European Community law would then depend on the particular approach taken by the judges in the various Member States. The Treaty of Rome or Community legislation might create rights which are enforced in, say, Germany and some other states, but not in Italy and the United Kingdom. The Community might be able to tolerate occasional differences of this type, but widespread divergence would make nonsense of the common market, let alone of the closer union which is the object of the Treaties of Rome and Maastricht.

(ii) Acceptance of Community Supremacy in the United Kingdom

How should judges in the United Kingdom approach conflicts between European Community law and Parliamentary legislation. They are given considerable guidance by the European Communities Act 1972, which was enacted in order to give legal effect in the United Kingdom to membership of the Community. Section 2(4) of the Act indicates that any legislation 'passed or to be passed . . . shall be construed and take effect subject to' the preceding terms of the section, one of which provides for the enforcement in the United Kingdom of directly effective rules of Community law. This opaque provision suggests that the courts should give such rules priority over inconsistent United Kingdom legislation, even when it is enacted after the European Communities Act 1972. Section 3 is much clearer; it imposes a duty on the courts to determine questions of Community law in accordance with the principles laid down by rulings of the ECJ. That indirectly requires them to accept the supremacy of Community law.

English and Scottish courts have accepted this principle in a number of cases, but it is only necessary to refer to one leading decision of the House of Lords. The *Factortame* case raised the question whether the English courts should suspend the enforcement of the Merchant Shipping Act 1988 until it was conclusively determined whether it violated the Treaty of Rome. The applicants, companies whose directors were Spanish nationals, claimed that the legislation infringed the prohibition in the Treaty of discrimination on the basis of nationality, inasmuch as it required British fishing vessels to be owned and controlled by United Kingdom citizens. Initially, the House of Lords had ruled that as a matter of constitutional law it was required to apply the Merchant Shipping Act 1988, in advance of any ruling of the European Court of Justice indicating that the statute violated Community law;[23] but the Lords referred to the ECJ the question whether it should, under Community law, suspend application of the statute, on the ground that there was a possible violation of the applicants' rights.

The European Court of Justice ruled that courts in the Member States must set aside national legislation (and other rules) which inhibited, even temporarily, the rights conferred by Community law. As a result, the House of Lords granted the applicants an interim order to stop enforcement of the Merchant Shipping legislation. In the course of his judgment Lord Bridge made this important statement of principle:[24]

> Under the terms of the Act of 1972 it has always been clear that it was the duty of a United Kingdom court, when delivering final judgment, to override any rule of national law found to be in conflict with any directly enforceable rule of Community law. . . . Thus, there is nothing in any way novel to according supremacy to rules of Community law in those areas to which they apply and to insist that, in the protection of rights under Community law, national courts must not be inhibited by rules of national law from granting interim relief in appropriate cases is no more than a logical recognition of that supremacy.

The decision in *Factortame* is particularly significant. The provisions of the 1988 statute were clearly intended to limit the rights of non-UK nationals, and the statute was, of course, enacted after the incorporation of the Treaty of Rome into United Kingdom law by the European Communities Act 1972. Normally, when there is a conflict between the terms of two statutes the courts must apply the later one, since it is understood to repeal the inconsistent provisions in earlier legislation— the principle of 'implied repeal'. But in this case the House of Lords decided it must give precedence to the Community rule over subsequent Parliamentary legislation. This does not entail that the latter is void or of no effect; the statute continues to apply to non-Community nationals, but it is inapplicable within the Community context.[25]

---

[23] *R* v. *Secretary of State for Transport, ex parte Factortame Ltd.* [1990] 2 AC 85. Subsequently, the ECJ ruled it was against Community law to make the nationality of its owner a condition for registering a vessel: [1992] QB 680.

[24] *Factortame Ltd.* v. *Secretary of State for Transport (No. 2)* [1991] 1 AC 603, 658.

[25] Also see Lord Keith in *Equal Opportunities Commission* v. *Secretary of State for Employment* [1994] 1 WLR 409, 418–9.

It is clear, therefore, that in relation to directly effective Community law, Parliament no longer enjoys legislative supremacy. The courts have decided not to apply statutes which conflict with directly effective provisions of Community law. The position would almost certainly be quite different if Parliament were to enact legislation expressly repealing the European Communities Act 1972, as a consequence of United Kingdom withdrawal from the Union. The courts would almost certainly apply that legislation over the Treaty of Rome and Community law. However, this expectation is not enough to support the view that Parliament still enjoys unqualified legislative supremacy. It does not while the United Kingdom remains a member of the European Union.

Lord Bridge emphasized in *Factortame* that Parliament had voluntarily accepted a limit on its legislative powers through passage of the European Communities Act 1972. Parliament had directed the courts, in sections 2 and 3 of the Act, to give priority to directly effective Community law. In effect it has itself qualified the apparently absolute principle of parliamentary legislative supremacy. This bears out the view, expressed earlier in this chapter, that the common law principle of parliamentary supremacy may constitutionally be modified by Parliament itself. Admittedly, it is possible to regard this qualification to the scope of parliamentary legislative supremacy as a 'legal revolution'. But that seems rather a melodramatic interpretation.[26] Rather, the European Communities Act 1972, like the Parliament Acts 1911–49, should be treated as amending the flexible constitution of the United Kingdom.

4. THE DELIBERATIVE FUNCTIONS OF PARLIAMENT

It would be a great mistake to conclude that the Westminster Parliament's only role is that of enacting legislation. Indeed, Bagehot thought it was subsidiary to its function of choosing the Prime Minister and government.[27] Related to that is its function of holding the government to account. Under the principle of ministerial responsibility, a government must resign if Parliament refuses to support it on a confidence motion. During the mid-nineteenth century, governments were frequently dismissed by Parliament under this principle. In theory Parliament, particularly the House of Commons, may also compel the

---

[26] See P. P. Craig, 'United Kingdom Sovereignty after *Factortame*' (1991) 11 *Yearbook of European Law* 221, 250–2, and T. R. S. Allan, 'Parliamentary Sovereignty: Law, Politics, and Revolution' (1997) 113 *LQR* 443.

[27] Bagehot, ch. IV, esp. 150–5.

resignation of individual ministers. These principles of collective and individual ministerial responsibility to Parliament are discussed in the next chapter.

We would now give more emphasis to other roles performed by the two Houses of Parliament, those described by Bagehot as the 'teaching' and 'informing' functions. Through debates and the questioning of ministers, and increasingly through their Select Committees, MPs and peers scrutinize the development of government policy, as well as examining aspects of the administration of that policy. The latter work has been considerably strengthened by the investigations of officers such as the Comptroller and Auditor General, who reports to the Public Accounts Committee, and the Parliamentary Commissioner for Administration (the Ombudsman), also responsible to a Select Committee of the House of Commons. The House of Lords in particular performs a valuable role in initiating discussion of contemporary social and ethical issues outside the scope of party politics; some of its committees, notably the Select Committee on the European Communities, have earned widespread respect.

In exercising these functions, the Houses of Parliament scrutinize and check the government. This work is characteristic of modern legislatures and their committees. It is quite different from their legislative function, which they discharge by the consideration and enactment of Bills. In the absence of a strong separation of powers principle in the United Kingdom, there are no constitutional objections to Parliament assuming deliberative, non-legislative functions; indeed, they provide a necessary check on government. Further, legislation may give the Houses of Parliament power to dismiss the holder of an office.[28] Statutes also frequently confer on the House of Commons and House of Lords authority to invalidate ministerial regulations by passing a negative resolution. Sometimes legislation requires the approval of the Houses to the application of government policy.

By comparison, legal difficulties may arise when a constitution is based on the separation of powers. In the United States Acts of Congress have been held unconstitutional when they gave it power to control the execution of the laws, a responsibility of the President under Article II of the Constitution. On this basis a majority of the Supreme Court invalidated an Act of Congress which had made provision for the two Houses (by Joint Resolution) to remove from office the Comptroller General, an officer who had an 'executive' power to order reductions in

---

[28] The Parliamentary Commissioner for Administration may be removed on a vote of both Houses: Parliamentary Commissioner Act 1967, s. 1(3).

departmental budgets. In the view of the majority, this procedure allowed Congress control over the execution of the laws; the Act, therefore, violated the separation of powers.[29] Equally controversial was a ruling to the effect that a procedure known as the 'legislative veto' was unconstitutional. Under this procedure Acts of Congress authorized one House of Congress to pass resolutions which invalidated executive decisions, in the particular case a decision by the Attorney-General to suspend the deportation of an alien.[30]

These constitutional problems cannot arise under the United Kingdom constitution. The 'legislative veto' procedure held unconstitutional in the United States is quite similar to the standard powers of each House of Parliament to veto ministerial regulations by negative resolution. The explanation for this difference is simply that Congress may only discharge the 'legislative powers' set out in the US Constitution, as interpreted by the Supreme Court; in contrast, the powers of the United Kingdom Parliament are not limited in this way. Legislation may, and often does, give it specific authority to participate in, or control, the implementation of laws by the executive.[31]

5. THE ROLE AND PRIVILEGES OF MEMBERS OF PARLIAMENT

Modern European constitutions frequently contain provisions about the rights and privileges of members of the legislature. Particularly common are rules, such as Article 9 of the Bill of Rights 1689, conferring immunity from prosecution or other legal proceedings in respect of anything said or done in the course of the Member's functions.[32] Their object is to secure uninhibited debate in the legislature. It is important for Members of Parliament not to be worried that anything they say, or write in a parliamentary report or other paper, might provide the basis for an action for defamation or a criminal prosecution. Absolute freedom of speech is not guaranteed primarily in favour of the individual Member, but in the interest of the House as a whole and the general public. So it may be proper for the legislative body to be able to protect its freedom of debate by taking proceedings against anyone who

---

[29] *Bowsher* v. *Synar*, 478 US 714 (1986).   [30] *INS* v. *Chadha*, 462 US 919 (1983).
[31] For the exercise by Parliament of judicial power, see Ch. 2, sect. 3 and Ch. 7, sects. 1 and 2.
[32] See Art. 26 of the French Fifth Republic Constitution, and Art. 46 of the German Basic Law.

attempts to interfere with that freedom. In the United Kingdom the House of Commons can protect its privileges, most notably its freedom of speech and debate, by taking disciplinary action in these circumstances against MPs or members of the public who, in its judgement, have interfered with their exercise. As will be explained, the courts are unwilling to control the exercise by the Houses and their members of these privileges, including the power of the Houses to take proceedings for breach of privilege and contempt.

It is common for constitutions to try to safeguard the independence of members of the legislature. The German rule is particularly striking:[33]

[Deputies to the German Bundestag] shall be representatives of the whole people, not bound by orders and instructions, and shall be subject only to their conscience.

There are similar provisions in the French and Italian Constitutions.[34] They reflect the classical principle of representative government, formulated by Edmund Burke in his speech to the electors of Bristol, that Members of Parliament are chosen to exercise their independent judgement. They are not delegates of the electorate. However, the phenomenon of modern party government which requires tight party discipline in the legislature is hard to reconcile with this principle. If Members exercised genuinely independent judgement on each Bill, a government would be unable to secure the passage of the programme on which it was elected, and for the same reason effective opposition with a clear alternative programme of measures would be difficult.

For the United Kingdom principles similar to the continental European provisions have been incorporated in various resolutions of the House of Commons. In 1947 Members of Parliament were forbidden by resolution from entering into an agreement with an outside body controlling their independence or requiring them to act as that body's parliamentary representative. The resolution affirmed that Members owed duties to their constituents and the country as a whole, rather than to any particular section of it.[35] In theory, both a Member of Parliament and an outside body, for example a company or trade union, could be reprimanded, if it threatened to withdraw financial support if he voted

---

[33] Art. 38(1) of the Basic Law.
[34] French Constitution, Art. 27; Italian Constitution, Art. 67.
[35] Resolution accepting Report of Committee of Privileges on *W. J. Brown, MP* (HC 118, 1947): 440 HC Deb. (5th ser.), col. 284.

against its interests. In extreme cases it is possible that the Member might be expelled from the House.[36] It is unclear whether these principles apply in the same way to parliamentary groups and to political parties or their local constituency associations. Government could not be sustained unless the backing of MPs from the majority party could be 'guaranteed' by the threat to withdraw the Party Whip in the event of failure to support it in the Commons. However, arguably the threat of the party outside Parliament to expel a Member if he voted in a particular way should be treated as a breach of the privileges of the House of Commons. Uncertainty concerning this point highlights the difficulties in applying traditional constitutional principles to modern mass party democracies.

The resolution of 1947 has been significantly strengthened by the House of Commons, following its acceptance of the first report of the Nolan Committee on Standards in Public Life.[37] Members are forbidden from engaging in any paid advocacy for an outside body by means, for example, of a Parliamentary Question or speech in a debate. Moreover, they must disclose the terms of any agreement with an outside organization and, in approximate terms, the level of remuneration paid for consultancy services. Enforcement of these rules will be helped by the appointment of a Parliamentary Commissioner for Standards responsible to the Commons Committee of Standards and Privileges. The rules encourage Members of Parliament to discharge their functions independently by exposing their consultancies to a degree of openness.

In the United Kingdom all questions concerning the conduct and payment of MPs are determined by the House of Commons itself. The courts play no part. They are even unwilling to intervene, for example, to determine whether the expulsion of a Member is lawful. The explanation for their reluctance is the long-standing common law rule that they should not question the manner in which the Houses of Parliament exercise their privileges, even if that may have involved an incorrect interpretation of the law.[38] The courts are prepared to decide whether

[36] The House of Commons still asserts, and conceivably could exercise, its power to exclude a properly elected Member from the House. This was last done in 1947 when Garry Allighan MP was expelled for contempt of the House.

[37] (1995) Cm 2850.

[38] e.g., see *Bradlaugh* v. *Gossett* (1884) 12 QBD 271, where the House refused to allow the plaintiff, an atheist elected for Northampton, to take the parliamentary oath and hence his seat. Although the House's interpretation of the legislation was wrong, the court refused to intervene.

a privilege exists in law and to determine its scope. But they will not go further to examine how it is exercised. This reluctance has led on occasion to odd results. In 1839 the Court of Queen's Bench ruled that the House of Commons could not grant Hansard, the publisher of authorized reports of its proceedings, immunity from a libel action;[39] that would have been an illegal extension of its privileges. However, when the Sheriff of Middlesex attempted to enforce judgment against Hansard, the House committed him for contempt, and the same court decided it could not do anything about this. The common law courts recognize the House's entitlement to punish Members or others who infringe its privileges or who commit a contempt of the House,[40] and they will not question the way in which the House exercises that power.

The courts are also unwilling to interfere with the internal proceedings of either House of Parliament. For instance, they have refused to entertain the argument that a Private Act of Parliament was obtained by fraud on the part of its promoter; any judicial intervention would have involved investigation of Parliamentary procedure.[41] Consequently, injustices may not be corrected. Moreover, in principle it is very unsatisfactory that the Houses can rule that there has been a breach of its privileges or contempt without any opportunity for the 'accused' to have legal representation or a right of appeal against the decision.

There is an argument for giving the courts power to determine whether there has been a breach of privilege or contempt of a House. There is a precedent for this step. Since 1868 disputes concerning the validity of election have been referred to an election court, in effect two judges. Previously they had been resolved by the Commons itself. The privileges of the two Houses of Parliament are of course quite separate from the doctrine of parliamentary supremacy. Under that principle the Queen in Parliament has authority to enact legislation and the courts must apply it. It does not follow that they should treat each House acting independently with the same respect.

Legal regulation of these matters is in fact possible as well as, on balance, desirable. The German Basic Law provides that deputies to the Bundestag are 'entitled to a remuneration adequate to ensure their independence'.[42] The Constitutional Court has held, among other matters,

---

[39] *Stockdale* v. *Hansard* (1839) 9 Ad. & E 1, 112 ER 1112.

[40] *Case of the Sheriff of Middlesex* (1840) 11 Ad. & E 273, 113 ER 419. But Lord Denman CJ suggested that the courts might intervene if the grounds given for contempt of the House were clearly insufficient for such proceedings.

[41] *British Railways Board* v. *Pickin* [1974] AC 765.   [42] Art. 48(3).

that legislation must provide deputies with salaries adequate to enable them to devote themselves fully to parliamentary responsibilities and to give up other sources of earned income. Moreover, legislation should prohibit any reliance by deputies on casual employment or consultancies which provide payment for services; such dependence might compromise their independence of judgement, guaranteed by the Basic Law.[43] In the United States the Supreme Court has held it can review a decision by the House of Representatives to exclude an elected member.[44] These are matters on which the Houses of the Westminster Parliament claim the last word, although they have nothing to do with its legislative supremacy. In principle, the scope of Parliamentary privileges should be set out so far as possible in statute, and the courts should have jurisdiction, at least to ensure that the House has exercised them on lawful grounds.

6. CONCLUSIONS

The principle of parliamentary supremacy is the foundation of the constitutional arrangements of the United Kingdom, taking the place occupied in other countries by the codified text. It has been modified by the European Communities Act 1972. But outside the context of conflicts with incompatible European Community law the principle asserts that Parliament is constitutionally free to enact any legislation it likes. If it were to enact a statute which violates fundamental principles of international law or which postpones the next general election, the courts would be required to apply it. Admittedly, under the Human Rights Act 1998, the courts may now rule that a legislative provision is incompatible with a right protected by the European Human Rights Convention. But the principle of parliamentary supremacy still prevents them holding that provision invalid. It is the courts which have accepted and formulated this principle; they determine its scope and its relationship with European Community law. Moreover, it is for the courts to determine the question whether Parliament is able to enact legislation which limits the freedom of later Parliaments. Perhaps, in an extreme case, a bold court might now refuse to apply evil legislation.

At the time of its development during the eighteenth and early nineteenth centuries, the doctrine of parliamentary legislative supremacy represented both a principle of constitutional law and a statement about

---

[43] 40 BVerfGE 296 (1975).   [44] *Powell* v. *McCormack*, 395 US 486 (1969).

the shift of political power from the Monarch to Parliament. Although there was still a balance of power between King and Parliament during the eighteenth century, increasingly Parliament, rather than the Crown, controlled the government. Moreover, during the course of the following century, it became increasingly clear that parliamentary supremacy really meant the supremacy of the House of Commons. This process was formally recognized by the enactment of the Parliament Act 1911, which significantly reduced the power of the House of Lords. Finally, in the twentieth century the supremacy of Parliament has to some extent become a fiction as far as political power is concerned. Although as a matter of constitutional law Parliament enjoys legislative supremacy, effective political power is now exercised by leaders of the political party which forms the government.

The major consequence of the doctrine of Parliamentary supremacy is that the government, and the political party from which it is drawn, can enact its manifesto without constitutional constraints. The courts may not invalidate legislation for infringing the separation of powers, nor, even after the passage of the Human Rights Act 1998, for violation of fundamental rights. The new Labour government is as wedded to the principle of parliamentary sovereignty as was its predecessors, despite its apparently ambitious programme of constitutional reform. The doctrine of parliamentary legislative supremacy is naturally popular with politicians, since it allows them more or less unlimited power when they are in government. But for that very reason it is contrary to the spirit of liberal constitutionalism.

6

Government and Executive Power

1. INTRODUCTION

IN modern constitutional democracies the executive is generally the most powerful of the three branches of government: legislative, executive, and judicial. The executive, or more precisely the government, formulates and conducts foreign and defence policy, while it also effectively determines which measures are enacted by the legislature. In the United Kingdom, and in many other countries, the government is formed from members of the majority political party (or coalition of parties) represented in the legislature. In one sense the legislature, therefore, chooses the executive. But the government, or more specifically the Prime Minister, may in turn be able to control the legislature through the power to dissolve it and call for fresh elections. The central place of the executive in modern democracies is indicated by the treatment of elections primarily as choices between two, or perhaps more, potential governments, rather than as the selection of Members of Parliament who then themselves freely decide its composition. The fusion of legislative and executive branches was identified by Walter Bagehot as '[t]he efficient secret of the English Constitution',[1] to be contrasted favourably, in his view, with the very different situation in the United States, where there is a strict separation of the legislative and executive branches of government. The President is elected separately from Congress, and neither he nor members of his Cabinet sit in the legislature.[2]

The executive is not only the most powerful, but it is the most difficult of the three branches of government to explain. In the first place, it is hard to describe exactly what are executive *functions*. They are much more varied than legislative and judicial functions. The choice of Prime Minister, the formation of governments, the dissolution of Parliament, the making of treaties, and the conduct of war all involve executive

---

[1] Bagehot, 65.
[2] Anomalously the Vice President presides over the Senate, but does not have a vote unless there is a tie: Art. I, S. 3.

decisions. The preparation of general economic and social policy, as well as its detailed administration, are equally executive functions. So also is the appointment of the heads of the civil service and of the armed forces, and of other civil servants. Executive functions and powers, therefore, range from the taking of crucial and sensitive political decisions to detailed administration involving little or no exercise of discretion. Indeed, it would perhaps be right to regard anything done by government or a public authority as executive, unless it falls within the categories of legislative or judicial power.

Similar difficulties occur when we come to describe the range of *institutions* and *persons* exercising executive functions. In the United Kingdom uncodified constitution, the Crown enjoys in law considerable executive power, though the reigning Monarch takes only a few decisions personally. Under constitutional conventions the vast majority of the Crown's executive functions and powers are exercised on the advice of ministers, in particular of the Prime Minister. Statutes frequently confer powers on a Secretary of State. In law the powers can be exercised by any of the persons holding this office, but in practice they are used by the minister responsible for the particular area of activity, e.g., the Secretary of State for Health or for Education. In contrast, the Prime Minister and Cabinet have no specific powers granted to them by statute. They are able to exercise political power, because the Crown exercises its legal powers on their advice. Other powers are conferred on a variety of authorities, commissions, and other institutions, such as the Post Office, the Atomic Energy Authority, the Independent Television Commission, and health authorities. These bodies certainly discharge executive and administrative functions, though it is less common to regard them as part of government. Indeed, many of them were set up in order to ensure that important executive functions were performed by independent public authorities not controlled by the government in power. Finally, the civil service, and perhaps the armed forces, should be included in the range of institutions and persons discharging executive functions.

In some countries the Head of State is the effective head of the executive branch of government. That is the position in the United States and under the post-1989 Constitution of the Russian Federation.[3] Both these countries have presidential executive systems. In other constitutions, such as those of the United Kingdom, Germany, Italy, and Spain,

---

[3] Arts. 80–93 of the Constitution of 1993.

the role of Head of State, whether President or Monarch, is largely, though not entirely, dignified and ceremonial. He or she represents the nation, but plays no part in determining political policy. In these countries there is a parliamentary executive system: the executive is composed of members of the legislature and is responsible to it.[4] Even in these countries the Head of State may in certain situations be called on to exercise some political judgement. This is true in the United Kingdom. We will see in section 3 that there are some circumstances where the King or Queen may still enjoy some personal discretion to take crucial decisions, for example, in the choice of Prime Minister or in refusing to grant a dissolution of Parliament.

Another comparative point should be made before we look at aspects of executive power in the United Kingdom in detail. Some constitutional texts refer to the role of the President as 'the guardian' or 'the guarantor' of the Constitution.[5] Others set out the oath which he must swear on assuming office; it contains among other commitments a promise to defend and uphold the constitution.[6] These provisions are not necessarily merely cosmetic. They are perhaps legacies of the view put forward by the great French constitutional theorist, Benjamin Constant, that every constitution needs a neutral authority to ensure that the various branches of government work smoothly together and to resolve disputes between them. A President such as the President of Germany, who is Head of State, rather than a political actor in his own right, is well suited for this role. It may, for instance, involve checking the constitutionality of legislation before its formal promulgation.[7] In contrast it seems less appropriate for a political President such as the Presidents of the United States or France to claim the role of a neutral authority.

It is a nice question whether the King or Queen has any role of this kind in the United Kingdom constitution. The following sections of this chapter discuss, among other topics, how much personal discretion the Monarch still enjoys in the exercise of her undoubted legal powers, or whether their conduct is entirely regulated by constitutional conventions.

---

[4] See Ch. 1, sect. 2 for the distinction between presidential and parliamentary constitutions.

[5] See the French Constitution, Art. 5, and the Russian Constitution, Art. 80.

[6] US Constitution, Art. II, S. 1; German Constitution, Art. 56; Russian Constitution, Art. 82.

[7] Art. 82 of the German Basic Law provides that laws 'enacted in accordance with the provisions of this Basic Law . . .' shall be signed by the President. This implies he has authority to check their constitutionality.

It will be argued that in some circumstances, for instance the choice of a Prime Minister after an inconclusive election, the Monarch's discretion is not limited by constitutional convention; the decisions taken by a King or Queen under this discretion may be regarded as an exercise of the neutral power identified by Benjamin Constant.

2. CROWN, GOVERNMENT, AND THE PREROGATIVE

(i) The Crown

The position of the Crown in constitutional law is complex, largely because the concept of 'the Crown' is itself ambivalent; it may be used to refer to the Monarch personally, to the government, or to some aspect of the state or of public authority. The bewildering variety of usage may be illustrated by two examples. The Crown Proceedings Act 1947 removes the immunity of the Crown as government from legal proceedings in tort and contract. In appropriate cases an action for negligence may now be brought against a government department if one of its officials has carelessly caused some damage. But the legislation preserves the personal immunity of the Monarch from legal proceedings.[8] Criminal prosecutions are brought by the Crown Prosecution Service, but clearly they do not involve the participation of either the Queen personally or the executive; it would indeed be quite improper for either of them to intervene. In this context, the use of the word 'Crown' refers to little more than the fact that the prosecution is public, rather than private.

These ambiguities are largely legacies of constitutional history. Until the sixteenth century there was little or no difference between the personal powers of the King and those of members of the government or executive who acted under his direction. Gradually, political powers were increasingly exercised by the Secretaries of State and by ministers, quite independently of the Monarch's personal wishes. Now statutes usually confer legal authority on a Secretary of State, rather than on the Crown; in these circumstances, it is clear that it is for the minister to take the executive decision. Constitutional difficulties may arise when important executive decisions are taken in areas which are not comprehensively regulated by statute: for example, the conduct of foreign policy, the choice of Prime Minister, the Monarch's Assent to Bills passed by Parliament, and the dissolution of Parliament.

[8] S. 40(1). For a discussion of this legislation, see H. W. R. Wade and C. F. Forsyth, *Administrative Law* (7th edn., Oxford, 1994), ch. 21.

(ii) Prerogative Powers

Many executive decisions are taken under common law rather than statutory powers. They are known as *prerogative* powers, to capture the point that they are special to the Crown. Historically these powers were of great importance, as the King could exercise them without recourse to Parliament. In *The Case of Proclamations*,[9] one of the great cases in constitutional history, the judges ruled that James I could not change the law, whether common law or statute, by the issue of a proclamation. The King only had the prerogative powers which the courts allowed him, and they did not include a power to change the common law or introduce new offences. Constitutionally the struggles of the seventeenth century, before and after the Civil War, concerned the limits of these powers, while politically they represented a contest between Parliament and the Stuart Kings. Parliament won that contest when James II fled the country, and it invited William and Mary to accede to the throne. The Bill of Rights 1689 expressed that victory in terms of constitutional law. It abolished some prerogative powers, making others exercisable only with the consent of Parliament. It was declared illegal for the King to suspend laws or dispense individuals from the obligation to comply with them; the Bill of Rights also forbade the raising of taxes for the Crown and the keeping of an army without Parliamentary consent.

Nevertheless, the Crown has retained a number of prerogative powers. They include some powers of great political significance, such as the choice of Prime Minister, the appointment and dismissal of Ministers, the power to create new peers, and the power to dissolve Parliament before the five-year term prescribed by statute has elapsed. Prerogative powers are particularly prominent in the conduct of foreign affairs, for example, treaty-making, the declaration of war, and the recognition of states. Others may be important to individuals, such as the power to grant and withdraw passports, the grant of pardons, and the award of honours, while a final group seem now rather quaint: for instance, the power to license the printing of versions of the Bible and the Book of Common Prayer, or the award of franchises for markets.[10]

As a matter of strict constitutional law, all these prerogatives may be exercised at the personal discretion of the Monarch. Dicey put the legal position in these terms:[11]

---

[9] (1611) 12 Co. Rep. 74.

[10] For a comprehensive treatment of the varieties of Royal Prerogative, see de Smith and Brazier, chs. 6 and 7; Bradley and Ewing, ch. 12.　　　　[11] Dicey, 424.

[T]he prerogative appears to be both historically and as a matter of fact nothing else than the residue of discretionary or arbitrary authority, which at any given time is legally left in the hands of the Crown.

But, as he explained, this gives an incomplete account of the *constitutional* realities. For the exercise of most of these prerogative powers is regulated by constitutional conventions, the most important of which requires the Queen to act on the advice of her ministers. Only a few examples need be given to illustrate this proposition. The decision to enter the European Community was taken under the foreign affairs and treaty-making prerogative power; it was not, of course, a decision of the Monarch. It is the Home Secretary, not the Monarch personally, who decides whether to pardon criminal offenders. Ministers are appointed and dismissed by the Prime Minister, though in law they are ministers of the Crown.

The constitutional position concerning the Royal Assent is perhaps more complex. In law the Queen could refuse to give Royal Assent to a Bill, but under a clear convention she is required to consent to its enactment. This convention has become gradually established over the last three centuries, though it is debatable whether the obligation it imposes is absolute in all circumstances. No Monarch has refused Assent since Queen Anne's reign. But it is well known that George V contemplated refusal in the case of the Irish Home Rule Bill in 1914;[12] he feared an insurrection in Ulster, if the Bill were to be enacted without the Province being excluded from its terms. It may be that even now a Monarch would be justified in withholding Royal Assent if its enactment were to pose a clear danger to public order, or if the two Houses of Parliament had passed without good reason a Bill to postpone a General Election. In both these cases the Monarch might be acting constitutionally if she ignored the government's advice, since Assent would be refused to preserve public order or, in the second situation, democratic values.

But these are fanciful hypotheses. In almost all conceivable circumstances the convention requires the Monarch to act on the advice of her ministers and assent to a Bill. Other important political prerogative powers concerning the appointment of the Prime Minister and the dissolution of Parliament are also largely, though not entirely, governed by convention.[13] Under the constitution, therefore, decisions taken in the

---

[12] See the account by V. Bogdanor, *The Monarchy and the Constitution* (Oxford, 1995), 122–35.
[13] See sect. 3 below.

exercise of prerogative powers are in reality taken by ministers. The Crown's prerogative provides a legal disguise which masks the practical political authority of the government.

(iii) Prime Minister and Cabinet

From a legal point of view the Prime Minister hardly appears in the constitution. His existence is mentioned in only a handful of statutes, mostly concerned with salaries and pension arrangements. If anything, the Cabinet receives even less statutory recognition. Yet the Prime Minister and Cabinet preside over the executive branch of government, determining the principal policies of the government to be implemented by particular departments and agencies. The absence of any legal statement of the powers of the Prime Minister and Cabinet shows very clearly the divorce in the United Kingdom between constitutional law and the operation of the constitution in practice.[14]

Further, United Kingdom constitutional law says nothing about the relationship of the Prime Minister to the Cabinet or to his ministers. By their nature these relationships are probably unsuitable for detailed coverage in a constitutional text, though there are some interesting provisions in some codified constitutions. The German Basic Law, for instance, provides that the Chancellor is to determine general policy guidelines, though within these principles each minister conducts the affairs of his department independently.[15] There is an even broader provision in the 1958 French Constitution to the effect that the Prime Minister directs the activities of the government and 'is responsible for national defence'; but '[h]e may delegate certain of his powers to ministers'.[16] However, the relationship of Prime Minister and President has given rise to constitutional difficulties in France. The text of the Constitution says little about their relationship, which in practice is regulated by an agreed convention.[17] The President has control of foreign affairs and defence, while the Prime Minister determines internal policy. Both represent France at international summits, though it is the President who has primary responsibility for negotiating with other European leaders the development of the European Union.[18] The need to formulate this convention shows that the allocation of important executive responsibilities should be left for negotiation from time to time by politicians rather than regulated by terms of the constitution. Though the complete absence of any mention of the Prime Minister in

---

[14] See Ch. 2, sect. 4 for discussion of this point.   [15] Basic Law, Art. 65.
[16] Art. 21.   [17] See Ch. 2, sect. 4.   [18] See Bell, 59–60.

a constitutional text would be surprising, it would be wrong to expect it to set out his functions in great detail.

In any case it would be surprising if the balance of powers within the political executive—between President and Prime Minister, or between individual ministers—were to become a matter for constitutional litigation. The character of these relationships will always be determined politically. In the United Kingdom, as in other countries, political factors and force of personality decide whether the Prime Minister individually or the Cabinet as a whole is dominant. It became common in the 1960s to argue that the Prime Minister had assumed a presidential role in all but name;[19] for many political commentators this perspective was confirmed during the period when Mrs Thatcher was Prime Minister. But when the governing party is strongly divided and it only has a small majority, as was the case for much of the time of Major's premiership, it may easier for ministers to act to some extent independently. In these circumstances, the Prime Minister may be little more than a chairman of the Cabinet; effectively there will be collective leadership of the executive. More importantly, the government is then in a weak position with regard to the legislature.

(iv) Judicial Review of the Executive

Although the courts in the United Kingdom are rarely, if ever, involved in umpiring disputes between ministers, they play an increasingly important part in controlling the scope and exercise of executive powers. In the first place they determine whether statutory powers are exercised legally. Judges may, for instance, rule that the Secretary of State or other authority has acted outside the scope of the powers conferred by Parliament. This is what is known in English and Scottish law as 'judicial review'; it should not be confused with the power of the courts to control the constitutionality of legislation, also described as 'judicial review' in other countries, notably the United States.[20] The English courts' powers extend beyond reviewing the technical legality of the administrative act or decision; they will review whether it is a grossly unreasonable or unfair exercise of the powers given by statute to the executive.[21]

---

[19] See the famous introduction by R. H. S. Crossman, himself a member of Harold Wilson's first Cabinet, to Bagehot, *The English Constitution* (1963).

[20] Ch. 1, sect. 4.

[21] The topic of judicial review is central to administrative law: see the discussion in, for example, Wade and Forsyth, n. 8 above, chs. 8–15.

Secondly, since *The Case of Proclamations*, the courts have determined the existence and scope of prerogative powers. They also determine whether a prerogative power has been abrogated by the enactment of a statute conferring an equivalent power on the executive.[22] But when the Crown does exercise a recognized prerogative power, the courts have until recently been unwilling to question whether it was exercised reasonably or fairly. The scope of judicial review in this context was, therefore, narrower than in cases when the exercise of statutory powers has been challenged. Now as a result of the *CCSU* case,[23] the courts will only decline to consider whether the Crown has abused its prerogative powers when in substance they are unsuitable for judicial review. For instance, judges will not question how the Crown exercises its power to make treaties or review the exercise of its power to dissolve Parliament. The formal distinction between statutory and prerogative powers has in effect been replaced by a distinction between powers which are capable of being controlled by the courts, and those which are unreviewable, because they are too political.[24]

With this limited exception of unreviewable prerogative powers, the courts do not hesitate to control the executive when it acts illegally. Two recent decisions of the House of Lords illustrate this proposition. In *M v. Home Office*[25] it held that the Home Secretary was liable for contempt of court for failing to comply with a court order that a refugee should not be deported until his application for asylum had been determined. While the Monarch personally remains immune from contempt proceedings, the law can be enforced against both the Crown as the executive branch of government and the individuals who preside over government departments. Two years later, in the *Criminal Injuries Compensation* case the House of Lords ruled that the Home Secretary acted illegally when he decided not to implement the Criminal Justice Act 1988, which put the scheme for compensating victims of criminal injuries on a statutory basis. Instead, he announced he would use his common law power to replace the existing system with a less generous scheme. The majority of the Lords held that the decision not to bring

---

[22] The leading case is *Att.-Gen.* v. *De Keyser's Royal Hotel* [1920] AC 508.

[23] *Council of Civil Service Unions* v. *Minister for the Civil Service* [1985] AC 374. The prerogative was exercised to prohibit staff at Government Communications Headquarters from membership of civil service unions; on the facts the decision not to consult the unions was not reviewable, as it was taken on grounds of national security.

[24] For further discussion of judicial review of prerogative powers, see Ch. 7, sects. 3 and 4.

[25] [1994] 1 AC 377.

the statutory scheme into operation was illegal; in effect the Home Secretary was improperly abandoning the discretion Parliament had given him to choose the date for bringing the statutory system into force.[26]

An important constitutional point is that the House of Lords rejected in both cases the argument that it would be improper for the courts to enforce the law against the executive and that reliance should be placed on the political accountability of ministers to Parliament. Admittedly, Lords Keith and Mustill dissented in the *Criminal Injuries Compensation* case, broadly on the ground that political, rather than judicial, control was more appropriate in these circumstances. But that is a bad point. Judicial control over the executive is necessary to prevent arbitrary government. It is misguided for the courts to place confidence in the accountability of ministers to Parliament. As we will see later in this chapter.[27] It is rare for the House of Commons to hold an individual minister to account; party discipline makes Members of Parliament from the governing party unwilling to compel the resignation of a minister merely because he has exceeded his powers. Courts may hesitate to invalidate legislation because judicial review can in that case be regarded as counter-majoritarian.[28] But that argument is hardly relevant when courts consider whether it is appropriate to review executive decisions.

3. THE FORMATION OF GOVERNMENTS

By convention the vast majority of the powers of the Crown must constitutionally be exercised on the advice of ministers, in particular the Prime Minister. But there is some dispute about the extent of the Monarch's discretion in the exercise of a few important prerogative powers. One context in which this question arises has been discussed already. The Royal Assent must in almost all circumstances be exercised on the advice of ministers, but conceivably there may be extreme circumstances in which the Monarch would be entitled to exercise her own judgement and refuse Assent. Should the same answer be given when the question whether the Monarch has some residual personal discretion is posed in other contexts: the choice of Prime Minister, the disso-

---

[26] *R v. Secretary of State for the Home Department, ex parte the Fire Brigades Union* [1995] 2 AC 513, and see E. Barendt, 'Constitutional Law and the Criminal Injuries Compensation Scheme' [1995] *Pub. Law* 357.

[27] S. 4.   [28] See Ch. 1, sect. 5.

lution of Parliament, the dismissal of a government, and the appointment of peers?[29]

Until relatively recently, the choice of Prime Minister was largely a matter for the Monarch, although in normal circumstances she would be expected to select a prominent person from the majority party represented in the House of Commons. On both the retirements of Eden in 1957 and Macmillan in 1963, the Queen consulted senior figures in the governing Conservative Party before inviting respectively Macmillan and Douglas-Home to form a government. But when Wilson announced his resignation in 1976, the Queen waited until the Labour Party had chosen Callaghan as its new Leader before appointing him Prime Minister. The same process occurred when Mrs Thatcher resigned as Conservative Prime Minister in 1990. There are, therefore, clear precedents for a convention requiring the Monarch to invite the elected leader of the majority party to form the government after the resignation (or death) of an incumbent Prime Minister.

Nobody doubts that the same rule applies in normal circumstances after a General Election. The leader of the party with the largest number of seats in the House of Commons should be invited to form the government. However, that cannot be an absolute rule. In the first place, a General Election may not produce a clear result. If it were known, for example, that the third and other minority parties would be willing to enter a coalition with the second party, but not with the largest party represented in Parliament after an election, the usual convention would almost certainly not apply; the Monarch would constitutionally be entitled to call on the leader of the second largest party to form an administration, whether or not he was Prime Minister before the Election. With the support of the other parties, he would be in a better position than the leader of the largest party to carry on effective government. On the other hand, it has been argued that in practice during the course of this century minority single-party government has been preferred to majority coalitions. That may be true, but it does not prove the existence of a convention *requiring* the Monarch to invite in all circumstances the leader of the largest party to form a government.[30] The existence and scope of relevant constitutional conventions are far from clear in this situation. It is also unclear what conventions, if any, apply

---

[29] The prerogative power to create new peers to help a reforming government secure the passage of legislation in the House of Lords has lost much of its importance after the removal of the Lords' power of veto: see Ch. 5, sect. 2.

[30] See Bogdanor, n. 12 above, ch. 6, esp. 151-7.

where minority parties might work with a prominent figure in the largest party to form a coalition, or at least give it support in the Commons, but they would not be prepared to work with its official leader. Again, in this situation, the Monarch would be entitled constitutionally to invite someone other than a party leader to form an administration, when this was the most realistic prospect of securing stable government.

In normal circumstances the Monarch is required by convention to accept the Prime Minister's advice to dissolve Parliament for a General Election. Prime Ministers use the threat of dissolution to impose some discipline on government back-benchers who might otherwise be tempted to vote against the government. The head of the executive is able in this way to check an unruly Parliament.[31] The better view is that the Monarch may constitutionally refuse a dissolution when it would clearly be contrary to the national interest to hold an election and an alternative government would command a majority in the House of Commons.[32] The convention requiring the Monarch to grant a dissolution is not absolute. An obvious case for departure from it would be if a Prime Minister defeated at a General Election were to recommend a dissolution in the hope that the result might be reversed at a second election.

It is even possible that the Crown retains a personal discretion in extreme circumstances to dismiss the Prime Minister and, perhaps, further to insist on a dissolution and general election. This power would probably only be exercisable at a time of constitutional crisis, say, when a government introduced a Bill to postpone the holding of a General Election or to repress an opposition political party. George V apparently considered this extreme course as an alternative to refusal of Royal Assent to the Bill granting Irish Home Rule in 1914. There are clearly obvious risks to the exercise of this power, as there are to the refusal of a request by the Prime Minister for a dissolution; in particular, there will be allegations that the Queen or King is favouring one political party over another through the exercise of a personal discretion which many people regard as outmoded in a modern democracy. There was an enormous controversy in Australia when the Governor-General dismissed Gough Whitlam as Prime Minister in 1975; Whitlam had

---

[31] The point is emphasized by Bagehot, 158–9, 221–4.

[32] See the discussion in de Smith and Brazier, 128–30, though they point out that the only recent precedents for a power to refuse a dissolution are from other Commonwealth countries.

refused to recommend the dissolution of both Houses of Parliament for a General Election to resolve the impasse which occurred when the Senate blocked necessary financial measures. The Governor-General had received assurances that the Opposition Leader, Malcolm Fraser, would recommend dissolution, and on that basis invited him to become Prime Minister. On the other hand, the exercise of personal discretion may be the only check against the exercise of capricious power by the Prime Minister or the emergence of something like a one-party state. It may be fanciful to imagine circumstances in which this ultimate safeguard of constitutional values need be invoked, but equally it would be wrong to argue against its existence altogether.

Constitutional convention confers on the United Kingdom Prime Minister enormous discretion to choose the most favourable time, for his party, to dissolve Parliament and hold an election. There is a statutory five-year limit on the length of a Parliament,[33] but no restriction on its earlier termination. In contrast, the German Basic Law significantly limits the circumstances in which the Bundestag may be dissolved before lapse of the four-year period prescribed by the Constitution.[34] The Federal President may only dissolve it early in two sets of circumstances. The first occurs when a Chancellor has been elected, on a third ballot of the Bundestag, on the basis of receipt of the largest number of votes, but he has failed to secure the support of a majority of its members. In this situation the President has the discretion to appoint him as Chancellor with minority support or to dissolve the Bundestag.[35] Secondly, the legislature may be dissolved at the Chancellor's request after he has lost a vote of confidence. The President has a discretion whether to accede to the request, though his power lapses if in the meantime the Bundestag elects another Chancellor.[36]

The Constitutional Court reviewed the scope of the second power, when in December 1982 Chancellor Kohl requested, and the President granted, a dissolution after the new CDU/CSU–FDP coalition had lost a vote of confidence.[37] The Court rejected the challenge to the President's dissolution of the Bundestag. The dissolution was constitutional, although it was clear that the procedure had been engineered by the coalition parties. But the Court did impose some limits on the powers of the Chancellor and President. The former is only entitled to recommend a dissolution when government with a stable majority has become impossible, as was the case at the end of 1982. He may not

---

[33] Parliament Act 1911, s. 7.   [34] Art. 39.   [35] Ibid., Art. 63.
[36] Ibid., Art. 68.   [37] 62 BVerfGE 1 (1983).

request it in order to increase an already adequate majority at the subsequent election. Nor may a Chancellor, elected by the Bundestag on a vote of no confidence in his predecessor,[38] request a dissolution and election, in an attempt to secure democratic, as well as constitutional, legitimacy. For his part the President must ensure that the Chancellor's request is made on constitutionally legitimate grounds; but he may not question the latter's view that an election is required to establish a stable government.

The Basic Law therefore imposes limits on the discretion of the Chancellor to call an election to suit party political advantage. Both the President and Constitutional Court check that dissolution has been requested with the object of establishing stable government after the election. In contrast, the only check on the freedom of the Prime Minister in the United Kingdom to choose the date of the election to suit his party is that which might be imposed by the Monarch. But constitutional convention almost certainly requires the Queen to accede to a request to dissolve Parliament, unless, as argued earlier, this would clearly be against the national interest. The absence of an effective check on prime ministerial power in this context is a major weakness in the United Kingdom constitution. It could largely be cured by the introduction of fixed term parliaments, with earlier dissolution if the government loses a confidence vote.[39]

4. MINISTERIAL RESPONSIBILITY

The principle of ministerial responsibility is a key feature of a parliamentary constitution where there is a fusion of legislative and executive powers. Under this system, unlike a presidential executive constitution such as that of the United States, the legislature chooses the government, in the sense that the latter is formed from members of the political parties or groups which have a majority in the elected Parliament. Moreover, ministers are almost always members of the legislature itself, generally of the Chamber directly elected by the people. The United Kingdom nicely illustrates this principle. Governments are formed from members of the majority political party in the House of Commons; with the exception of the Lord Chancellor, it is very rare for a senior minis-

---

[38] Basic Law, Art. 67. Under this provision (constructive vote of no confidence) the Bundestag can only express its lack of confidence in a Chancellor by electing a successor.

[39] The Constitution drafted by the Institute of Public Policy Research in 1991 contained provisions along these lines: Art. 60.

ter not to sit in that House. If a government loses the confidence of the legislature, it must resign. That is the position, at least in the case where it is defeated on a formal vote of no confidence or on a censure motion. In the United States, on the other hand, there is no constitutional contradiction in the co-existence, say, of a Congress under the control of the Republicans and a Democrat President. The President and his Cabinet are not in any sense responsible to Congress, though he will be much weaker politically if it is dominated by the other party.

However, beyond these relatively straightforward propositions, there is much uncertainty about the status and meaning of ministerial responsibility in the United Kingdom constitution. Indeed, the only clear point is that it is not a rule of constitutional law. It is in fact possible to incorporate some rules in a constitutional text, as is shown in the Constitution of the Fifth French Republic.[40] Article 49 sets out the procedure for a censure motion in the National Assembly on the government; under Article 50 the Prime Minister must offer the government's resignation, if the Assembly has passed such a motion or disapproves its programme or general policy. It is hard to imagine that rules of this kind could be legally enforced, but the formulation of the principles in the constitution itself may not be without significance. At least it expresses in an authoritative form the dependence of the government on the continued confidence of a majority of Parliament.

Under the United Kingdom constitutional arrangements there are two broad types of ministerial responsibility: *collective* and *individual*. The former refers to the overall responsibility of the government to Parliament, particularly the House of Commons, and the duty of each minister to support government policy, even when he may privately disagree with it. It is doubtful, however, whether all aspects of the doctrine of collective responsibility should now be regarded as regulated by conventions binding on the government and its ministers. One should probably distinguish, from other aspects of the doctrine, the rule requiring a government to resign if it is defeated in the House of Commons on a motion of censure or of no confidence: that is almost certainly a binding convention. It was illustrated most recently in 1979 when the Labour government lost a vote of no confidence on an opposition motion. But government defeats on their legislative programme or on individual Bills, or on any matter in the House of Lords, impose no such obligation. Governments may be outvoted in these ways, but may

---

[40] Also see Italian Constitution of 1948, Art. 94.

soldier on, perhaps after winning a motion of confidence tabled by the Prime Minister and other leading members of the Cabinet.

Apart from the obligation to resign on a no confidence motion, the principles of Cabinet and ministerial solidarity and confidentiality now appear little more than political practices or usages which may be departed from whenever this is convenient to the government. For example, Harold Wilson as Prime Minister suspended the principle that Cabinet ministers must support its majority view when he allowed dissenters in the government to argue against membership of the European Community during the 1975 Referendum campaign. Ministers frequently leak the terms of their discussions when it suits them, so the principle of Cabinet confidentiality seems to be as much honoured in its breach as in its observance. Of course, it is possible to say in both these circumstances that a convention exists, but that it is often broken.[41] But that point concedes the weakness of reliance on constitutional conventions as a significant constraint on political behaviour.[42] As these examples show, it is easy for Prime Ministers and other ministers to manipulate them without attracting the censure that would follow a breach of clear rules of constitutional law.

The principle of individual ministerial responsibility is equally uncertain in its scope. Experts differ with regard to its general formulation. Broadly, under the principle a minister is responsible to Parliament for the conduct of the department of which he is the political head. That means at least that he must provide accurate information to Parliament about the department's policies and actions, and answer questions about these matters on the floor of the House or in written answers to parliamentary questions; in particular a minister must not mislead the House. Clearly, this is a matter of political, rather than legal, responsibility. But it is far from clear when, if ever, the principle of ministerial responsibility requires a minister to resign for departmental maladministration. The sanction of resignation may be appropriate where the minister has personal responsibility for blameworthy conduct by his department. Further, there are some precedents which may show the existence of a convention requiring a minister to resign for serious incompetence or maladministration within his department, whether or not he was per-

---

[41] The convention of collective Cabinet responsibility was recognized by Lord Widgery CJ in *Att.-Gen.* v. *Jonathan Cape Ltd.*, [1976] QB 752 as the basis for finding that ministers owed a legal duty to keep their discussions confidential.

[42] See Ch. 2, sect. 4.

sonally at fault.[43] Ministers in the last few years have sometimes resigned after the press has disclosed details of their sexual affairs, but this has nothing to do with a minister's political responsibility for his department.

Recently a distinction has been drawn between ministerial *responsibility* and *accountability*.[44] It is said that the minister is only responsible, and potentially liable to criticism, for matters, particularly of policy, over which he was personally in charge. The duty to account to Parliament is much wider. It imposes an obligation to provide accurate and truthful information about matters of detailed administration conducted by his department, and an obligation to undertake to put matters right when mistakes have been made. Ministers should be as open as possible with Parliament, though they may refuse to provide information when it would not be in the public interest to disclose it.[45] (On the other hand, a minister is not answerable to the same extent for the activities of the recently created executive agencies, such as the Prison Service and the Benefits and Highways Agencies, which have some independence from day-to-day ministerial control.) It is doubtful, however, whether the distinction between ministerial responsibility and accountability is particularly helpful when it is considered that, even in the former set of circumstances—where the minister is *responsible*—it is most unusual for him to be under serious pressure to resign. What is important is that ministers give as much information as possible concerning their policies and the conduct of their departments, and that the House of Commons, armed with that information, is able effectively to scrutinize this conduct and where appropriate criticize the individual minister. It is immaterial whether this liability and power are regarded as aspects of the traditional principle of ministerial responsibility or whether instead they fall under a separate principle of accountability.

It is in fact far from clear that a convention was ever firmly established that a minister should resign if he had been personally at fault or

[43] The best known example is the resignation in 1956 of Sir Thomas Dugdale as Minister of Agriculture for maladministration by his department in the Crichel Down affair. Lord Carrington resigned as Foreign Secretary in 1982 for incompetence by the Foreign Office in failing to anticipate the invasion of the Falklands. But these cases are rare: 2nd Report of Public Service Committee, *Ministerial Accountability and Responsibility 1995–6*, HC 313, paras. 22–6.

[44] In particular, see ibid., and the Government's Response to this Report, 1996–7 HC 67. Also see the Scott Report on Arms to Iraq, 1995–6 HC 115, paras. K8.15–16, where the distinction is accepted.

[45] Resolution of 19 Mar. 1997 on ministerial responsibility approved by the Commons: 292 HC Deb. (6th. series), cols. 1046–7.

his department had been guilty of serious maladministration.[46] At all events it is doubtful whether the convention exists now. Any convention that did exist has been destroyed by modern party politics. The survival of a minister, even one who has lied to the House of Commons, depends largely on whether his colleagues, and in particular the Prime Minister, continue to support him, and whether his resignation would be politically damaging to the party. The resolution put forward by the government and approved by the House of Commons in March 1997 seems to recognize this reality: if ministers knowingly mislead the House, it will expect them to offer their resignation to the Prime Minister.[47] Resignation is not to be automatic, as it would be under a strong convention, designed to impose effective control on the executive. The principle of individual ministerial responsibility has, therefore, been modified by the exigencies of party, just as the doctrine of collective responsibility may be waived when that suits the interests of the party in government.

5. THE CIVIL SERVICE AND THE ARMED FORCES

In practice the overwhelming majority of executive decisions, even many of a significant policy character, are taken by civil servants. As a matter of constitutional law, they are taken in the name of the Secretary of State or other minister. Generally the courts are not concerned whether a decision has been taken by the minister personally or by a civil servant on his behalf. Nor does it matter whether authority to take the decision has been formally delegated to the official.[48] In this way, the courts recognize the realities of practical government, which make it impossible for a minster to give personal consideration to more than a handful of the decisions taken by his department. However, the theory is that civil servants act under political control; as explained earlier, ministers are responsible to Parliament for their conduct, at least in the sense that they must give information and answer Parliamentary Questions.

The armed forces are also subject to the control of the elected government, though legally they are directed by the Crown under its

[46] A classic article by S. E. Finer, 'The Individual Responsibility of Ministers' (1956) 34 *Public Administration* 377 strongly disputed its existence.
    [47] For the text of, and commentary on, this resolution, see D. Woodhouse, 'Ministerial Responsibility: Something Old, Something New' [1997] *Pub. Law* 262.
    [48] *Carltona* v. *Commissioners of Works* [1943] 2 All ER 543.

prerogative powers. Moreover, since enactment of the Bill of Rights of 1689 it has been illegal for the Crown to keep an army in the country in peace-time without Parliament's consent. This principle has necessitated the periodic enactment of legislation to provide a basis for the continued existence of an army and, more recently, the air force.[49] In only the exceptional circumstances of a national emergency may the armed forces act autonomously, without the direction or approval of the elected government: this state is known as one of 'martial law', and is discussed in Chapter 9.

Civil servants and members of the armed forces are Crown employees or, in the quaint phrase used in law reports and books, 'Crown servants'. They are employed under the Crown's prerogative powers, so that at common law they are liable to summary dismissal irrespective of the terms of their contract of employment. However, civil servants, but not members of the armed forces, do now enjoy statutory protection against unfair dismissal.[50] Indeed, in practice they enjoy much the same degree of security and general employment rights as other workers; the fact that they are employed under the prerogative is in most respects of little importance.

However, it is significant that civil servants' duties are owed to the Crown, whether they are imposed by contract or under the prerogative. For, as under constitutional convention, the government of the day represents the Crown, it follows that civil servants are answerable to ministers, who then in their turn are responsible to Parliament. Civil servants owe no separate duty to give information to the public, unless either a statute or the government directs them to supply it. (That is also implicit in the French constitutional provision to the effect that the government 'has at its disposal the public service and the armed forces'.[51]) This position may have legal implications. One was highlighted by the direction of the judge, McGowan J, in a prosecution for breach of the official secrets legislation.[52] Clive Ponting, an official in the Ministry of Defence, was prosecuted under the Official Secrets Act 1911 for leaking confidential documents to a Member of Parliament, a member of the Commons Select Committee which was then investigating incidents during the Falklands War. The judge said it was

---

[49] In contrast the navy is for the most part regulated under the prerogative power. For details of the constitutional status of the armed forces, see de Smith and Brazier, ch. 11, esp. 223–6; Bradley and Ewing, ch. 16.

[50] For the details of this area of law, see Wade and Forsyth, n. 8 above, 68–79.

[51] Art. 20(2).   [52] *R* v. *Ponting* [1985] Crim. L. Rev. 318.

unacceptable for the defence to argue that it was 'in the interest of the State' to send documents to the Member.[53] As a matter of law, he directed the jury, it is for the government of the day to determine the interests of the state. (Despite this ruling, the jury acquitted Ponting.) The consequence is that civil servants cannot argue that it is in the public interest for information to be made available; that decision is for the government.

More recently there has been much disquiet at the part played by civil servants in the Arms to Iraq affair investigated by Sir Richard Scott. It is clear from his Report that many officials knew that the government's answers to Parliamentary Questions were incomplete, or, on one interpretation, dishonest; indeed, it was they who drafted these answers. The new Civil Service Code issued at the end of 1995 affirms the duty of officials to serve the elected government and its ministers. It also provides that a civil servant may report any impropriety under departmental procedures, in particular if he is asked to do anything illegal or unethical. If he is dissatisfied with the response from the head of his department, he may refer to the matter to the Civil Service Commissioners.[54] However, he is not free to disclose to the public what he considers to be government wrong-doing; he must either comply with his instructions or resign from the service.

A related issue is whether civil servants should be free, or even required, to give information which discloses, say, policy differences within a department or the shortcomings of government policy. The last Conservative government resisted attempts to encourage the direct accountability of civil servants to Select Committees.[55] It opposed a proposal that the Chief Executives of the new Executive Agencies, such as the Prison Service and the Highways Agency, be allowed to appear before Committees and answer questions independently of the minister. In the government's view, civil servants who testify to a Committee do so on behalf of the minister, and it is the minister, not the civil servant, who is accountable to Parliament.

The difficulty in accepting this position is that it enables governments too easily to escape scrutiny. There is no effective safeguard against a minister directing officials to supply incomplete and misleading infor-

[53] This defence is not available in the otherwise less restrictive Official Secrets Act 1989.
[54] (1995) Cm 2748, discussed in Bradley and Ewing, 310–12.
[55] Government Response to 2nd Report of Public Service Committee, *Ministerial Accountability and Responsibility*, 1996–7 HC 67.

mation, and then prohibiting them from answering questions from a Select Committee which might exposure this economy with the truth.[56] Equally, there are arguments against recognizing a higher duty of civil servants to the public, or even to Parliament itself. Traditionally, the executive has not been as open and as exposed to public scrutiny as the legislature and the courts. A government might be tempted to react to a change requiring greater openness by appointing more political advisers to senior positions or by promoting sympathetic civil servants who could be relied on support its case. That might in effect destroy the traditional neutrality of the civil service. In short, executive government might become more difficult if civil servants were wholly free to explore policy options with Members of Parliament.

But it is possible to exaggerate the strength of these arguments. In Sweden civil servants have traditionally been required to make available to the media or any member of the public all official documents, except for a limited category of material. Other democracies provide different compromise solutions to the conflicting interests in open government and in respect for the confidentiality of executive procedure. This is shown in the terms of freedom of information legislation which usually exempts from disclosure Cabinet minutes, confidential commercial and private information, and documents relevant to defence and foreign policy and other sensitive matters. These exemptions are likely to be incorporated in the freedom of information legislation which the Labour government proposes to introduce in 1998. The White Paper also suggests that the advice of civil servants need not be disclosed under the legislation, where disclosure would cause harm; the importance of frank open discussion and the need to preserve the political impartiality of officials would be among the relevant factors in determining whether disclosure was appropriate.[57]

One valuable constitutional reform would be to institute a formal appeals board, headed by a judge, to which civil servants could have recourse if they considered that they were required to behave unethically. It is surely wrong to allow the civil service itself, or even the Civil Service Commissioners, the final word on this matter. More importantly, the introduction into United Kingdom law of freedom of

---

[56] See I. Leigh and L. Lustgarten, 'Five Volumes in Search of Accountability: The Scott Report' (1996) 59 *MLR* 695, 710–15.

[57] *Your Right to Know* (1997) Cm 3818. For freedom of information generally, see R. Austin, 'Freedom of Information: The Constitutional Impact' in J. Jowell and D. Oliver (eds.), *The Changing Constitution* (3rd. edn., Oxford, 1994), ch. 14.

information legislation should do much to redress the balance of power between the legislative and executive branches of government, as well as enabling the citizen to make more informed judgements about the wisdom of government policy. But it is rare for a constitution itself to provide a right of access to official information. Moreover, typically it is silent about the liberties of civil servants. That is almost certainly because constitutions have not come to terms with the enormous increase in power government has acquired during the twentieth century, just as they have generally failed to address the phenomenon of mass political parties and their impact on the relationship between executive and legislature.

7

The Courts and Judicial Power

1. THE SEPARATION OF JUDICIAL POWER

ALEXANDER Hamilton, one of the authors of the *Federalist Papers*, described the judiciary as the 'least dangerous' branch of government.[1] He meant that it cannot significantly damage the rights of citizens. The courts do not enjoy the wide law-making power of the legislature or the capacity of the executive to implement political policies. They are dependent on the government for financial support. Further, they may not be able to enforce their judgments without the assistance of bailiffs and other executive officials. Hamilton shared Montesquieu's view that judges are relatively weak. It is, however, more interesting that he also agreed with the French jurist's opinion that 'there is no liberty, if the judiciary power be not separated from the legislative and executive.'[2] Otherwise there might be arbitrary government; Parliament or the executive would be able to determine when its laws had been broken. Hamilton concluded that an independent judiciary, under a duty to declare the nullity of unconstitutional laws, was 'essential in a limited Constitution', so anticipating the conclusion reached by the Supreme Court in *Marbury* v. *Madison*.[3] There is general agreement in the United Kingdom on the importance of the independence of the judiciary, if not over the wisdom of constitutional review of legislation. But it is unclear what independence of the judiciary really means.

As observed in Chapter 2, the United Kingdom constitution observes the separation of powers principle in the context of judicial powers more carefully than it does with respect to the legislative and executive branches. For instance, a full-time judge, whether of the High Court or a Circuit Court, cannot sit in the House of Commons.[4] Rules of the

---

[1] No. 78. The description provided the title for one of the great books on US constitutional law, Alexander Bickel's *The Least Dangerous Branch: The Supreme Court at the Bar of Politics* (Indianapolis, Ind., 1962).

[2] *The Spirit of the Laws*, Book XI, ch. 6 (in translation, introd. by F. Neumann, New York, 1949), 152

[3] See Ch. 1, sect. 4.   [4] House of Commons Disqualification Act 1975.

House significantly limit the freedom of MPs to criticize the judiciary or to discuss cases pending before the courts, and hence influence their decisions.[5] The most important guarantee of judicial independence is that senior judges hold their position 'during good behaviour, subject to a power of removal [by the Crown] on an address . . . presented by both Houses of Parliament'.[6] No judge has been removed under this procedure since 1830; in practice it is more or less inconceivable that the government and the majority of both Houses would agree to a judge's dismissal because they disliked his decisions in politically controversial cases.

But this does not mean that the independence of the judiciary is fully guaranteed in the United Kingdom. In many important respects the arrangements, particularly with regard to its appointment, seem less effective for this purpose than the provisions in the constitutions of other countries. The absence of comprehensive guarantees is wrong in principle, even though the consequences in practice may not be very significant. This topic is explored further in the next section. At this stage something more should be said about the functions of the judiciary in the context of the separation of powers principle.

The principal concern of the separation of powers principle is to prevent the concentration of authority in the hands of one person or body.[7] The separation of judicial power from the two other branches of government is particularly crucial in a constitution such as that of the United Kingdom where the legislative and executive powers are fused, in the sense that members of the government sit in Parliament and, through the governing political party, are effectively able to control the legislature. There is no system of 'checks and balances' as there is under the United States Constitution, or as there may be in France when the President and National Assembly represent different political parties. English and Scottish judges retain a capacity to challenge the government which the legislature has largely lost. (They may be more inclined to exercise it during a period when one party is in power for a sustained period, as happened under the long period of Conservative government from 1979 to 1997.) It is crucial, therefore, that the judiciary is independent of control by the legislature or by the executive for the reasons identified by Montesquieu and Hamilton.

[5] For discussion of these rules, see R. Brazier, *Constitutional Practice* (2nd edn., Oxford, 1994), 274–80.

[6] This provision, originally part of the Act of Settlement 1701, is now in the Supreme Court Act 1981, s. 11.

[7] See Ch. 1, sect. 3 and Ch. 2, sect. 3.

The independence of the judiciary, therefore, requires constitutional provisions for the appointment and dismissal of judges, appropriate to insulate them from political influence. But a liberal constitution should also say something in broad terms about the functions or, to use a common legal term, the jurisdiction of the courts. Otherwise a government, through legislation or executive order, would be able, for example, to set up specialist tribunals to decide certain types of case, for instance, criminal prosecutions which traditionally have been decided by the ordinary courts. Such a move would surely amount to an infringement of judicial power.[8] This would be particularly clear if members of the new specialist tribunals were appointed or elected on political grounds. It would then be immaterial that the judges in the ordinary courts, deprived of their jurisdiction over criminal cases, were wholly independent and performed their remaining functions impartially.

Under the separation of powers principle, therefore, constitutions should allocate *judicial functions* to independent courts. It is not enough for them simply to guarantee judicial independence. The Privy Council took this point in *Liyanage* v. *The Queen*.[9] The Parliament of Ceylon (now Sri Lanka) had enacted legislation specifically to deal with the leaders of an unsuccessful insurrection. It widened the scope of the criminal law, prescribed minimum sentences, and set up a special court and rules of procedure for the trial of the 'offenders', who had even been named in a government White Paper. The legislation did not apply after the trial. The Privy Council held it invalid, regarding it as eroding the judicial power. It was, in the words of Lord Pearce, 'a grave and deliberate incursion into the judicial sphere'.[10] What really troubled the Privy Council was that Parliament was more or less taking over characteristic functions of the courts, determining guilt or innocence and prescribing the offenders' sentence. It is worth noting that the judges remained independent, and indeed acquitted some of the defendants. But independence of the judiciary is of little value if the courts lose some of their significant functions.

But what are *judicial* functions? There are no easy answers to this question, though some will be suggested in this chapter. In the United Kingdom, as in other countries, many decisions which could be left to the courts are allocated by statutes to tribunals and administrative authorities. For example, this is the position with regard to the award

---

[8] It is clear that this would be unconstitutional in Germany; the Basic Law, Art. 92 provides, 'Judicial power shall be vested in the judges . . .'. See p. 140 below.
[9] [1967] 1 AC 259.   [10] Ibid., 290.

of social security and other welfare benefits, the grant of planning permission, and the issue of a wide range of licences and permits. There are good reasons for allocating decisions of this character to specialist institutions; they are more able than the ordinary courts to handle a large number of applications informally, speedily, and cheaply. But the High Court ensures that tribunals and administrative authorities keep within the scope of their powers and act fairly, in some cases requiring them to follow procedures very similar to those which the courts have developed in criminal and civil cases. In particular, they are unwilling to hold that Parliament has excluded their power of judicial review even when that seems to be what the statute intended. In the *Anisminic* case, one of the landmark decisions in modern administrative law, the House of Lords ruled that it was entitled to review the legality of decisions of the Foreign Compensation Commission, even though legislation setting up the Commission had expressly provided that its decisions 'shall not be called in question in any court of law'.[11] Yet on a literal interpretation of these words in the statute the judges had no business reviewing the Commission's decisions.

Though the grounds of judicial review, at issue in *Anisminic*, are a central part of administrative law,[12] the right of the courts to intervene is fundamentally based on constitutional principles, among them the separation of powers. That doctrine requires that independent courts have the final power of decision on questions of law in particular cases, even when, as frequently happens, Parliament provides that the initial decision is taken by an administrative tribunal, such as the Foreign Compensation Commission, or by some other authority. Moreover, traditionally some types of case, for example, criminal prosecutions and civil actions for damages, are determined by the courts. It would make nonsense of the existence of a separate independent judicial power for these cases to be allocated to administrative authorities or tribunals, closely linked with the executive. Conceivably in the United Kingdom, where the separation of powers doctrine gives way to the principle of parliamentary legislative supremacy, a statute could confer these powers on other institutions and provide that they could not be reviewed by the ordinary courts. But even in this country, access to the courts is regarded as a constitutional right. The *Anisminic* case and many others show that judges in the United Kingdom will disregard a statute which,

---

[11] *Anisminic Ltd. v. Foreign Compensation Commission* [1969] 2 AC 147.
[12] For a detailed discussion, see H. W. R. Wade and C. F. Forsyth, *Administrative Law* (7th edn., Oxford, 1994), esp. 301–6.

on its plain meaning, would appear to exclude such access. The courts give prominence to this right for a sound constitutional reason, the crucial importance of preserving the judicial power as a check on the other branches of government.

2. THE INDEPENDENCE OF THE JUDICIARY

Constitutions attempt to guarantee judicial independence in a variety of ways. The German Basic Law states the principle quite explicitly: '[t]he judges shall be independent and subject only to the law.'[13] However, it is probably of more value to ensure, in so far as this is possible, that the appointments process does not give rise to a politically biased bench of judges, and that they are free from political pressure. A number of different procedures can be adopted to neutralize the part inevitably played by political considerations in their appointment. In the United States, the President nominates the members of the Supreme Court and other federal judges, but their appointment may be blocked in the Senate; two-thirds of its members must concur in the nomination. This procedure gives Senators the opportunity to examine whether the candidate has the right qualifications to sit on the Court, or has been nominated by the President to carry out his political agenda. President Reagan's nomination of Judge Bork was blocked by the Senate in 1987, because of its fears that the judge was committed to a conservative political programme which he intended to implement on the Supreme Court.[14]

In contrast, European constitutions usually endeavour to ensure a balanced court by provisions excluding monopoly rights to nominate its members. For example, the French Constitution provides that three members of the Constitutional Council are to be appointed by the President of the Republic, three by the President of the National Assembly, and three by the President of the Senate.[15] Moreover, a third of the Council's membership is to be replaced every three years. Unless, therefore, one party controls both the Presidency and the legislature over a sustained period, there is little chance that all members of the Council will be chosen by representatives of one party. It is fairly clear, however, that political factors have influenced the nomination procedure, most notoriously when President Mitterrand chose the Minister

[13] Art. 97(1).
[14] For an admittedly partial account of this event, see R. Dworkin, 'What Bork's Defeat Meant' in his *Freedom's Law* (Oxford, 1996), 276.
[15] Art. 56.

of Justice, Robert Badinter, as President of the Council, shortly before the expected Socialist defeat at the Elections of 1986, after which, it was rightly anticipated, the majority of new appointments would be made by Gaullists.[16] In Germany too, appointments to the Bundesverfassungs-gericht are highly political. But balance is ensured to some extent by the provision that half its members are elected by a committee of the Bundestag and half by the Bundesrat, the State Council composed of representatives of the *Länder*.[17] The Constitutional Court Statute requires a judge to be elected by either two-thirds of the Bundestag Committee or two-thirds of the votes in the Bundesrat, as the case may be, a rule which in effect enables the opposition to bargain with the government, since it can always block the latter's favoured candidate.[18]

Regrettably there are no provisions of this character in the United Kingdom. English High Court and Circuit judges are appointed by the Lord Chancellor, a member of the Cabinet, while the Lords Justice of Appeal who sit in the Court of Appeal, and the judges in the House of Lords are chosen by the Prime Minister. (In practice the Lord Chancellor also exercises great influence in their appointment.) There is admittedly no evidence that party political considerations play any part in this process; Lord Mackay, the last Conservative Lord Chancellor, appointed some judges who were known to have liberal, left-wing sympathies. But it is difficult to mount a principled defence of the government's monopoly power of appointment, which moreover is exercised in private, without public scrutiny. It would be preferable to set up a body such as a Judicial Services Commission, with judicial and lay members, with powers to appoint the judges and to discharge other functions, for instance, considering complaints and perhaps dismissing judges in extreme cases.[19]

Under the separation of powers doctrine no person should exercise more than one of the three functions of government, the separation of persons principle. As Viscount Simonds said in a Privy Council ruling on the separation of powers in Australia, '[t]o vest in the same body executive and judicial power is to remove a vital constitutional safeguard'.[20] It would obviously be wrong for a minister or MP to sit as a judge. This is a standard constitutional rule, sometimes described as the

---

[16] See Bell, 34–41.   [17] Basic Law, Art. 94(1).

[18] Law of 11 Aug. 1993, ss. 6(5) and 7.

[19] See the Draft Constitution of the Institute for Public Policy Research (1991). For a contrary view, see S. Shetreet, *Judges on Trial* (Amsterdam, 1976), 394–404.

[20] *Att.-Gen. for Australia* v. *The Queen & The Boilermakers' Soc. of Australia* [1957] AC 288.

'incompatibility principle'.[21] But there are awkward questions about its scope: is it, for example, a breach of the principle for a judge to preside over a commission of inquiry into a major accident or industrial dispute, as frequently occurs in this country?[22] In Germany the principle is taken to extreme lengths. Constitutional Court judges are precluded from doing any other work, apart from teaching at a German university.[23] In this respect the British arrangements are much laxer. For a start, the position of the Lord Chancellor is a constitutional anomaly. He is a member of the Cabinet, with responsibility for appointing senior judges, is Speaker of the House of Lords as a legislative body, and may sit as a member of the Lords in its role as final appeal court. In short, he participates in all three branches of government, a flagrant breach of the incompatibility principle. Admittedly, in practice most Lord Chancellors rarely sit as a judge. It would certainly now be regarded as shocking for him to do this in a politically sensitive case as distinct from one involving points of private law. But it is far from clear that there is a convention forbidding him to sit as a judge in an appeal to the House of Lords on a question of constitutional law.[24]

Should we view with the same disquiet the common practice of a judge presiding over Royal Commissions or commissions of inquiry? In these circumstances he is performing broadly an executive, policy-making function, albeit in an advisory capacity. Another difficulty arises when Law Lords exercise their freedom to speak in debates in the House of Lords on topics such as sentencing, reform of the legal profession, or the desirability of incorporating the European Convention on Human Rights into British law. On occasion Law Lords have spoken on more political issues, most notoriously perhaps when Lord Carson campaigned both in and outside the House of Lords against the Irish Free State Bill in 1922. Arguably, these practices are contrary to

---

[21] See, for instance, Art. 4 of the Organic Law on the French Constitutional Council: '[t]he functions of members of the Conseil . . . are incompatible with those of being a member of the Government, or of Parliament, or of the Economic and Social Council.'

[22] Lord Wilberforce, for instance, presided over inquiries to settle miners' strikes, while judges have headed inquiries into matters as diverse as the collapse of an insurance company and multiple deaths at a football ground.

[23] Law of 11 Aug. 1993, s. 3(4), extending the incompatibility rule in the Basic Law, Art. 94.

[24] Lord Simon sat as Lord Chancellor in *Duncan* v. *Cammell, Laird & Co. Ltd.* [1942] AC 624, where the Lords held that the courts must accept a claim by the Crown that it was against the public interest to disclose sensitive documents for legal proceedings. This principle has been reversed: *Conway* v. *Rimmer* [1968] AC 910.

the separation of powers.[25] Certainly they are in conflict with a strict incompatibility rule, and would be unconstitutional in Germany. They infringe that aspect of the pure separation of powers doctrine which asserts that each branch of government has only one function and must stick rigidly to its discharge. But it would be hard to argue that these practices really upset the balance of powers between the three branches of government. At most they could compromise an individual judge, if they undermined the confidence of the public in his ability to consider cases impartially when he has already adopted a general position about the types of issue they raise—for instance, the right of unions to call a strike or sentencing policy. Above all, it should be emphasized that these practices do not represent systematic attempts by the judiciary to take over the legislative or executive functions of government. They pose much less danger to individual freedom and the other values of a liberal constitution than, say, attempts by the government or legislators to pack a court with its supporters or to influence the judicial process in a particular case.

In contrast, arrangements for the payment of judicial salaries do raise questions about judicial independence and the balance of powers between the branches of government. The question was raised with commendable frankness by Hamilton in the *Federalist Papers*. 'Next to permanency in office, nothing can contribute more to the independence of the judges than a fixed provision for their support. . . . In the general course of human nature, *a power over a man's subsistence amounts to a power over his will*.'[26] So the United States Constitution prohibits the diminishing of judicial salaries.[27]

It is difficult to present the history of this topic in the United Kingdom in a sympathetic light.[28] Salaries used to be fixed by Act of Parliament, but they were not increased from 1832 until 1954. Indeed, in the early 1930s the judges were briefly required to take a cut in salary under the National Economy Act. Whatever the merits of this reduction in circumstances of economic crisis, there is a clear constitutional objection to the ability of the legislature, in effect the government, to lower

---

[25] See R. Stevens, *The Independence of the Judiciary* (Oxford, 1997), 168–73, and 'Judges, Politics, Politicians and the Confusing Role of the Judiciary' in K. Hawkins (ed.), *The Human Face of the Law* (Essays in honour of Donald Harris, Oxford, 1997).

[26] No. 79 (italics are in the original text).

[27] Art. III, S. 1. It is unclear whether this imposes an obligation to revise salaries with inflation.

[28] A full account is given in Stevens, n. 25 above, chs. 3 and 7.

judicial salaries.[29] The present position is, if anything, even odder. The Lord Chancellor has power to increase, though not lower, salaries with the consent of the Minister for the Civil Service, but without any involvement of Parliament. By what may amount to a constitutional convention, the government always implements the recommendations of the Top Salaries Review Body; however, the spirit of the convention, if that is what the practice amounts to, was perhaps broken by the Prime Minister, John Major, when he announced, shortly before the General Election of 1992, that the Review Body's proposals for a substantial increase in judicial salaries would not be implemented immediately.

Important though they are, salary arrangements are less crucial to the independence of the judiciary than its security of tenure. Judges should be appointed for a reasonable length of time and be protected against arbitrary removal by a government. At one extreme is the position in the United States, where judges hold office 'during good behaviour' without any retirement age. Life tenancy certainly gives security, but it also creates the risk that judges may stay in post when their best years are over. Some Supreme Court judges, notably Chief Justice Taft and recently Brennan and Marshall JJ, have remained on the Court, largely to prevent the President replacing them with judges of a different constitutional perspective. This was a factor in the notorious Court-packing controversy in the United States in the 1930s. President Roosevelt was confronted by a Supreme Court dominated by conservative judges, most of them over 70 years old who had in a series of cases held much of the New Deal welfare legislation unconstitutional. The President introduced a Bill which would have increased the size of the Court from nine to fifteen judges. This was a threat to the Court's independence, and the crisis only abated when the Court began to adopt a more sympathetic attitude to welfare legislation, the famous 'switch-in-time that saved nine'.

The German arrangements for security of tenure are quite different. Federal Constitutional Court judges are appointed for a term of twelve years, without any possibility of renewal. This has the disadvantage of limiting the contribution that a great judge may be able to make to the development of constitutional law, but it is certainly a long enough period to establish judicial independence. A more important contrast with the United States Constitution is that judges may only be dismissed, suspended, or given a different position by a *judicial*

---

[29] See W. Holdsworth, 'The Constitutional Position of the Judges' (1932) 48 *LQR* 25.

decision.[30] It is hard to imagine a more secure guarantee of their independence than that.

The position in the United Kingdom has already been mentioned.[31] The senior judiciary hold office 'during good behaviour', as in the United States, but may be removed by the Crown upon an address of both Houses of Parliament. The general view is that by constitutional convention an address of both Houses is necessary for a High Court (or other senior) judge to be dismissed, and it is only appropriate to take this step for gross misconduct in office. Once an address has been passed, it is doubtful whether the Crown could constitutionally refuse to act on it, and it is unlikely that the courts would be prepared to intervene by judicial review.[32] However, the government is most unlikely to allow time in Parliament for an address to be debated unless it favours dismissal. A motion in 1973 supported by 187 Labour Members of Parliament for an address to remove Sir John Donaldson, then President of the Industrial Relations Court, was never debated. The Speaker is reluctant to allow criticism of individual judges outside a formal motion, so it is very difficult for MPs to criticize judges in the House of Commons itself.

Other members of the judiciary enjoy less security of tenure than the senior judges. The Lord Chancellor may dismiss Circuit Judges and Recorders for incapacity or misbehaviour, while the independence of the latter is in theory compromised by their appointment for short periods, with a possibility of renewal. Lay magistrates can be removed at any time. A hearing is given before dismissal, a procedure which the courts themselves would enforce, if necessary. But it is doubtful if they would entertain an argument by, say, a Circuit Judge that the Lord Chancellor had dismissed him for political reasons. In principle, he should have a right of appeal in these circumstances to an independent court.

The independence of the judiciary in this country, as in other genuine constitutional democracies, is now rarely much of a problem. But in the United Kingdom this is largely owing to convention and practice, rather than constitutional law, as it is in Germany and the United States. The role of judges outside the court-room raises interesting questions, but they are hardly of central importance. The crucial constitutional issue is: what questions should judges decide as judges? In other words, what is the scope of the judicial power?

---

[30] Basic Law, Art. 97(2). Under the US Constitution, federal judges may be removed by impeachment in the Senate: Art. I, S. 3.

[31] See sect. 1 above.

[32] See Shetreet, n. 19 above, ch. IV for the fullest discussion of these difficult points.

3. THE SCOPE OF JUDICIAL POWER

The United States Constitution provides the beginning of an answer to the question posed at the end of the previous section. Under Article III, Section 2 the judicial power 'shall extend to all Cases, arising in Law and Equity, under this Constitution, the Laws of the United States, and Treaties . . .', and, among things, to 'Controversies' between states and between one state and the citizens of another. The judicial power is vested in a Supreme Court, and other lower courts which have been established by Congress. However, their power is not exclusive; authority to decide disputes may be conferred on administrative agencies and tribunals, provided they are subject to the control of the courts. Moreover, the grant of judicial power to the Supreme Court did not tell it how it was to use its power. In particular, Article III left open the question, answered affirmatively in *Marbury* v. *Madison*, whether the Court is entitled to review the constitutionality of legislation passed by Congress.

The Supreme Court has inferred from the 'Case or Controversy' provision that it should not give advisory opinions on general constitutional questions at the request of the President or other parts of the Executive.[33] So when President Washington wanted the Court's advice on various issues of international law in 1793, it refused to help him. The German Constitutional Court has adopted the same approach.[34] As a result its authority to give advisory opinions on a joint request of the legislature and executive was withdrawn by statute in 1956. On the other hand, it has jurisdiction to determine the constitutionality of enacted legislation outside the context of a particular case (the 'abstract review of laws') and to determine disputes between the federal and state governments.[35] Both these jurisdictions go way beyond the scope of the powers conferred on the US Supreme Court by the Case or Controversy Clause.

When a court gives its legal opinion to the government or Parliament, it is assisting in the discharge of an executive (or legislative) function. This is particularly clear if its opinion need not be accepted as binding; judges are then in effect doing the work of government legal advisers. Even if the constitution gives the court the last word, there are good reasons for it to be cautious. Giving an advisory opinion on the constitutionality of a measure may lead the judges into intense conflict with

---

[33] *Hayburn's Case*, 2 Dall. (2 US) 408 (1792); *Muskrat* v. *US*, 219 US 346 (1911).
[34] 2 BVerfGE 79, 86 (1952).   [35] Basic Law, Art. 93.

the government (or Parliament) at the very time when the latter is intending to introduce it. There is less pressure on the judges when they consider a question of constitutional law (perhaps many years) later, if it arises as an issue in the course of conventional litigation. Moreover, judges prefer to examine a statute or executive decision in the light of a particular case; it is easier then to appreciate the circumstances in which it is applied and see its possible defects.

However, some constitutions do allow courts to give advisory opinions. In the United Kingdom the Judicial Committee of the Privy Council may be asked both by the Crown and by the House of Commons to give non-binding advice on constitutional issues.[36] The French Constitution gives the Conseil constitutionnel an advisory role when the President takes measures in a state of emergency.[37] More fundamentally, its principal function—pronouncing on the constitutionality of a Bill before it is officially promulgated—would be regarded in the United States as falling outside the 'Case or Controversy' requirement, and inappropriate for a court. The Treaty of Rome gives the European Court of Justice (ECJ) jurisdiction to give an opinion whether an international agreement between the Community and another state or other organization would be compatible with the Treaty.[38] The jurisdiction only arises when an opinion is requested by the Council, Commission, or a Member State. This is a significant point. Constitutional courts (and the ECJ) give advisory opinions, and hence perhaps trespass into the territory of another part of government, when they are invited to do so by a political institution. The latter in effect consents to any infringement of the separation of powers which takes place.

Constitutions usually leave open the extent to which cases may be allocated to other tribunals and authorities, or alternatively whether there are some questions which the courts should not decide because they are inherently too political for the judiciary. The Case or Controversy Clause, for instance, does not resolve these difficulties. They are fundamental questions which have to be decided, even in the United Kingdom, where of course the courts must proceed without the help of a constitutional text. In contrast, the German Constitutional Court derives considerable assistance from the Basic Law. Admittedly, Article 92 merely provides for the vesting of judicial power in the

---

[36] Judicial Committee Act 1833, s. 4. In re *Parliamentary Privilege Act 1770* [1958] AC 331 it gave advice to the Commons on the impact of the statute on freedom of speech in Parliament.
[37] Art. 16: see Ch. 9 below.   [38] Art. 228.

judges. But Article 101 forbids the institution of extraordinary courts and the withdrawal of disputes from the courts. Moreover, only judges are entitled to rule on the deprivation of personal liberty,[39] while there must be recourse to the courts—judicial review, to use the Anglo-American legal term—for any violation of rights by a public authority.[40] It is for the Constitutional Court itself to decide the scope of judicial power.[41] It held that any other view would make nonsense of the separation of powers, and the allocation by the Basic Law of the judicial power to independent courts. The Court, therefore, invalidated statutory provisions which enabled administrative authorities to impose fines for tax offences. In a statement of general principle, the Court said the Basic Law allocated what it described as the 'traditional' responsibilities of the courts to the judiciary, in particular the determination of criminal and civil liability.

English courts have in fact taken a similar approach to the protection of their own jurisdiction. Mention has already been made of the *Anisminic* case, where the House of Lords ruled that decisions of the Foreign Compensation Commission could be challenged in the courts, even though on a literal interpretation of its wording the statute would appear to have excluded judicial review. Another example of this approach is the decision that the Customs and Excise Commissioners could not give themselves authority by regulation to determine conclusively the amount of purchase tax which should be paid; the courts must have the final word on tax liability.[42] Access to the courts has been described as a 'basic' or 'constitutional' right. Prisoners must, for instance, be free to correspond with their solicitor, without interference from the prison governor.[43] The Divisional Court has held the Lord Chancellor acted unlawfully, when he introduced an Order under the Supreme Court Act 1981 requiring litigants to pay minimum court fees irrespective of their income.[44] The legislation had not explicitly authorized the levying of fees in circumstances which would have the effect of depriving some people of access to the courts; the judges held that the constitutional right could not be abrogated, unless Parliament made it absolutely clear by express words that this is what it intended to do.

---

[39] Basic Law, Art. 104(2).   [40] Ibid., Art. 19(4).
[41] 22 BVerfGE 49 (1967).
[42] *Commissioners of Customs and Excise* v. *Cure and Deeley Ltd.* [1962] 1 QB (Sachs J).
[43] *Raymond* v. *Honey* [1983] 1 AC 1; *R* v. *Secretary of State for the Home Department, ex parte Leech (No. 2)* [1994] QB 198.
[44] *R* v. *Lord Chancellor, ex parte Witham* [1997] 2 All ER 779.

These decisions show that the judiciary protects the right of access to the courts at least as fully as other fundamental rights, such as freedom of expression and association.[45] Its concern is to preserve, so far as it can, the judicial power as a balance to the executive and the legislature. Obviously, however, under the doctrine of parliamentary legislative supremacy the courts in Britain, unlike the German Constitutional Court, may not strike down legislation which deprives them of 'traditional' areas of jurisdiction.

The constitutional position in this country can be illustrated by a brief reference to recent controversies concerning the power to sentence criminal offenders. Although Parliament has on occasion fixed a sentence for a type of offence—notably, the mandatory life sentence for murder— and lays down maximum and minimum sentences for certain categories of offence, traditionally the courts are responsible for sentencing particular offenders in the light of the circumstances. Recently Parliament curtailed this judicial discretion by imposing mandatory life sentences for persons convicted for the second time of a 'serious offence', as defined in the legislation.[46] Some senior judges criticized the removal of their discretion on the ground that it infringed the separation of powers; the legislature was treading in an area which historically has been a judicial responsibility. Whatever the merits of this argument as a matter of political principle, it could not be used to attack the legislation in the courts.

On the other hand, the judicial power has been protected by a ruling of the European Court of Human Rights.[47] Since 1983 a 'tariff period' has been fixed as the minimum period which a life prisoner will have to serve in prison in order to satisfy the requirements of retribution and deterrence. Subsequent to that period his release may be ordered if this is consonant with public safety. Originally the tariff was determined by the Home Secretary in all types of cases.[48] But the European Court ruled that in the case of *discretionary* life prisoners (e.g. those convicted of manslaughter or rape), a court (or similar body independent of the executive) should determine both the length of the tariff period and whether detention after that period was justified. The Criminal Justice

---

[45] See Laws J in *ex parte Witham* [1997] 2 All ER 779, 787.

[46] Crime (Sentences) Act 1997, s. 2. The courts have a limited discretion not to impose a life sentence in 'exceptional circumstances'.

[47] *Thynne* v. *UK* (1991) 13 EHRR 666.

[48] In *R* v. *Secretary of State for the Home Department, ex parte Venables* [1997] 3 All ER 97, 147, Lord Steyn said that in fixing a tariff the Home Secretary is carrying out a 'classic judicial function' contrary to the separation of powers.

Act 1991 accordingly gave powers to the trial judge to determine the tariff, and to the Parole Board to determine subsequent detention or release.

4. NON-JUSTICIABLE POLITICAL QUESTIONS

Are there some issues which courts should not be prepared to resolve because they are too political and are therefore inappropriate for judicial resolution? Or, put more simply, are some issues 'non-justiciable'? This question has surfaced in a number of cases in this country, as well as spawning some complex constitutional law in the United States, where the courts have traditionally abstained from determining what they term 'political questions'. In contrast, the concepts of 'justiciable' and 'non-justiciable' issues are relatively new in this country. But arguably they explain why United Kingdom courts are reluctant to intervene in some cases, despite their general jurisdiction to review unlawful administrative action. For example, they are unwilling to entertain an action, at least when brought by non-British subjects, in respect of executive conduct which can be justified as an 'act of state', that is an act of policy in the field of foreign affairs.[49] The courts also do not allow anyone to challenge the exercise by the Crown of its prerogative power to make a treaty with a foreign country or international organization. That is the reason litigants have had no success in contesting UK accession to treaties with the European Community.[50]

Until recently, the courts also automatically abstained from reviewing the exercise of prerogative (as distinct from statutory) powers in the domestic field.[51] In the *Council of Civil Service Unions (CCSU)* case, the majority of the House of Lords abandoned this position. It held that an individual should be able to challenge in the courts an executive decision which affects his rights, irrespective whether it was taken under statutory or prerogative powers. But this does not apply where the character of the particular power, whether statutory or prerogative, make it unsuitable for review. As Lord Roskill explained:[52]

---

[49] The leading modern case is *Nissan* v. *Att.-Gen.* [1970] AC 179, which regrettably failed to resolve the question whether act of state can be argued where the claim is brought by a British subject.

[50] *Blackburn* v. *Attorney-General* [1971] 1 WLR 1037; *R* v. *Foreign Secretary, ex parte Rees-Mogg* [1994] QB 552.

[51] For prerogative powers, see Ch. 6, sect. 2 above.

[52] *Council of Civil Service Unions* v. *Minister for the Civil Service* [1985] AC 374, 418.

Prerogative powers such as those relating to the making of treaties, the defence of the realm, the prerogative of mercy, the grant of honours, the dissolution of Parliament and the appointment of ministers as well as others are not . . . susceptible to judicial review because their nature and subject matter are such as not to be amenable to the judicial process.

It would be too difficult for the courts to formulate standards in these sensitive areas, on the basis of which they could decide whether the minister had abused his power.

Later cases show the difficulty in drawing a sharp line between justiciable and non-justiciable issues. In *R* v. *Home Secretary, ex parte Bentley*,[53] the Divisional Court held, despite Lord Roskill's remarks in *CCSU*, that in some circumstances it could review the refusal by the Home Secretary to exercise the prerogative of mercy. The courts could review, for instance, a refusal to grant a pardon, if it was based on the convicted person's race or religion. On the other hand, it was beyond the competence of the judges to formulate the criteria for granting a free pardon. Watkins LJ said that was a matter of non-justiciable policy. The Court of Appeal declined to hold that an application for judicial review of the rules of the Criminal Injuries Compensation scheme was non-justiciable; it was immaterial that a successful application, leading to more awards of compensation, would have consequences for public expenditure.[54] In *R* v. *Ministry of Defence, ex parte Smith*,[55] it took the same view of a challenge, brought by four former serving members, to the policy of discharging from the armed forces anyone of homosexual orientation. The policy had nothing to do with national security, and, in the judges' view, it was not beyond their capacity to review it. An important factor was its clear impact on the applicants' human rights, in particular the right to respect for their private life. Sir Thomas Bingham MR emphasized the 'constitutional role and duty' of the courts to scrutinize the government's decisions when human rights are in issue. However, having held that it was entitled to review the discriminatory policy, the Court of Appeal in *Smith* surprisingly refused to uphold the challenge to its rationality.

English courts do not really need to draw a sharp line between justiciable and non-justiciable issues in judicial review cases when a challenge is brought on the ground that the minister has exercised his statutory powers in a grossly unreasonably or irrational way. Judges are

---

[53] [1994] QB 349.
[54] *R* v. *Criminal Injuries Compensation Board, ex parte P* [1995] 1 WLR 845.
[55] [1996] QB 517.

particularly hesitant to question the rationality of a government decision involving the formulation and application of national economic policy; in these circumstances it would be difficult to formulate standards on the basis of which a court could comfortably conclude that the decision was irrational. The House of Lords has, therefore, refused to consider this ground of challenge to decisions which had designated local authorities as having excessive budgets for the purpose of limiting the amount of poll tax they could levy.[56] The courts are only prepared to invalidate decisions of this kind, if they were patently absurd or were clearly taken in bad faith. A separate doctrine of 'non-justiciable' decisions is redundant in these cases. Furthermore, it would be inappropriate to invoke the doctrine when courts are asked to protect fundamental human rights, except possibly in cases involving genuine national security or emergency considerations.[57] Indeed, the House of Lords scrutinizes administrative decisions impinging on fundamental human rights, such as the right of asylum and freedom of speech, particularly carefully to check whether they have been taken within the powers granted by Parliament.[58]

In the United States the principle that courts should not question the constitutionality of non-justiciable 'political questions' has given rise to similar difficulties. The Supreme Court has applied the principle in a handful of cases. Two examples will be given. In one case, the Court refused to consider an application by members of the Kansas legislature that it was too late for that state in 1937 to ratify an Amendment to the Constitution which had been proposed by Congress in 1924 (in order to validate restrictions on child labour).[59] The Court held that it was for Congress itself to determine if a proposed Amendment had lapsed, because it had become too late, in view of the changes in social and economic circumstances, for a state to ratify it. There were no standards on the basis of which the Supreme Court could decide this question. In *Goldwater* v. *Carter*,[60] four members of the Court gave the 'political questions' doctrine as justification for its refusal to entertain an action by Senator Goldwater and other Senators to restrain President Carter from ending a Mutual Defense Treaty with Taiwan without a two-thirds vote

---

[56] See Lord Scarman in *R* v. *Secretary of State for the Environment, ex parte Nottinghamshire CC* [1986] AC 240, 247, and Lord Bridge in *R* v. *Secretary of State for the Environment, ex parte Hammersmith and Fulham LBC* [1991] 1 AC 521, 597.
[57] See Ch. 9.
[58] See *R* v. *Secretary of State for the Home Department, ex parte Bugdaycay* [1987] AC 514; *R* v. *Secretary of State for the Home Department, ex parte Brind* [1991] 1 AC 696.
[59] *Coleman* v. *Miller*, 307 US 433 (1939).   [60] 444 US 996 (1979).

of the Senate. (The US Constitution requires such a vote to ratify a Treaty, but says nothing about termination.)

One view of these cases is that the Court simply held that on a correct interpretation the Constitution allocated these decisions to the other branches of government, in the first example to Congress, and in *Goldwater* to the President. On this approach there is no need for a distinct 'political questions' doctrine, just as it is unnecessary for English courts to invoke a principle of non-justiciability in most judicial review cases. Certainly, in recent years the Supreme Court has become more reluctant to invoke the doctrine. In *Baker* v. *Carr*[61] the Court held it did not preclude judicial review of the fixing of electoral boundaries for the Tennessee General Assembly. Voters argued that the Assembly's use of boundaries which had been determined as long ago as 1901 violated their rights under the Equal Protection Clause of the Constitution; the votes of the electorate in heavily populated electoral districts were not given equal value to those of the electorate in sparsely populated areas.[62] The Court overruled its earlier decision that 'it ought not to enter this political thicket'.[63]

Two points can be made to justify judicial review in this case. First, the Court was called on to protect an individual right, the right to equality guaranteed by the Equal Protection Clause of the Fourteenth Amendment. This factor distinguishes *Baker* v. *Carr* from the two cases mentioned in an earlier paragraph where no individual rights were at stake. Secondly, it was clear that the voters would not get redress from the Tennessee Assembly, many members of which had no interest in revision of the unequal electoral boundaries. Courts are right to assert judicial power to protect constitutional rights, particularly when the legislature or executive is unwilling to defend them. Moreover, the ruling shows, as did the earlier and equally famous decision in *Brown* requiring desegregation of state schools,[64] that the courts may correct the *omission* of the legislature to take appropriate steps to protect fundamental rights, as well as invalidating *acts* and *positive decisions* which infringe them. It is quite wrong to regard the judicial power as solely a negative check on the legislature and government. That does not do justice to its functions in the context of a constitution which guarantees rights to equality and privacy, and other rights which may require state action for their full protection.

[61] 369 US 186 (1962). [62] For further discussion, see Ch. 8, sect. 3(ii).
[63] Frankfurter J in *Colegrove* v. *Green*, 328 US 549, 567 (1946).
[64] *Brown* v. *Board of Education*, 347 US 483 (1954).

One bad argument for a 'political questions' or comparable non-justiciability principle is that it is undesirable for the courts in politically sensitive cases to come to a different conclusion from that of the legislature or executive. The argument is misconceived, because if it were taken seriously it would preclude judicial review in any case where the government would be seriously inconvenienced by an adverse ruling. Courts should not hesitate to protect fundamental rights, even when their decisions disturb majority opinion or may be thought to weaken another branch of government. Equally, they are rightly prepared to prevent the abuse of executive power. The House of Lords, for instance, held illegal the Home Secretary's decision not to implement an Act of Parliament which had put the criminal injuries compensation scheme on a statutory footing; by introducing under the prerogative a cheaper scheme inconsistent with the statutory scheme, he was improperly abandoning his discretion to bring the latter into effect.[65] In a dissenting speech Lord Keith in effect invoked a 'political questions' principle: the Home Secretary's decision was 'unsuitable' for judicial review and he was answerable only to Parliament. That would be profoundly unsatisfactory. As we saw in the previous chapter, the principles of ministerial responsibility which Lord Keith had in mind are enforced, if at all, only by weak constitutional conventions. Judicial review is necessary to prevent arbitrary government in these circumstances.

As a matter of constitutional law, therefore, judges should themselves determine the scope of the judicial power. Moreover, as far as possible they should protect access to the courts for individuals to challenge the constitutionality of executive acts and legislation, particularly when this infringes fundamental rights. There is little justification for a distinct principle of 'non-justiciable political questions', though in some cases courts may decide that the constitution gives the government wide, indeed almost unlimited, discretion to take the decision it considers appropriate. The United Kingdom judiciary has gone a long way to assert its authority, even in the absence of constitutional provisions similar to those contained in the US Constitution and the German Basic Law.

But why should the courts be entitled to fix the boundaries of the judicial power, as well as the frontiers between the powers of the legislature and the executive, when a similar capacity is denied these other branches of government? There is no simple answer to this question. It

---

[65] *R* v. *Secretary of State for the Home Department, ex parte Fire Brigades Union* [1995] 2 AC 513: see Ch. 2, sect. 1, and Ch. 6, sect. 2.

is worth recalling, however, that judges are usually appointed by the legislature, or the government, or a committee of these institutions; moreover, outside the United States they do not enjoy life tenure. The government can, and sometimes does, exercise an indirect influence on the general direction of judicial decisions through the appointment process. However weak this influence is, it does counteract the judicial power. In short, the judiciary is independent, but its independence is not absolute. More importantly, a court can only intervene when a litigant brings a case to it. Unlike Parliament or the government, it cannot draw up a programme or set its own agenda. Its impact on government is episodic, rather than constant. Nor can it do anything if its judgments are ignored. As Hamilton said, it is 'the least dangerous' part of government. For that reason there is little cause for anxiety, if a constitution gives it, and it alone, the authority to determine the scope of its powers.

8

Political Parties and Elections

1. PARTIES AND THE CONSTITUTION

POLITICAL parties play a key role in modern democracies. Governments are formed from one party or from a coalition or loose alliance of parties; others constitute the opposition. Indeed, it would be difficult to carry on stable government without them. Parties are essential to translate the views of individuals and pressure groups into political programmes, which in their turn constitute the policy of the executive government and provide the basis of legislation. The parties' role is particularly important in parliamentary systems like that of the United Kingdom, where the government is formed from members of the majority party sitting in the legislative assembly. Party solidarity makes the Members of Parliament of that party extremely reluctant to vote against the government, or even to hold individual ministers to account, if that would embarrass it. These inhibitions have rendered increasingly dated the traditional account of ministerial responsibility; they have consequently upset the balance of powers between the Parliament on the one hand and the Crown and ministers on the other. If one party controls both the legislature and the executive, and also enjoys a monopoly power of appointment to the judiciary, the separation of powers is significantly weakened as a check on arbitrary government. Ultimately the ambitions of a strong cohesive party can only be checked by the possibility of its removal from power at a general election.

One might, therefore, expect constitutions to lay down some framework rules for political parties, at least to prevent them adopting totalitarian policies and to safeguard the rights of individual members. But constitutions rarely say much about parties, while some have totally ignored their existence. The United States Constitution has never taken any notice of them, an attitude which is shared by the uncodified arrangements in the United Kingdom.[1] These particular omissions are

---

[1] For British law, see K. Ewing, *The Funding of Political Parties in Britain* (Cambridge, 1987), ch. 1, and H. F. Rawlings, *Law and the Electoral Process* (London, 1988), ch. 4.

not surprising. Mass political parties, with their discipline and emphasis on group solidarity, are largely a phenomenon of the twentieth century. In the previous 200 years individual Members of Parliament in Britain were relatively free from party restraint, and as a consequence governments were frequently defeated on the floor of the House of Commons. There were no national party organizations until the 1880s; even after their formation MPs were rarely treated as responsible to them or to their local constituency associations. In Britain the political parties have been regarded as private organizations, governed by the law of contract and by the rules which apply to other unincorporated associations, such as religious bodies and trades unions.[2] There is no register of political parties, nor are they required by law to publish their accounts or to disclose their sources of funding. They can choose the procedures for selection of their candidates at elections,[3] and they are free to disband a local constituency association or expel a member, provided they observe the procedural rules of natural justice.[4]

Although the United States Constitution says nothing about political parties, this does not mean that its framers were unaware of their significance. Madison wrote about the dangers of the state legislatures being dominated by parties and factions which might exercise power in their own interest without regard to the general welfare.[5] He advocated the separation of powers and the establishment of the federation to avoid these perils. The former would balance strong executive governments against Congress and the state legislatures, while under a federal system power would be shared between the centre and the states.

The implementation of these principles in the US Constitution has had the consequences desired by Madison. The President is elected separately from the Congress; he may be a Republican at a time when Congress is dominated by the Democratic party. The House of Representatives and the Senate may be controlled by different parties. The President is not entitled to dissolve either House and call for a fresh election, so he lacks the power which enables the head of the executive in a parliamentary system to keep his party colleagues under control.

---

[2] The national Conservative Party, as distinct from local associations, does not exist as a distinct legal entity: see *Conservative Central Office* v. *Burrell* [1982] 2 All ER 1.

[3] But see *Jepson* v. *Labour Party* [1996] IRLR 116, where an industrial tribunal held that the policy of all-women short-lists for certain constituencies was contrary to the Sex Discrimination Act 1975.

[4] *John* v. *Rees* [1970] Ch. 345 held the Labour Party must give a local association a hearing before disaffiliating it from the party.

[5] *The Federalist Papers*, No. 10.

Under these arrangements it is very hard for one party to exercise the degree of power which is usual in the United Kingdom. Further, the geographical area of the United States has made difficult the development of tightly organized parties. Subsequent developments, in particular the institution in many states of primary elections, have further reduced party cohesiveness. Primaries remove the power of the party bosses to determine the candidates for state and federal elections; the voters who have registered with a particular political party elect them.[6]

Many post-war European constitutions have however recognized the constitutional role of political parties. The most comprehensive provision is that in Article 21 of the German Basic Law, the first paragraph of which states:

> The political parties shall participate in the forming of the political will of the people. They may be freely established. Their internal organization must conform to democratic principles. They must publicly account for the sources and spending of their funds as well as their financial resources,

Article 21(2) provides that parties which seek the overthrow of the democratic order or endanger the existence of Germany are unconstitutional. But only the Federal Constitutional Court may rule on this question; neither the Bundestag nor the government can dissolve a political party. This gives parties a degree of protection beyond that extended to other associations, which may be banned by executive order if they have criminal or anti-constitutional aims.[7] In principle it is right for a court to determine the constitutionality of political parties, as there is an obvious risk that the government might otherwise be tempted to proscribe an opposition party on the pretext that it has extremist policies. In fact the Constitutional Court has banned only two parties, the neo-Nazi Socialist Reich party and the Communist party, in each case after a careful examination of its philosophy, organization, and political activities.[8] The equivalent provision in the French Constitution of 1958 is much simpler. Parties may be formed freely, but they 'must respect the principles of national sovereignty and democracy'.[9] In contrast to the Basic Law, the French Constitution leaves unclear the procedure for dissolution of a totalitarian political party. But the Constitutional Council has ruled that the National Assembly lacks authority to determine whether

---

[6] See S. G. Calabresi, 'Political Parties as Mediating Institutions', 61 *U Chicago L Rev.* 1479 (1994).
[7] Basic Law, Art. 9(2).   [8] 2 BVerfGE 1 (1952); 5 BVerfGE 85 (1956).
[9] Art. 4.

a party respects democratic principles, and hence should be recognized for parliamentary purposes.[10]

The German Constitutional Court has clarified the constitutional role of political parties in a number of decisions. As bodies recognized by the Basic Law, they can protect their rights directly by taking proceedings before the Court against, say, the Federal or a state government, or Parliament.[11] (It is in contrast unclear whether a political party, or its leader, has standing in English law to challenge administrative decisions.[12]) The Court regards the multi-party system as a fundamental principle of the Constitution, as is the equal opportunity of all political parties to participate in democratic life and their right to form an effective opposition.[13] These principles are so important that they cannot be amended under the Constitution.[14] It is for these reasons that it has become common to characterize modern Germany as a party-state (*Parteienstaat*) where the role of political parties is in effect constitutionally entrenched.

Provisions of this type recognize the importance of mass political parties which are characterized, at least in principle, by a large membership, tight discipline, and clear political programmes. Other constitutional clauses, however, may be inspired by the older tradition of representative democracy, which gives emphasis to the independence of members of the legislature and their freedom from external instructions. For instance, under Article 38 of the Basic Law, members of the Bundestag are 'representatives of the whole people, not bound by orders and instructions, and shall be subject only to their conscience'.[15] It may be difficult to reconcile this provision with the practice of mass parties which expect their parliamentary members to implement their programme and follow group decisions. Clearly they are entitled not to re-elect a deputy who has failed to support the party in the legislature. But equally while he remains a member, he is free to defy the party whip, and even to transfer to another party without submitting himself to a fresh election. United Kingdom practice allows an MP to do that; a handful of members have 'crossed the floor' to join another party in the

---

[10] Decision 59–2 DC of 17, 18, and 24 June 1959, Rec. 58 (Favoreu and Philip, 34).
[11] 4 BVerfGE 27 (1954).
[12] The standing of Michael Foot as Leader of the Labour Party to challenge Boundary Commission proposals was doubted by Oliver LJ in the Divisional Court in *R* v. *Boundary Commission, ex parte Foot* [1983] 1 QB 600.
[13] *Socialist Reich Party case*, 2 BVerfGE 1, 13 (1952).   [14] Basic Law, Art. 79(3).
[15] There are similar rules in Art. 27 of the 1958 French Constitution and in Art. 67 of the post-war Italian Constitution.

last fifty years.[16] This is perfectly constitutional under the classic principle of Edmund Burke that a Member of Parliament is a representative, and not a delegate, of his electors; he is free to form his own judgement which party to support in the House of Commons. Constitutional provisions may be supplemented by legislation, for example, the German Parties Law (*Parteiengesetz*). This contains detailed rules about their internal order, the rights of members, the election and responsibilities of party executives, the arbitration of internal disputes, public and private financing, and the obligations to disclose the source and amount of contributions and to publish accounts.[17] It is of course necessary in such a law to define a political party in order to distinguish it from pressure groups and other associations which do not enjoy the same constitutional and legal privileges and responsibilities. The German statute requires the full and abbreviated name of a political party to be clearly distinguished from those of its rivals, a position which is not always achieved in Britain.[18]

Constitutional tradition in the United Kingdom has been hostile to regulation of this character, particularly on the sensitive topic of party financing, discussed in the next section of this chapter. Political parties are, as already mentioned, subject to the general law of contract and the rules governing unincorporated associations. (The absence of special legislation, tailored to the needs of political parties, is perhaps an aspect of the traditional British reluctance to formulate basic civil liberties in a constitutional document.) Broadly, the justification for this perspective is that parties are essentially private bodies; it would be wrong in principle for their organization, financing, and activities to be regulated, provided they conform to the general law. Moreover, governments might abuse their regulatory power to control opposition parties. However, this argument leaves out of account the fact that parties enjoy considerable privileges; for example, they have access to free broadcasting time and to other facilities at elections. It is not right, therefore, to regard them simply as ordinary private bodies. More fundamentally, it is legitimate to require them to be organized democratically and to adopt open financial arrangements in view of the enormous power they wield. Otherwise a few party bosses, secretly financed by major corporations,

---

[16] See P. Cowley, '"Crossing the Floor": Representative Theory and Practice in Britain' [1996] *Pub. Law* 214.

[17] The Parties Law of 31 Jan. 1994 contains 40 articles.

[18] Ibid., s. 4. A UK political party could not stop another using the same name through an action for passing-off: see *Kean* v. *McGivan* [1982] Fleet Street Reports 119.

would be able to dominate them, and so indirectly control the political branches of government.[19] Finally, the abuse by government of its regulatory power can be controlled by independent courts.

Constitutions should, therefore, certainly cover political parties along the lines of the provisions contained in the German Basic Law, although these principles need to be supplemented by more specific laws. But this is subject to an important proviso. Some types of party regulation might have the effect of fossilizing the existing party system. The same is true about aspects of election laws. For example, if state financial aid or the opportunities for election broadcasts were allocated only to parties already represented in the legislature, the development of new parties and groups would be inhibited, with the consequent impoverishment of political debate. Moreover, electoral systems or regulations, for instance a requirement that a candidate be nominated by 1,000 electors, could produce similar results; this topic is explored in the third section of this chapter. However, this proviso does not amount to a persuasive argument against the coverage by constitutions of political parties and of the basic electoral rules. Rather, it strengthens the case for judicial supervision of the detailed rules on the basis of principles set out in the constitution. The courts can exercise their power of judicial review to prevent the framing of party and election laws which favour the interests of the established majority groups to the cost of minorities. Equally, it is right for constitutional courts to take account of the need for stability in the party system. This may justify the more generous treatment of those parties likely to form a government than of minority parties; we will see in the other sections of this chapter how courts in continental Europe have attempted to balance these considerations in their treatment of party funding and election broadcasting regulations.

2. THE FUNDING OF POLITICAL PARTIES

The funding of political parties has given rise to great constitutional dispute in a number of countries. The United States Supreme Court in a landmark ruling held that the imposition by Act of Congress of limits on the expenditure by, or on behalf of, election candidates violated the First Amendment to the Constitution, the guarantee of freedom of speech.[20] But a ceiling of $1,000 dollars on contributions to candidates was approved as necessary to deter corruption and its appearance. For

---

[19] See sect. 2 of this chapter for development of this idea.
[20] *Buckley* v. *Valeo*, 424 US 1 (1976).

the same reasons the Court also upheld provisions requiring candidates to disclose the source of all contributions of more than $10. Finally, the Court held constitutional a complex scheme of public subsidies to parties and individual candidates, under which more federal money would be available to major parties (defined as those which had received over 25 per cent of the vote in the preceding presidential election) than to minor and newly established parties. It rejected the argument that it was impermissible to treat minor parties less generously than the Republicans and Democrats, holding it was appropriate for the legislation not to 'foster frivolous candidates, create a system of splintered parties, and encourage unrestrained factionalism'.[21]

Both the German and French Constitutional Courts have ruled several times on the constitutionality of party funding laws. German constitutional law in this area is governed by two fundamental principles. The first is that the parties must be free from state control (*Staatsfreiheit*), while secondly they must have equal opportunity (*Chancengleichheit*) to participate in the political process. In 1992 the Court held that public funding need not be confined to the reimbursement of election expenses. But the *Staatsfreiheit* principle precluded total, as opposed to partial, public funding; its level should not exceed the party's income from private sources. It was also constitutional to fix a threshold of 2 per cent of the popular vote to qualify for public funding and to allocate it in proportion to the party's election results. The principle of *Chancengleichheit* did not require the state to compensate for existing financial inequalities between the parties, but it did preclude their aggravation by tax concessions which disproportionately benefited individuals in high income groups and corporations, and consequently the parties supported by these donors. The implication of the constitutional obligation to account for the sources of party income was that the Basic Law is as concerned to prevent private and corporate influence as it is to preclude state control.[22]

Similar concerns have been felt in France. The Conseil constitutionnel has approved legislation providing public funding for political parties, on condition that it does not make them dependent on the state and that it respects the need for open political debate. It would, therefore, be unconstitutional to fund only the parties already represented in the National Assembly; further, the Conseil held invalid a rule that a party must obtain 5 per cent of the votes in each constituency to be eligible

[21] Ibid. 101.   [22] 85 BVerfGE 268 (1992).

for assistance, because this requirement would hinder the development of new parties and political views.[23] On the other hand, it was legitimate to require, as a condition of eligibility, that the party put candidates up in at least seventy-five constituencies. Legislation subsequently reduced the requirement to the nomination of candidates for fifty seats.

In the last few years French law has exercised increasingly strict control over private contributions in an attempt to minimize the risk of corruption. Legislation in 1990 prohibited donations from foreign governments and corporations, while three years later the Conseil constitutionnel approved a statute requiring disclosure of lists of donors to parties and candidates. In its view the requirement did not interfere with freedom of expression or the freedom of political parties guaranteed by Article 4 of the 1968 Constitution.[24] Legislation in 1995 prohibits all corporate support for political parties and election campaigns.

The position in the United Kingdom has been in marked contrast to these rules.[25] There is some public financial support in terms of the 'Short money' allocated by the House of Commons to help opposition parties in their work in Parliament. (This is named after Edward Short, Leader of the House of Commons, who introduced the system in 1975.) Election candidates are allowed free of charge the use of public rooms for meetings and the postal delivery of election addresses. Most importantly, parties enjoy free access to the BBC and some commercial channels for political and election broadcasts, a topic discussed further in the next section of this chapter. But there is no general public financial support for political parties. Its introduction was recommended in 1976 by the majority of the Houghton Committee in its report, *Financial Aid to Political Parties*.[26] But no proposal for legislation was made by the Labour government of the time, largely because the Conservative Party was opposed to it. In 1994 the Conservative majority on the Home Affairs Committee of the House of Commons restated the Party's opposition to state funding.[27]

Opponents of public funding of political parties raise three principal objections. The first is that it would breach the traditional constitutional understanding of the parties as private voluntary associations. It would compel members of the public to subsidize the activities of parties, the aims of which they might strongly disapprove: why should Labour party

---

[23] Decision 89–271 DC of 11 Jan. 1990, Rec. 21.
[24] Decision 92–316 DC of 20 Jan. 1993, RJC I–516.
[25] See Ewing, n. 1 above, esp. chs. 5–6.   [26] Cmd. 6601.
[27] *Funding of Political Parties*, HC 301, 1993–4.

voters subsidize the Conservative party or the Liberal Democrats? Secondly, the government might use the introduction of public provision to justify the imposition of restrictions on private contributions. Finally, parties would have less incentive to recruit members and look for private funding, if they enjoyed state support.

None of these arguments is convincing. With regard to the first point, members of the public are often obliged through taxation to support activities they oppose. Taxpaying pacifists, for instance, must support the armed forces. Further, the more enlightened supporters of, say, the present government should appreciate the need for healthy opposition parties. Secondly, there is a powerful case for limiting the amount of private contributions; as has been recognized in France and the United States, large gifts give their donors a potentially corrupting influence over the party concerned. The third argument fails because there is no evidence that state aid would necessarily lead to a decline in membership; the risk can be reduced, as it is in Germany, by limiting public funding to the level which matches the sums raised privately from members and donors.

With regard to private funding, the most significant features of the position in the United Kingdom are the absence of any legal limits on the amounts corporations and individuals may give and of any requirement on the parties to disclose the identity of donors. The Conservative Party has regarded the freedom to give unlimited money to a political party in complete anonymity as a democratic right which is, in its view, also an aspect of the right to privacy.[28] It has argued that not only are legal restraints undesirable in principle, but they could easily be evaded, by, for instance, making donations to political foundations. For the Conservatives it has been important to retain a degree of trust in the integrity of individuals and political parties. However, the introduction of disclosure rules would reduce the risk of corruption, even if they did not entirely eliminate it. (Both the Labour and Conservative parties have now decided to publish the names of substantial donors, if not the precise sums they have given.) Contribution limits serve the same purpose. To some extent they may also prevent the distortion of the political process which occurs when policies are framed in the interests of those with the deepest pocket. Constitutional democracy does not only entail an equal right to vote, but equal opportunities to persuade by rational argument. These values are compromised if individuals or companies

[28] Ibid., paras. 73 and 81.

can in effect purchase influence by giving a party enough money to make it dependent on its donors.

Even opponents of reform recognize that the funding of political parties is a constitutional issue. For example, the Minority Report of the Houghton Committee argued that state aid would represent a departure from the established constitutional practice that political organization is voluntary. The Home Affairs Committee of the House of Commons has reviewed the funding of political parties as an aspect of its responsibility for constitutional affairs. It seems, therefore, that defenders of the traditional understanding of political parties as essentially private associations do not regard them as entirely outside the purview of the constitution. The question is rather what sort of arrangements for their regulation and funding are constitutionally appropriate. The matter has recently been referred to the Committee on Standards in Public Life, now under the chairmanship of Lord Neill.

The parties exercise real political power through their ability to control at the same time the legislative and executive branches of government. Under a liberal constitution, it is, therefore, as legitimate to regulate the funding of parties as it is to require individual MPs to register their financial interests; neither can reasonably argue that this is solely a private matter. If the sources of private funding are limited, it may then become expedient to introduce some public financial assistance to compensate for funds which have been lost and to provide some basic support for less well endowed minor parties. The allocation of public funding should be subject to judicial review to guarantee that this sensitive task is discharged with due regard to constitutional principles, in particular to ensure that the parties are not vulnerable to state control.

3. ELECTIONS

(i) Regular, Free, and Direct Elections

Liberal constitutions should set out the basic principles for elections, although they may leave many important questions to the legislature, including even the decision whether to adopt the plurality, or first-past-the-post, system used in Britain for general and local elections, or some other method such as a proportional representation system. A constitution should prescribe regular, free, equal, and secret elections;[29] in cer-

[29] The First Protocol to the European Human Rights Convention, Art. 3, requires states 'to hold free elections at reasonable intervals by secret ballot . . .'. Also see IPPR Constitution, Art. 83.1.

tain cases at least, the courts should be willing to enforce these requirements, for otherwise there will be no safeguard against the party or fac-
tion in government perpetuating its hold on power by manipulating the
electoral system. A governing party might, for instance, attempt to
secure for itself exclusive power to use the mass media during elections,
or it might gerrymander constituencies so that it was able to win a
majority of seats with a minority of the electorate's votes.

The United Kingdom constitution recognizes the importance of *regular* elections. The Parliament Act 1911 reduced the maximum length
of a Parliament from seven to five years, while preserving the power of
the House of Lords to veto any Bill which extended this five-year limit.
Some constitutional theorists, notably Tom Paine,[30] have advocated
annual elections of at least part of the legislature as a constitutional
check, though this possibility was rejected by Madison in the *Federal
Papers*.[31] Elections in the United Kingdom are *free* in the sense that it
is easy for anyone to present himself as a candidate; there are only minimal nomination requirements,[32] though the requirement to pay a
deposit, not refundable if the candidate does not secure 5 per cent of
the vote, may deter some people from standing. In the United States in
contrast, states frequently impose restrictions on the freedom of smaller
parties and individuals to secure access to the ballot, by, for instance,
requiring independent candidates to be nominated by 5 per cent (or
more) of registered voters. On occasion the Supreme Court has upheld
the constitutionality of these rules as promoting the state's substantial
interest in avoiding voter confusion and a stable political process.[33]

United Kingdom elections are *direct*: voters elect Members of
Parliament and local authority councillors themselves, rather than
choosing a body of electors who then vote for the legislature. That is
also true now of the election of Members of the European Parliament;
it was initially composed of members selected by national legislatures.[34]
Both the German Basic Law[35] and the US Constitution[36] provide for
direct elections for the legislature, but the Constitution of the French

---

[30] *Rights of Man* (1791–2, Penguin ed., 1985), 201.

[31] No. 49. The election every two years of the US House of Representatives represents
a constitutional entrenchment of this principle: US Const., Art. I, S. 2, cl. 1.

[32] Only persons serving a sentence of imprisonment of more than one year cannot even
be nominated, though many others, e.g. Peers, aliens, and civil servants, cannot sit as MPs.

[33] See *Jenness* v. *Fortson*, 403 US 431 (1971) and *Storer* v. *Brown*, 415 US 724 (1974).

[34] Direct elections were held for the first time in 1979 under a Council Decision of
1976, implementing EC Art. 138(3).

[35] Art. 38(1).

[36] The 17th Amendment (1913) introduced direct elections to the Senate.

Fifth Republic permits direct or indirect suffrage.[37] The Senate is still chosen by a complex electoral body consisting largely of the elected National Assembly Deputies, Regional Councillors for the *départements*, and representatives chosen by municipal councils.[38] The United States President, as a matter of strict constitutional law, is elected indirectly by the electoral college composed of representatives of the states, but by convention they are bound by the popular vote in the state they represent. In effect the President is elected directly. Indirect election obviously compromises the democratic and egalitarian character of a constitution, giving added voice to national and local politicians.

(ii) Equal Elections

The hardest questions of constitutional law in this area concern the principle of *equal* elections. There is no problem now concerning 'one person, one vote'. With the extension of the franchise to all sane adults, irrespective of race, religion, and gender, that requirement of equality is easily satisfied. What is much more difficult is whether elections, particularly those conducted under a first-past-the-post system, give equal value to each vote and whether a failure to give it equal value violates the constitution. Arguably, votes in a constituency with a numerous electorate have less value than those in one with fewer voters. If the difference is significant and it is reproduced in a large number of constituencies, it becomes hard to argue that an election is really equal. Moreover, unless it is checked by a court or some other independent body, a governing political party with command of the legislature may be tempted to fix elections in advance by, say, grouping its supporters into smaller but more numerous constituencies.

The position in the United Kingdom is that four Boundary Commissions (one each for England, Wales, Scotland, and Northern Ireland) draw up proposals periodically for the number and size of Parliamentary constituencies, subject to rules and guidelines set out in legislation. Their proposals are submitted to the Home Secretary, who must then table them with a draft Order to give effect to them, with or without modification. If confirmed, the Order cannot be challenged in the courts.[39] The Boundary Commissions are directed to take account, among other rules, of a principle that constituencies should not cross

---

[37] Art. 3.

[38] See D. Lavroff, *Le droit constitutionnel de la V. République* (2nd edn., Paris, 1997), 278–9.

[39] For a full account of the complex procedure, see Rawlings, n. 1 above, chs. 1 and 2.

county or London borough boundaries, and also a principle of equal constituency electorates so far 'as is practicable' if regard is paid to the other rules; it is clear that they should give more weight to the former principle, unless this would lead to 'excessive disparity' in the number of voters.[40]

Two constitutional issues clearly arise in this context. The first is the independence and powers of the Boundary Commissions. Their members are appointed by ministers in consultation with the opposition parties; there is little anxiety about their impartiality. In principle, however, it is wrong for the government in effect to have the final word on constituency boundaries. In 1969 the Labour Home Secretary, James Callaghan, delayed laying the Commissions' proposals before Parliament; eventually he tabled them with a draft Order, but recommended that Parliament, in which naturally his party had a majority, should vote them down. Consequently the General Election in the following year was fought on constituency boundaries drawn in 1954. A valuable reform would be to remove authority for the determination of these boundaries entirely from government and Parliament, and leave it with the Commissions, subject only to judicial review.

The second issue is less clear. The rules in the United Kingdom do not give priority to the principle of equal value for each vote, but direct the Boundary Commissions instead to give greater weight to local authority boundaries when determining the size and shape of constituencies. Further, Scotland and Wales have both been over-represented in the Westminster Parliament, relative to their population. This reflects the tradition that Members of Parliament represent geographical and social communities, rather than simply sets of individuals. Further, from a practical point of view, it can be argued that a constituency in a sparsely populated area such as Northumberland or the Scottish Highlands would have to be of enormous area if its electorate were to be brought near to the average. That might make it difficult for its Member to represent his constituents satisfactorily.

There are, therefore, powerful arguments against insistence as a matter of constitutional law on the principle of equal value for each vote. Nevertheless, some constitutional courts are reluctant to tolerate departure from this principle, which they see as paramount under constitutions committed by their text to the treatment of individuals with equal

---

[40] Parliamentary Constituencies Act 1982, Sch. 2, rr. 4 and 5. See *R* v. *Boundary Commission for England, ex parte Foot* [1983] QB 600, the leading case on the interpretation of the rules.

respect and to elections which are equal. This is most clear in the United States. After deciding in *Baker* v. *Carr*[41] that the apportionment of constituencies for state elections was not a political question totally immune from judicial review, the Supreme Court ruled in a number of cases that the Equal Protection Clause of the Constitution required states to draw up equal districts for elections to both Houses of their legislatures.[42] Some deviation from the equal value principle might be permitted in order to respect local authority boundaries, but the mere size and character of an area would not support departure from it. Easier transport, in the Court's view, made it harder to warrant more generous treatment of less populated areas. Warren CJ gave the classic answer to the communitarian argument for departing from the equal value rule: '[l]egislators represent people, not trees or acres. Legislators are elected by voters, not farms or cities or economic interests.'[43] Against this approach, Stewart J, dissenting in one case, said that the logical implication of the majority judgment was that legislatures should be elected by a system of proportional representation.[44] In his view, a state was constitutionally entitled to opt for electoral districts representing distinctive social and economic communities, provided that the overall apportionment was rational and balanced.

The French Constitutional Council too is wedded to the principle of equal value for each vote. The equal suffrage prescribed by Article 3 of the 1958 Constitution requires the election of the National Assembly on an essentially demographic basis. An electoral law may depart from this principle only to a limited extent for reasons of clear public interest. On this basis the Council held invalid a measure which clearly overrepresented the non-white population in New Caledonia to the prejudice of the white settlers.[45]

Obviously the primacy given to the equal value principle in the United States and France can be questioned. The British tradition, as already mentioned, has given more weight to the representation of communities than to the rights of individuals to exercise an equal voice. (The over-representation of Scotland and Wales has also been defended on the basis that it has provided some compensation for their absorp-

---

[41] 369 US 186 (1962), discussed in Ch. 7, sect. 4 above.
[42] The leading case is *Reynolds* v. *Sims*, 377 US 533 (1964).
[43] Ibid. 562.   [44] *WMCA* v. *Lomenzo*, 377 US 633 (1964).
[45] Decision 85–196 DC of 8 Aug. 1985, Rec. 63 (Favoreu and Philip, 626). On the other hand, the Council upheld the Bill for elections in mainland France, allowing for a limited departure from the equal value principle: Decision 86–208 DC of 1 July 1986, Rec. 78 (Favoreu and Philip, 679).

tion in the unitary United Kingdom dominated by England. Interestingly, the Scotland Act 1998 provides for the number of Scottish constituencies to be reduced and calculated on the same basis as those in England.) Moreover, it would be understandable if courts were reluctant to shape electoral systems on the basis of such abstract principles as the right to equality. But it is surely right for the courts not to abandon the last word to the legislature; they should intervene if the apportionment is plainly irrational or there is strong evidence that boundaries have been gerrymandered to give more weight to particular factional interests.

(iii) Proportional Systems

The application of constitutional principles to more proportional election systems may be no easier. Germany has adopted what is known as the Additional Member System.[46] Each voter has two votes, one to elect a candidate for a particular seat, the other for a political party. The parties each present a list of candidates for this second ballot. Half the number of members of the Bundestag are elected for single-member constituencies on the first-past-the-post system. The other half are elected on the basis of the proportion of votes the party has obtained nationally; the highest ranking candidates on the party list will enter the legislature, unless they have already been elected for a particular seat on the first-past-the-post ballot. However, in order to be represented in the legislature there is a threshold requirement that the party must have obtained at least 5 per cent of the votes in the second ballot or won three seats nationally. One difficulty has been whether the choice and ranking of candidates on the list by the political parties infringes the constitutional requirement of *direct* elections. The Constitutional Court has upheld the constitutionality of party lists on the basis that voters retain the decisive choice whether to vote for a party and its candidates; but it is impermissible for a party to change the order of its candidates on the list after the election has taken place (for example, for the purpose of replacing a successful candidate who had resigned for health reasons[47]).

The threshold requirement for entry into the Bundestag has given rise to constitutional litigation. Arguably the condition unreasonably

---

[46] The Constitutional Court in an early case said this was a matter of choice, not constitutional obligation: 1 BVerfGE 208, 246 (1962). The European Court of Human Rights has held that Art. 3 of the First Protocol to the Convention does not require any particular voting system: *Mathieu-Mohin* v. *Belgium* (1988) 10 EHRR 1.

[47] 7 BVerfGE 77 (1957).

prejudices the chances of minority parties to secure representation in the legislature and infringes the principle of equal value for each vote. The votes for parties which secure, say, only 3 or 4 per cent of the national vote are in effect wholly discounted, though no more so, it might be said, than they are under a plurality voting system. The Constitutional Court has recognized the force of this argument, but has also referred to the danger that it may be difficult for a Parliament composed of a number of small parties to form a stable government.[48] Elections are held to choose governments, as well as to represent the different strands of opinion among the electorate. A threshold of 7.5 per cent has been held to be too high, but generally the Court has approved the standard threshold requirement that a party obtain 5 per cent of the national vote. However, it was unconstitutional to apply this rule to parties rooted in the former East Germany for the first national election after reunification, in view of the difficulty they would have had in satisfying the requirement; in these circumstances it was enough for them to obtain 5 per cent of the vote in the former East German states.[49]

The German Court's approach in these cases represents a necessary compromise. Under the Basic Law voters and parties have rights to participate in equal elections; that entails respect for the interests of minority parties and their supporters. Equally, the electorate votes in order to choose the government and a Parliament which will support it. The constitution must be interpreted to accommodate both of these purposes.

(iv) Election Broadcasts

Similar principles apply in another contentious area, the allocation of election broadcasts. A party denied fair opportunity to present its case on television (and in the other media) will be unable to mount an effective campaign. A denial may contravene a constitutional requirement of free and equal elections. On the other hand, the freedom of the press and of the broadcasting media is at stake. As a matter of constitutional law in some countries, newspapers are free to campaign for a particular party and are not required to provide space for its opponents. But broadcasters have been more tightly regulated. Public broadcasters in particular are required to treat the parties impartially and to allow time for election broadcasts.[50] The United Kingdom practice in this area has

---

[48] 1 BVerfGE 208, 247–8 (1952).　　　　　　[49] 82 BVerfGE 322 (1990).
[50] For a comparative discussion of this topic, see E. Barendt, *Broadcasting Law* (Oxford, 1995), ch. VIII.

until recently been characteristically informal. The number of party election (and annual political) broadcasts has been agreed by a Party Political Broadcasting Committee composed of representatives of the major parties and the two broadcasting bodies, the BBC and the Independent Television Commission (ITC). This is now the legal responsibility of the ITC in the case of commercial television,[51] though the parties are still consulted. Broadcasts are allocated on the basis of the party's support in previous elections and the number of candidates it puts forward; any party with at least fifty candidates is 'entitled' to one five-minute broadcast. The allocation has frequently given rise to litigation, and is particularly difficult in Scotland and Wales, where the nationalist parties argue they should be entitled to the same number of broadcasts as the major parties which campaign throughout Britain.[52]

In other countries this litigation would probably raise constitutional questions. Reference will only be made to the leading German case, decided in 1962.[53] The third party, the Free Democrats, argued that the public broadcasting channel in North Rhine-Westphalia had infringed the constitutional principle of equal opportunities for all parties when it was allocated significantly fewer broadcasting slots than the two major parties, the Christian Democratic Union and the Social Democratic Party. Rejecting the complaint, the Court held it was permissible for the broadcaster to give weight to the relative importance of the parties and the seats they had won in previous elections. But it should also take account of factors other than these results, since otherwise new parties would inevitably be excluded from broadcasting facilities. Even small parties should be allowed some access. On the other hand, little importance should be attached to the number of candidates a party put up, since that did not provide a reliable indication of its strength. Within these minimal constraints, the broadcasting body enjoyed considerable discretion, and the Court found there was no constitutional objection to the way in which it had been exercised.

This decision nicely illustrates some key points of this chapter. It is appropriate for constitutions to cover political parties and elections, for they play an essential, and a linked, role in the conduct of a constitutional democracy. A liberal constitution should not ignore fundamental questions relating to the funding of political parties and the conduct of

---

[51] Broadcasting Act 1990, s. 36.
[52] See the unsuccessful challenge brought by the Scottish National Party: *Wilson* v. *IBA (No. 2)*, 1988 SLT 276.
[53] 14 BVerfGE 121 (1962).

free and equal elections. If it does, it may fail to control authoritarian power. On the other hand, it is usually difficult for constitutional courts to do more than lay down broad principles in these contexts. Judges are understandably reluctant to question the manner in which the legislature, Boundary and Electoral Commissions, or the broadcasting authorities apply these principles in particular circumstances. The decisions, notably of the US Supreme Court, on the equal value of each vote are an exception to this reluctance; they can perhaps be justified as respecting the equal rights of individual voters.

9

Constitutions in Times of War and Emergency

1. GENERAL PRINCIPLES

ONE theme of this book has been that modern liberal constitutions are generally characterized by a separation of powers between distinct branches of government and by a concern to guarantee basic human rights. Indeed, it is these features which distinguish such constitutions from those systems of despotic or totalitarian rule which at most erect a constitutional façade behind which the government can do whatever it wants. But there are some situations in which even the most enlightened government finds it necessary to exercise power free from the normal constraints, in particular those imposed by the separation of powers and the need to respect the full range of individual liberties. Liberal constitutional principles may appear a luxury when a nation faces invasion or terrorism.

It is common to confer special powers on the government during wartime, as the United Kingdom Parliament did during both the First and Second World Wars.[1] Emergency powers are also frequently granted to deal with terrorism, actual or threatened insurrection or subversion, strikes in essential services, and natural disasters. In the last thirty years a number of statutes have been passed in the United Kingdom to deal with terrorism in the context of the continuing troubles in Northern Ireland. In contrast, a general statute, the Emergency Powers Act 1920, gives the government authority to proclaim a state of emergency when events, typically industrial disputes, are likely to deprive the community of essential services. Additionally, statutes now regulate the Security Service and the Secret Intelligence Service, while the Interception of Communications Act 1985 gives the Home Secretary authority to issue warrants in certain circumstances to tap telephones and intercept the post. The laws belonging to this final category are designed to deal not

---

[1] See sect. 2 of this chapter.

only with subversive activity, but also some serious criminal offences which may be committed from time to time in peaceful societies. It is, therefore, perhaps difficult to characterize them as emergency measures in the true sense, since they are in force in all circumstances. They were not enacted to deal with any particular danger.

Genuine emergency provisions have two principal features. First, they concentrate power in the hands of the executive, by enabling it to issue regulations on a wide variety of matters or by giving it more extensive powers, for instance of arrest, search, and detention, than those it enjoys in normal circumstances. In some extreme instances, the executive or military forces may even be allowed to supplant the judicial power by setting up special courts for the trial and sentencing of rebels and terrorists. This may be tolerated in the United Kingdom, in so far as constitutional law recognizes the controversial principle of 'martial law', which is discussed in the next section. Secondly, it is usual to limit the scope of civil liberties during a state of war or other emergency. Not only are the police or army given special arrest and search powers, but the government may take power to limit freedom of movement, disband political parties and other associations suspected of disloyalty, and even to restrict freedom of speech and of the press.

Emergency powers may be abused. In the first place a government may succumb to the temptation to proclaim or declare a state of emergency, when objectively such a step is unwarranted. Secondly, a state of emergency may be artificially prolonged when the war, or other danger to national security and public order, is over. Arguably, this has happened in the United Kingdom with the annual renewal for the last twenty-five years of the Prevention of Terrorism (Temporary Provisions) Act. This measure was first enacted after only a few hours' debate in 1974 in the wake of an IRA pub bombing in Birmingham which created widespread apprehension of further terrorist attacks. A third danger is that, in its anxiety to deal ruthlessly with terrorism and subversion, the government will impose excessive restrictions on the exercise of civil liberties; moreover, in war-time or other state of emergency, the courts may be more reluctant to protect them than they are in normal circumstances. This danger is discussed in section 3 of the chapter.

Some constitutions attempt to reduce these risks by imposing limits on the executive's freedom to act unilaterally during periods of emergency. For instance, the US Constitution gives Congress, rather than the President, authority to suspend habeas corpus when public safety requires this extreme step to deal with invasion or rebellion.[2] The President cannot suspend habeas corpus,[3] nor may he authorize military tribunals to try civilians for breach of martial law regulations.[4] Equally, when the German Basic Law was amended in 1968 to deal with terrorist episodes, it gave the Bundestag, and not the government, power to determine the existence of a state of tension; this is defined broadly as circumstances in which an attack or terrorist outrage is feared.[5] The more serious state of defence can only be determined at the request of the government by a two-thirds majority of the votes cast in the Bundestag (including a majority of its members, whether voting or not).[6] Moreover, the Constitutional Court is to continue to perform its functions unimpaired during the state of defence.[7] With the consent of the Bundesrat (the Council of States), it is for the Bundestag to decide when the state of defence is over. The Basic Law gives a decisive voice to the legislature in determining when the situation calls for emergency powers, and guarantees constitutional review of measures taken during this period.

The South African Constitution of 1996 provides particularly strong safeguards against the abuse of executive powers.[8] First, a state of emergency may be declared by an Act of Parliament only in the circumstances detailed in the Constitution itself: the life of the nation must be threatened by war, invasion, insurrection, disorder, or natural disaster, and the assumption of emergency powers must be necessary to restore order. Initially, the declaration (and legislation enacted in consequence of it) may be effective for only twenty-one days, though it may be renewed on subsequent occasions. Any court, not only the Constitutional Court, may rule on the validity of both the declaration of the emergency and of any legislation or executive action taken under emergency powers. Finally, there are strict limits on the extent to which emergency legislation may derogate from the rights guaranteed by the Constitution.

In contrast, the French Constitution of 1958 confers wide powers on the President of the Republic. He is given authority to take appropriate measures to deal with serious and immediate threats to the institutions of the Republic, national independence and territorial integrity, where 'the proper functioning of constitutional public authorities is interrupted

---

[2] Art. I, S. 9.   [3] *Ex parte Merryman*, 17 Fed. Cases 144 (1861).
[4] *Ex parte Milligan*, 4 Wall. (71 US) 2 (1867).   [5] Art. 80a.
[6] Art. 115a. A state of defence may be called only when the federal territory is under attack by armed forces or such an attack is imminent.
[7] Art. 115g.   [8] Art. 37.

. . .'.[9] However, there are some safeguards against abuse of this power. The President must consult the Prime Minister, the Presidents of the two chambers of Parliament, and the Constitutional Council before assuming special powers. The Council must also be consulted when particular emergency measures are taken. De Gaulle assumed emergency powers when there was an army revolt in Algeria in the spring of 1961; its leaders took a member of the lawful government prisoner and took steps to regulate civilian life. The Council published its Opinion that these circumstances warranted the President's assumption of emergency powers to protect the Republic. But it is unclear what the constitutional position would have been if it had not taken that view.[10] Unlike its decisions on the constitutionality of legislation, the Opinion of the Council in this context does not bind public authorities. The constitutional restraints on the President's freedom to assume special powers are, therefore, relatively weak. Further, there is no restriction on the duration of an emergency; de Gaulle's emergency measures lasted for five months, though the crisis had passed after a few weeks. Article 16 does, however, provide for the National Assembly to sit throughout the period, a provision which at least means that an undue prolongation of a state of emergency should be subject to political criticism.

There are no equivalent constitutional restraints on the assumption or exercise of emergency powers in the United Kingdom. Parliament is legally free to confer unlimited powers on the executive during wartime, a period of emergency, or indeed at any time. Since the executive invariably controls the House of Commons, if not the House of Lords, it is in effect free to assume emergency powers without restraint. Moreover, there is no constitutional distinction between those periods of war and national emergency when it may well be justifiable to grant the executive some special powers, and other periods when their grant would be less appropriate.

Indeed, one of the unfortunate aspects of United Kingdom constitutional law in this context is that it provides no guarantee against the indefinite prolongation of emergency powers. Many of the emergency powers assumed by government during the Second World War were preserved, or renewed, for a number of years after 1945. As already mentioned, the so-called Prevention of Terrorism (Temporary Provisions) legislation, first enacted in 1974, has been renewed annually, so that it has become a permanent feature of the constitutional land-

[9] Art. 16. [10] Opinion of 23 Apr. 1961, 1961 Rec. 69 (Favoreu and Philip, 126).

scape. Admittedly the government has instigated a number of independent reviews of the terrorism legislation, but it retains the final word on whether to propose that it should be given further life. Moreover, in the absence of any special constitutional procedure for the enactment of emergency measures, the terrorism legislation may be renewed by simple majority. There is no provision comparable to that in the South African Constitution of 1996, requiring extension of a state of emergency to be approved by a special majority of the members of Parliament.[11]

The only legal constraints on the freedom of the UK government are imposed by the European Convention of Human Rights (ECHR). Article 15(1) of the ECHR provides:

> In time of war or other public emergency threatening the life of the nation any [State] may take measures derogating from its obligations under this Convention to the extent strictly required by the exigencies of the situation, provided that such measures are not inconsistent with its other obligations under international law.

As will be explained in section 3 of the chapter, a state may not derogate from its obligation to observe some of the most fundamental rights guaranteed by the ECHR, such as the right not to be tortured. With regard to derogation from its observance of other rights, it must notify the Council of Europe of the measures it has taken and the reasons for them.[12]

The European Court is prepared to review independently whether the facts justify the state's derogation, and further whether the specific measures taken by it are required by the emergency. In a leading case, the Court held that the term 'public emergency' refers to an exceptional crisis affecting the whole population, amounting to a threat to its organized life.[13] But it is prepared to allow states a wide 'margin of appreciation' when they proclaim a state of emergency and when they take measures in response to it. For example, in *Brannigan* v. *United Kingdom*[14] the Court rejected a challenge to the United Kingdom's derogation from its obligation under Article 5 of the ECHR to bring detained suspects 'promptly' before a judicial officer. Under the Prevention of Terrorism legislation the Secretary of State has power to detain terrorist suspects for seven days, a power the Court had earlier ruled to be in breach of

---

[11] Art. 37. Second and further extensions of a state of emergency, every three months, must be approved by 60% of Assembly members.

[12] ECHR, Art. 15(3).   [13] *Lawless* v. *Ireland (No. 3)* (1961) 1 EHRR 15.

[14] (1994) 17 EHRR 539.

the obligation imposed by Article 5.[15] In response to that decision, the UK government derogated from this obligation; it argued successfully that the detention provision in the Prevention of Terrorism legislation was required by the exigencies of the situation in Northern Ireland.

Although the effectiveness of the Convention in this context is open to doubt, it provides one lesson for UK constitutional law. If the European Court of Human Rights, at least in theory, is willing to review independently whether there is an emergency justifying derogation from observance of fundamental rights, the courts in the United Kingdom (and other states) should surely be equally prepared to question executive decisions in this context. Indeed, they should be less hesitant than a supra-national court to intervene. Unlike the European Court, they are in a relatively good position to assess whether special powers have been obtained in good faith to deal with a real emergency and whether the measures taken in response are appropriate. As a matter of principle, judges should not simply accept the word of the executive that, say, national security or terrorism warrants the exercise of emergency powers. Otherwise, constitutional government may too easily slide into something like arbitrary rule.

2. MARTIAL LAW AND EMERGENCY LEGISLATION

The most extreme form of emergency power is military rule under which army commanders regulate and restrict civilian life in order to restore some system of public order. They may go so far as to stage trials and execute people found guilty of insurrection or other offences; even if the ordinary courts continue to sit during this period, they make no attempt to control the use of military power. This state of affairs is known as 'martial law'. (It should be distinguished from the body of military law applicable in all circumstances to members of the armed forces which has been enforced by courts-martial.) Martial law in the true sense seems to have been prohibited by the Petition of Right of 1628, which received the reluctant assent of Charles I. It is unclear whether the Petition outlawed martial law only in times of peace or also precluded its use during war and other serious disturbances.[16] In any event martial law has not been proclaimed by an army commander in Great Britain since the early seventeenth century, nor has it been declared during the troubles in Northern Ireland during the last thirty years.

[15] *Brogan* v. *UK* (1988) 11 EHRR 117.
[16] Dicey boasted that the term was unknown in English law: see Dicey, 287.

Its uncertain constitutional position has been clarified in cases arising from the Boer War in South Africa and the suppression of disorder in Ireland in 1920–1.[17] Usually these cases concerned applications to the ordinary courts to release civilian prisoners condemned to death by military tribunals set up after a proclamation of martial law. They show that it is for the courts themselves to decide whether a state of war exist. The military commander cannot establish a state of martial law merely by proclaiming it. On the other hand, once the courts have recognized that a state of war does exist, they will not interfere with the armed forces during the emergency. The military authorities may even impose the death sentence without interference from the ordinary courts. But after the war is over, members of the forces may be criminally or civilly liable if they go beyond what was reasonably necessary to restore public order. In fact, Parliament has usually passed Acts of Indemnity to validate retrospectively acts done by the armed forces. On the basis of these cases martial law is best seen as 'an extension of the ordinary common law power to meet force with force'.[18]

The major reason martial law is now of no constitutional importance in the United Kingdom is that Parliament enacts emergency legislation to give the executive and armed forces the sweeping powers they may need in time of war. There is no need to invoke a state of martial law, even if it is theoretically still possible to do so.[19] Special powers legislation is a much more effective tool. Unlike martial law, it confers explicit powers on the executive. More importantly, under the principle of parliamentary supremacy the courts are unwilling to challenge the fundamental legislative decision that it is appropriate for the government to be given special powers, including those which may be used to restrict normal civil liberties.

In both the First and Second World Wars wide emergency powers were given to the executive to make general regulations, as well as to take a range of administrative decisions restricting civil liberties. The Defence of the Realm Consolidation Act 1914 conferred on the government power to issue regulations for securing public safety and to authorize trial by courts-martial of civilians committing offences against these regulations. There was no explicit grant of power to make regulations

---

[17] In particular, see *Ex parte Marais* [1902] AC 109; *R* v. *Allen* [1921] 2 Irish Reports 241.

[18] See R. F. V. Heuston, *Essays in Constitutional Law* (2nd edn., London, 1964), 159.

[19] Martial law is not declared under the Royal Prerogative, so the power to proclaim it would not be abrogated by the enactment of legislation conferring similar powers: see Ch. 6, sect. 2(iv).

authorizing detention and internment. However, a majority of the House of Lords in *Ex parte Zadig* held that the grant of power in the legislation was wide enough to support a regulation enabling the Home Secretary to intern a person whose detention was considered necessary in view of his hostile origin or associations.[20] Lord Shaw dissented vigorously. He argued that, on the majority's interpretation of the legislation, the government in effect enjoyed authority to dispense with civil liberties altogether by use of its emergency regulatory powers. Regulations could be made, for instance, to authorize the detention of all Roman Catholics or Jews on the ground that this was appropriate to secure public safety. In response, Lord Dunedin, one of the majority in the Lords, pointed out that constitutionally Parliament was indeed free to confer such absolute power on the executive.

The emergency legislation enacted at the outset of the Second World War was, if anything, even broader in its scope. The Emergency Powers (Defence) Act 1939 specifically authorized the making of regulations to empower the Home Secretary to detain persons without trial in certain circumstances.[21] The Treasury was given power to impose charges in connection with any scheme authorized by Defence Regulations, a departure from the provision in the Bill of Rights 1689 that only the legislature is entitled to impose taxation.[22]

The 1939 legislation also provided that the statutory powers were in addition to, and not intended to displace, the prerogative powers. In fact, it has never been authoritatively established what prerogative powers the Crown does enjoy in order to deal with a serious emergency or, for that matter, disorder falling short of that. However, the recent decision of the Court of Appeal in the *Northumbria Police* case[23] recognized wide prerogative powers to take steps to preserve public order at all times, and not only during a state of emergency. So the Court held it lawful for the Home Secretary to make plastic baton rounds and CS gas available to local police forces, irrespective of the wishes of the police authority. The decision bears out the point that in the United Kingdom there is no sharp line between the powers the executive enjoys during a genuine emergency and those it may exercise during normal conditions. Just as Parliament is free to enact emergency legislation whenever it likes

---

[20] *R* v. *Halliday, ex parte Zadig* [1917] AC 260. The Lord Chancellor, Lord Finlay, presided in the House, a clear breach of the separation of judicial power: see Ch. 7, sect. 2.

[21] See sect. 3 for further discussion of this power.

[22] Emergency Powers (Defence) Act 1939, s. 2(1).

[23] *R* v. *Home Secretary, ex parte Northumbria Police Authority* [1989] QB 26.

(subject to the limits imposed under the European Convention), so the Court of Appeal recognised a wide prerogative power to take step to preserve the peace, irrespective whether there was an actual or apprehended emergency.

States of emergency outside times of war and insurrection are covered by the Emergency Powers Act 1920 and various other enactments.[24] Under the 1920 legislation, the Crown, in effect the government, may proclaim a state of emergency, if it considers that events have occurred, or may occur, which are calculated to deprive the community of the essentials of life by interfering with the supply of food, water, fuel, or light, or the movement of transport. Parliament must be notified. If it is not sitting, it must meet within five days. The government has wide power to make regulations to secure the community with the essentials of life. But they are not to continue in force unless both Houses of Parliament have passed resolutions to provide for this. Moreover, the proclamation is not to remain in force for more than a month. The legislation was originally enacted to give the government sweeping, though not unlimited, powers to deal with strikes in essential service industries; it now covers natural disasters and any other event which is likely to bring about serious disruption to community life.

Two linked points of constitutional law are raised by this legislation and other enactments giving the government wide emergency powers in the context of serious industrial disputes and natural disasters. The first is that the legislation does provide for Parliamentary control over the exercise of the regulatory power, and indirectly over the decision to proclaim, or to continue the proclamation of, the state of emergency. But this is ineffective, largely because the government will always be able to induce its own supporters in the House of Commons to approve its action. That leaves the courts as the only significant safeguard against abuse by government of its peace-time emergency powers. The risk of such abuse should not be ignored. For instance, a government may be tempted to invoke its emergency powers under the 1920 legislation purely in order to break a strike. But the decision of the House of Lords in *Ex parte Zadig*, and other rulings discussed in the following section, show how reluctant the courts are to review the exercise of emergency powers. Often their reluctance is justified by the argument that the government is responsible to Parliament; it would be inappropriate, it is said, for the courts to review a regulation which has been approved by

---

[24] Bradley and Ewing, 677–9; G. S. Morris, 'The Emergency Powers Act 1920' [1979] *Pub. Law* 317.

the Houses of Parliament. This argument is no more convincing during times of emergency than it is in other contexts. In effect, it leads to an abandonment of any control over the executive.

3. CIVIL LIBERTIES IN TIMES OF EMERGENCY

The European Human Rights Convention recognizes that in times of war and other public emergency states are free to derogate from their obligations to respect the Convention rights. But their freedom is qualified. First, states may not derogate from their obligation to respect the most fundamental of those rights: the right to life (except in respect of death resulting from lawful acts of war), the rights not to be tortured or subjected to inhuman treatment, and the right not to held in slavery. Nor may a state invoke an emergency to justify the enactment of retrospective criminal legislation. Secondly, states are only entitled to take those measures, in derogation from their obligations to respect the less fundamental rights, which are strictly required by the emergency. There can be no indiscriminate interference with the rights, say, to freedom of expression, association, or to personal liberty against arbitrary arrest and detention. Moreover, the European Court itself reviews whether the derogating measures were strictly required, although it allows states a wide margin of discretion in this context to determine what is appropriate. It is clear that there is no room for martial law under the Convention, for that allows the armed forces to execute civilians after summary trial without judicial control during the state of war.

The English courts generally defer to the judgement of the executive in times of emergency even when civil liberties are at stake. Mention has already been made of the First World War decision in *Ex parte Zadig*, where the House of Lords upheld a regulation enabling the Home Secretary to intern anyone he considered to be of hostile association. Only Lord Shaw took the view that the liberty of the person and freedom of movement should be protected, unless legislation explicitly authorized the issue of regulations to limit these basic rights. The same deference to the executive was shown by the House of Lords in the notorious Second World War case, *Liversidge* v. *Anderson*.[25] Under the Defence Regulations the Home Secretary had power to detain anyone whom he had 'reasonable cause to believe' to be hostile or to have been involved in acts prejudicial to public safety. Influenced by the fact that

---

[25] [1942] AC 206.

he was required to report monthly to Parliament on the number of detainees, the majority of the House held that it was for the Home Secretary himself to decide whether there was 'reasonable cause' for his belief; in other words, the courts would not examine whether there were any grounds amounting to 'reasonable cause' for the minister to exercise his powers of detention. In an eloquent dissent Lord Atkin protested against this abdication of the courts' responsibility to protect the liberty of the individual and the distortion of the plain meaning of the words of the Defence Regulation.

Emergency legislation enacted to combat terrorism and to preserve order in Northern Ireland has curtailed the exercise of many civil liberties traditionally enjoyed in the United Kingdom.[26] For instance, the Prevention of Terrorism (Temporary Provisions) 1989 restricts freedom of association by banning specified terrorist organizations and by empowering the Secretary of State to ban others which in his view encourage terrorism in Northern Ireland. Freedom of movement within the United Kingdom is limited by the Secretary of State's power to issue exclusion orders to prevent terrorism; these orders may be made to stop someone entering or being in Britain, or entering or being in Northern Ireland. The Secretary of State may detain anyone arrested under this legislation for up to a week, compared to the maximum period of ninety-six hours detention allowed by the Police and Criminal Evidence Act 1984 (PACE), the general statute regulating powers of detention in England and Wales. While the detention of suspects under PACE beyond thirty-six hours must be authorized by a magistrate, there is no independent judicial scrutiny of the detention of terrorist suspects. After the European Human Rights Court had ruled that this power of detention violated the Convention requirement to bring detained persons 'promptly' before a judge or other officer exercising judicial power,[27] the United Kingdom derogated from this obligation in order to preserve the power of detention for up to a week.[28]

Other legislation applicable only in Northern Ireland does away with trial by jury for various offences, confers wide powers of arrest on the police and armed forces, and contains powers to introduce internment of terrorists and those suspected of being terrorists.[29] These provisions

---

[26] See C. Gearty, 'Political Violence and Civil Liberties', in C. McCrudden and G. Chambers (eds.), *Individual Rights and the Law in Britain* (Oxford, 1994), 145; Bradley and Ewing, ch. 25.

[27] *Brogan* v. *UK* (1989) 11 EHRR 117.   [28] See sect. 2 above.

[29] Northern Ireland (Emergency Provisions) Act 1996. This legislation was first enacted in 1973 and has been amended on a number of occasions in the last 25 years.

constitute much greater restrictions on civil liberties than those experienced in the rest of the United Kingdom. The armed forces, for example, need not comply with the usual obligation, incumbent on police officers, to give reasons for an arrest; it is enough for soldiers to state that they are acting as members of the forces.[30] (Outside Northern Ireland they do not have any special powers of arrest beyond those enjoyed by all members of the public.) To give one more example, under powers conferred on him by broadcasting legislation, from 1988 until 1994 the Home Secretary imposed a ban on the radio and television transmission of interviews with members and supporters of various political groups in Northern Ireland, including Sinn Fein. The ban amounted to an interference with freedom of expression.

The courts have generally accepted the legality of the limits imposed on civil liberties during the Northern Ireland troubles. The broadcasting ban was upheld as a reasonable exercise of the Home Secretary's powers; the House of Lords refused to consider whether it was compatible with the ECHR's guarantee of freedom of expression, since the Convention was not then incorporated into United Kingdom law.[31] In a case decided before the imposition of direct rule in Northern Ireland by Westminster, a majority of the House of Lords upheld a regulation of the Northern Ireland Minister for Home Affairs making it an offence to be a member of a Republican club or 'any like organisation howsoever described'.[32] Although the regulation clearly limited freedom of association and was extremely vague in its coverage, the majority accepted that the Minister could lawfully issue it under his statutory power to make regulations to keep the peace. In another case, the House took a broad view of the scope of the arrest powers of army officers, holding that they were not required, unlike police officers in normal circumstances, to inform the occupant of a house that she was under arrest at the time she was first restrained.[33]

It would be wrong to imply that the English courts are unique in their deference to the executive in this context. Constitutional courts in other countries have sometimes been equally hesitant to give full protection to civil liberties during periods of emergency or of terrorism.[34] In the

---

[30] Northern Ireland (Emergency Provisions) Act 1996, s. 19(2).

[31] *R* v. *Home Secretary, ex parte Brind* [1991] 1 AC 696: see Ch. 2, sect. 5 above.

[32] *McEldowney* v. *Forde* [1971] AC 632.

[33] *Murray* v. *Ministry of Defence* [1988] 1 WLR 692.

[34] G. J. Alexander, 'The Illusory Protection of Human Rights by National Courts during Periods of Emergency' (1984) 5 *Human Rights Law Jo.* 1.

Korematsu case,[35] a majority of the United States Supreme Court upheld the conviction of a US citizen of Japanese ancestry for failing to report to a control station, from which he would be removed for internment. Normally the Court would have regarded the internment order as an unconstitutional infringement of the Fourteenth Amendment prohibition of discrimination on the basis of race, nationality, or national origin. Clearly it singled out individuals of Japanese origin for internment, whatever their attitude to the war and whether or not they posed a danger to public security. However, in the Court's view Korematsu was not detained because of his ancestry, but because the military authorities, acting under statutory powers, feared an invasion of the west coast of the United States and thought internment an appropriate security measure. In France the Constitutional Council has upheld the constitutionality of provisions in a criminal law statute providing that for terrorist offences there should be no jury, but a panel of seven judges who could decide by a simple majority.[36] The Council pointed out, however, that the requirements of due process were met, since the judges provided an impartial tribunal.

There is some justification for judicial caution during periods of war and emergency. It is difficult for judges to question, say, the reasonableness of the decision to proclaim an emergency or of the particular decisions of the police or armed forces. They do not have the same information as the executive does, though that may be because the latter does not make it fully available to the court. In extreme circumstances a court might even feel its survival would be in danger if it forfeited the confidence of the government and the public by decisions which appeared to pay more attention to the protection of civil liberties than to the current national crisis or war effort. Moreover, because it may take some time to get a case to court, its intervention may be too late to be effective; in one US case during the Second World War, the Court released a woman of Japanese ancestry two and a half years after she had been unlawfully interned.[37]

Equally, when a constitutional court decides that the executive or armed forces have acted lawfully, the effect of its ruling may be to give some respectability to the suppression of civil liberties during an emergency period. This point was made by Jackson J in his dissent in *Korematsu*; the danger of the majority judgment was that, by legitimating

[35] *Korematsu* v. *US*, 323 US 214 (1944).
[36] Decision 86–213 of 3 Sept. 1986, Rec. 122.
[37] *Ex parte Endo*, 323 US 283 (1944).

racial discrimination in that case, it would create a precedent which would affect the development of the law after the war was over. (Happily, this did not happen. Courts are generally prepared to resume more critical scrutiny of government action in peace-time.) The implication of Jackson J's remarks may be that it would be wiser for courts to invoke principles like the 'political questions' doctrine considered in Chapter 7, and for them to decline to entertain challenges to executive action during war-time and other extreme emergencies. A ruling that a court lacks jurisdiction to interfere with the armed forces at least avoids the danger of legitimating the suppression of civil liberties.

However, this course would amount to an abdication of the judicial responsibility. Courts should be able to balance the need for strong executive government during an emergency and their duty, so far as possible, to protect civil liberties. It is right for judges to allow the government a wider margin of discretion during these periods than in normal circumstances; equally, they should usually insist that the executive provides some evidence or reasons to justify its action. What cannot be defended is a total surrender to executive discretion, as happened in some of the House of Lords decisions during the two world wars and during the Irish troubles. We should remember the words of a Supreme Court judge in one of the Second World War cases: '[f]rom time immemorial despots have used real or imagined threats to the public welfare as an excuse for needlessly abrogating human rights.'[38] No emergency is so grave that the courts should abandon their duty to protect civil liberties.

[38] Murphy J in *Duncan* v. *Kahanumuku*, 327 US 304, 330 (1945).

Select Bibliography

GENERAL WORKS

United Kingdom

Every student should be encouraged to read some chapters of two classic works: A. V. Dicey, *Introduction to the Study of the Law of the Constitution* (10th edn., London, 1961), and Sir Ivor Jennings, *The Law and the Constitution* (5th edn., London, 1959). W. Bagehot, *The English Constitution* (Fontana edn. with introd. by R. H. S. Crossman, London, 1963) remains a marvellous introduction to the constitution from a political perspective. There are a number of good textbooks, among which are S. de Smith and R. Brazier, *Constitutional and Administrative Law* (7th edn., London, 1994), and A. W. Bradley and K. D. Ewing, *Constitutional and Administrative Law* (12th edn., London, 1997).

The Changing Constitution, ed. by J. Jowell and D. Oliver (3rd. edn., Oxford, 1994) is a collection of stimulating essays. Also recommended are the Radcliffe lectures by Lord Nolan and Sir Stephen Sedley, *The Making and Remaking of the British Constitution* (London, 1997). G. Marshall, *Constitutional Theory* (Oxford, 1971) and T. R. S. Allan, *Law, Liberty, and Justice* (Oxford, 1993) explore the principles underlying constitutional law; both books will reward ambitious students.

France

J. Bell, *French Constitutional Law* (Oxford, 1992) is a lucid introduction to this subject; it also contains translated extracts from some decisions of the Conseil constitutionnel. L. Favoreu and L. Philip, *Les grandes décisions du Conseil constitutionnel* (7th edn., Paris, 1993) provides the text of many important rulings, with a full discussion of their significance.

Germany

The best book in English on German constitutional law is D. P. Currie, *The Constitution of the Federal Republic of Germany* (Chicago, Ill., 1994). D. P. Kommers, *The Constitutional Jurisprudence of the Federal Republic of Germany* (Durham and London, 1989) provides translated extracts from many Constitutional Court decisions, together with a valuable commentary on them. There is a two-volume collection of these decisions edited by two members of the Court, D. Grimm and P. Kirchhof, *Entscheidungen des Bundesverfassungsgerichts* (Tübingen, 1993).

United States of America

Strangely, there is a dearth of good short introductions to US constitutional law. R. G. McLoskey, *The American Supreme Court* (Chicago, Ill., 1960) is a classic, if dated, history of the Court. A. M. Bickel, *The Least Dangerous Branch* (Indianapolis, Ind., 1962) and S. M. Griffin, *American Constitutionalism* (Princeton, NJ, 1996) discuss, among other topics, whether judicial review can be reconciled with a commitment to democratic government.

Comparative Works

Three books should be mentioned: K. C. Wheare, *Modern Constitutions* (Oxford, 1966); R. C. van Caenegem, *An Historical Introduction to Western Constitutional Law* (Cambridge, 1995); S. E. Finer, V. Bogdanor, and B. Rudden, *Comparing Constitutions* (Oxford, 1995). The last-named of these books contains the texts of the Constitutions of the USA, Germany, France, and Russia, as well as extracts from the European Human Rights Convention and the European Community/Union Treaties.

WORKS ON SPECIFIC TOPICS

Constitutionalism

C. H. McIlwain, *Constitutionalism: Ancient and Modern* (New York, 1947) is a good introduction to the history of constitutionalism. G. Sartori, 'Constitutionalism: A Preliminary Discussion' (1962) 56 *American Political Science Rev.* 853 explores its significance.

Separation of Powers

The best comparative study is M. J. C. Vile, *Constitutionalism and the Separation of Powers* (Oxford, 1967). M. P. Sharp, 'The Classical American Doctrine of the Separation of Powers' (1935) 2 *U Chicago L Rev.* 385 describes the history of the principle in the United States. P. L. Strauss, 'The Place of Agencies in Government: Separation of Powers and the Fourth Branch' (1984) 84 *Columbia Law Rev.* 573 reinterprets the separation principle in the context of modern government.

For a recent assessment of its significance, see E. M. Barendt, 'Separation of Powers and Constitutional Government' [1995] *Public Law* 599.

Federalism

K. C. Wheare, *Federal Government* (3rd edn., Oxford, 1953) and G. Sawyer, *Modern Federalism* (Carlton, Victoria, 1976) are magisterial surveys of the varieties of federalism. See K. Lenaerts, 'Constitutionalism and the Many Faces of Federalism' (1990) 38 *American Jo. of Comp. Law* 205 for discussion of its relevance to analysis of the European Community. For US federalism, see A. R. Amar, 'Of Sovereignty and Federalism' (1987) 96 *Yale LJ* 1425, and for a comparative treatment, see J. E. Finn, 'Federalism in Perpetuity: West German and United States Federalism in Comparative Perspective' (1989) 22 *New York Univ. Jo. of International Law and Politics* 1.

The Constitution of the European Union

Most textbooks on the fundamentals of European Union law have chapters on this topic. The article by J. H. Weiler, 'The Transformation of Europe' (1991) 100 *Yale LJ* 2403 is the most penetrating analysis of the constitutional development of the Community. Also recommended are: T. C. Hartley, 'Federalism, Courts, and Legal Systems: The Emerging Constitution of the European Community' (1986) 34 *American Jo. of Comp. Law* 229; G. F. Mancini and D. T. Keeling, 'Democracy and the European Court of Justice' (1994) 57 *MLR* 175; B. De Witte, 'Sovereignty and European Integration: The Weight of Legal Tradition' (1995) 2 *Maastricht Jo. of European and Comp. Law* 145.

Parliamentary legislative supremacy

The classic defence of Dicey's principle is by H. W. R. Wade, 'The Legal Basis of Sovereignty' [1955] *CLJ* 172, to which R. F. V. Heuston, 'Sovereignty' in his *Essays in Constitutional Law* (2nd, edn., London, 1964) is an eloquent reply. N. MacCormick, 'Does the United Kingdom have a Constitution? Reflections on *MacCormick* v. *Lord Advocate*' (1978) 29 *Northern Ireland LQ* 1 is stimulating. P. P. Craig, 'Sovereignty of the United Kingdom Parliament after *Factortame*' (1991) 11 *Yearbook of European Law* 221 discusses the impact of Community law on the principle.

The Crown, Executive, and Constitutional Conventions

R. Brazier's books, *Ministers of the Crown* (Oxford, 1997) and *Constitutional Practice* (2nd edn., Oxford, 1994) are very helpful on these complex topics. V. Bogdanor, *The Monarchy and the Constitution* (Oxford, 1995) offers fresh insights on the constitutional role of the Monarch. G. Marshall, *Constitutional Conventions* (Oxford, 1984) is the leading study of this subject; see also C. R. Munro, 'Laws and Conventions Distinguished' (1975) 91 *LQR* 218.

The Courts

J. A. G. Griffith, *The Politics of the Judiciary* (5th edn., London, 1997) is very critical of the English judiciary for their conservative disposition and reluctance to defend civil liberties. Other aspects of the constitutional position of the English courts are examined by S. Shetreet, *Judges on Trial: A Study in the Appointment and Accountability of the English Judiciary* (Amsterdam, 1976), and by R. Stevens, *The Independence of the Judiciary* (Oxford, 1993). President Roosevelt's plan to pack the Supreme Court is described in W. E. Leuchtenburg, *The Supreme Court Reborn* (New York, 1995), chapters 4 and 5.

Political Parties

K. D. Ewing, *The Funding of Political Parties in Britain* (Cambridge, 1987) is the authoritative study in the UK context. For comparative studies, see G. Casper, '*Williams* v. *Rhodes* and Public Financing of Political Parties under the American and German Constitutions' [1969] *Supreme Court Rev.* 271, and S. G. Calabresi, 'Political Parties as Mediating Institutions', (1994) 61 *U Chicago L Rev.* 1471.

Constitutions in Time of War and Emergency

There is a broad discussion of constitutional issues by M. P. Boyle, 'Emergency Situations and the Protection of Human Rights: A Model Derogation Provision for a Northern Ireland Bill of Rights' (1977) 28 *Northern Ireland LQ* 160. For a comparative survey, see G. J. Alexander, 'The Illusory Protection of Human Rights by National Courts during Periods of Emergency' (1984) 5 *Human Rights Law Jo.* 1.

Index

Printed in Australia
AUHW021413301121
356243AU00004B/69

9 780198 762546